T0203414

NOT QUITE WHITE

"Delves into what it's like growing up mixed race in the UK".—**Mashable**

"Charts the pain and confusion of growing up while grappling with a complicated, mixed ethnic identity . . . a memoir that many mixed-race people will easily relate to".—**Dazed**

"Intimate, powerful and nuanced reflection of exploring one's identity, understanding and embracing mixedness. . . . Laila has created a space for so many people to feel seen".
—**Diverse Bookshelf**

"Woozeer creates an environment in the reader's mind that allows us to learn more about ourselves. . . . This is the real gift to readers".—**Brown Girl Bookshelf**

"A moving piece of literature . . . an eloquent portrayal of self-discovery and building your identity in a society that is eager to dismantle your existence at every turn".
—**Wales Art Review**

"An insight into what it's like growing up mixed race".—**MyLondon News**

"One of the most relatable [books] I've read on the mixed experience".
—**Mixed Messages**

"Laila's book serves as a blanket of comfort, validation and hope".—**Read With Samia**

"Heartbreaking, vivid, lyrical, and very smart. . . . I was so grateful to Laila giving us the understanding of this quite complex topic".—**Book Reccos podcast**

"Magnetically moving, poetically written and enigmatically captivating, Laila has created a mastery of their life with this book".
—**DaisyButter Book Review**

"A pulsing exploration of the self, this book hands you the privilege to observe Laila find meaning, and it oozes with vulnerability, hope, beauty and story. When I'm older I want to write like Laila".—**Gina Martin, writer and activist**

"A lyrical odyssey of self-discovery, told with folkloric flair. In charting her journey across Welsh mountains and Mauritian seas, Laila Woozeer offers a map that can guide us all, regardless of our origins, to unearth the treasure that lies within. A must-read for anyone in search of themselves".
—**Jassa Ahluwalia, writer and activist**

"Anyone who wants to learn how our racial identity impacts not only our experience of the world but also how we understand ourselves should pick up this book. Gorgeously written, too".—**Natasha Devon, author and broadcaster**

"The most nuanced and moving account of mixed race identity I've read".
—**htmljones, influencer and musician**

"This book is a gem. I genuinely couldn't stop turning the pages. Laila is an essential voice in today's important issues of race, identity and belonging".
—**Kai Samra, comic and writer**

"This book is a treat, asking timely questions about race, who we are and how we define ourselves, but through such exquisite prose you get utterly pulled in".
—**Rosie Holt, writer and comedian**

NOT QUITE QUITE
WHITE

A MEMOIR

LAILA WOOZEER

RED ⚡ LIGHTNING BOOKS

This book is a publication of

Red Lightning Books
1320 East 10th Street
Bloomington, Indiana 47405 USA

redlightningbooks.com

© 2024 by Laila Woozeer
Originally published in Great Britain by Gallery Books in 2022

All rights reserved
No part of this book may be reproduced or utilized in any form or
by any means, electronic or mechanical, including photocopying
and recording, or by any information storage and retrieval system,
without permission in writing from the publisher.

First Printing 2024

ISBN 978-1-68435-227-2 (pbk.)
ISBN 978-1-68435-228-9 (web PDF)

For the Fourth

A NOTE TO THE READER

This book features my own experiences of racism and will contain references to, and direct mentions of, racial slurs. Some may be triggering to read.

Contents

Prologue Two Moons Time   1

1   Princess Jasmine was the Only One
    in Trousers   3
2   Last of the Dragon's Blood   29
3   We Throw the Burned Ones Out   51
4   Mum Never had a Moustache   85
5   Remembering Pluto   119
6   Across From Ghosts   144
7   Now Collecting All the Colours on
    the Canvas   179
8   Everywhere Birds   207
9   The Tree that Blooms the Whole
    Year Through   241
10   A Ceaseless Sequence of Stars   270

Epilogue For Fur   296

Afterword Letter from Laila   299
Appendix The Snow Queen   302
Acknowledgements   305

Not Quite White

Prologue

Two Moons Time

. . . actually it all started when I lost myself.

March, 2018. It is 2am on a Saturday night and I am sat cross-legged on my bed, rumpled duvet and a notebook full of chords, at the dawn of a new project, searching for something I forgot to remember at the time. My long hair falls forward on my papers as I write, and my rescue snake slumbers round my ankles, curled up in a hug. Sometimes, she explores the pages and pencils littering the bed; but it's late, so she stays close. As I type out half-remembered memories onto my dads's old iPad and email them to my phone to place in order (my laptop broke last year and I can't afford to repair it), I start to map out moments. And so begins my current task: to untangle the threads of myself and weave them together into something coherent. But also, to remind myself of who I was, when I was a version of myself still seeking; and to remind myself that I am here now, found, in this small safe room by this single square window, with my view of the tree that blooms each spring and a dim buzzing sound from the streetlights.

Cradled in the sanctuary of the twilight hours, of the quiet when all the city sleeps, I sit down and think backwards to the beginning, or my beginning, or this story's beginning at least, and somewhere beyond I see the spark of a sentence. I begin, at last, to write. Outside in the densest of clouds London so rarely knows, a cold snow blows past the moon; the wind whispers and a comet crackles, and through falling snowflakes comes the tender glance of stars. And one day – not yet, but one day, somewhere near the end – I'll recall this particular moment as the one that started the rest.

When did you first realise you didn't exist?

Chapter One

Princess Jasmine was the Only One in Trousers

October 1994. I sit on top of a mountain in rural North Wales on a stiff-backed chair in a small classroom. Classmates chatter around me as I silently search a red plastic box for a crayon to draw myself. Other children at the table are busy colouring bright pink people with yellow hair; technicolored stick figures on green grass strips below blue scribble skies. But I haven't got that far yet; I am still searching. I need to draw myself. I stare blankly at my forearms then back to the box of crayons. The skin-coloured hue I need does not appear to exist. I want to find the warm coppery fawn colour that I see when I look at my small limbs, which are speckled with a handful of faint freckles and downy black hair, like the proverbial ugly duckling. But I cannot find the crayon I need.

I am four years old, and I know the eight other children in this room as well as I know myself. Our separate selves blur together at the edges as we grow up nestled in the safety of rural life, raised like a litter in increasingly sized rooms. Two years ago, we ran around in circles in the community centre on the hill, singing along to a cassette of nursery rhymes and practising skids when our parents weren't looking. Last year, we played in the room next door to this one, taking turns to cram into the playhouse, finger paint, and nap. Now we are a 'year group', older, in a bigger class, sat on slightly higher chairs, with more mature obligations. Like today's assignment: drawing pictures of our family.

It should be simple, really. I have drawn my mother with the requisite pink crayon, in a blue triangle dress with stick arms and legs, and I have drawn my father entirely in black crayon, a monochrome man, more line arms and legs, and a loopy squiggle of hair. I have drawn our yellow house on the side of a hill and our old grey car sat faithfully in front. And now, I am trying to draw myself and complete the scene. But even though I have tuned out the chitchat of the classroom and thoroughly raked through the box, I still can't find the right crayon.

At this point, it's not a negative thing, it's just one of those simplistic, state-the-obvious kid facts. *Grass is green; sky is blue; my skin is not a colour of crayon.* It is not a fact with baggage attached, but a plain and simple truth. We learn everything quickly when we're young, then spend the rest of our time unlearning as those early facts suddenly bloom into sprawling, nuanced worlds of meaning. Grass is green, brown, yellow, pink, dull purple, bleached gold, coarse orange, scuffed jade. The sky is blue, black, lavender, peach, deep crimson, shot silver, bright violet, dove grey.

I searched for a brown crayon without understanding the implication of what that could mean. No indication of the struggle ahead and the hunt for validation that would occupy my teenage years; of the identity crisis that would define all my adult work; of the terse conversations with strangers over where I was really from and the thousand times I'd have to spell my name out to a frowning face with a quizzical expression. I didn't know what was to come, what I would unlearn and what would bloom. I just couldn't find the right crayon to draw myself with.

At the age of four, my world was small: home, school and the community around me. Home was where I lived with my mum and sometimes, dad, high up in an ex-mining village – a single rubble road curving round the side of a mountain, around which houses occurred in no particular order or design, simply appearing on a whim like the foxgloves and ferns. School was two villages over, a cheerful red-roofed building in another tiny village. My relatively large year group had nine pupils, the same kids I'd known since we were toddlers.

Most of the mountain where I lived was rolling rock face, abandoned mines and dense, ancient forest; all around was the smell of damp moss and dirt, the sound of gentle rustling and creaking wood. The landscape was punctuated by occasional slate roofs that turned from grey to soft mauve in the rain. Our house was a crooked old stone building that had long ago been two. It loomed against the steep mountain, with metre-thick walls to keep the winds out and a long passage at the back where tired horses once rested. The building was constructed apparently before construction existed (no right angles or bricks) and had been haphazardly adapted over time, the structure hinting at long-ago things that could no longer be known. The house swallowed up sounds and only occasionally allowed light in from strange directions. There were four towering chimneys for three huge stone fireplaces, one with a giant log-burning stove. Uneven walls were punctuated by peculiar brackets and empty doorframes, with a trapdoor in the living room that led to a blocked off passage in the cellar and a step up on one side of the house without a corresponding step on the other side.[1] Nobody minded these quirks because it was home. Mum filled the empty fireplaces with dried flowers in jugs and Dad kept his keys on a bit of exposed rock overhanging his desk under the stairs – and the sloping floor in the kitchen made a great ramp for my tricycle. It wasn't a big house but it was a house you could get lost in.

I was born in London, where Dad worked when he wasn't with us and where my big brother lived, but Wales was my home and the mountain was my world. Surrounding the few houses was the forest, which was old and knew things. Air stayed green through the leaves and wispy specks sailed through with a curious weightlessness, as though rules of the normal realm didn't apply: soft white fluffkins drifted around, flying sparks sprang in all directions, bright secrets scuttled overhead and dark flashes dashed underfoot. Only the sunlight was bound by gravity, lying in jagged fragments on the floor.

And within this world our neighbours became family. Our across-the-road neighbours had three kids – Lisa, Dawn and Jake – and our down-the-road neighbours had two kids: Kayleigh and Martin. Our house was built into the mountain,

---

1. Later in life, I'd see optical illusions and geometrical designs of impossible architecture with walls and floors adjoining where they shouldn't, depicting what was remarkably similar to our ground floor.

with a garden that stretched up the mountainside. Kayleigh and Martin's house started on the same level as our house but went down instead of up, ending much lower than ours. Jake, Lisa and Dawn's house was built *down* the mountain, at the bottom of a steep driveway, so that the pointed roof was lower than the bottom of our house. When we played at each other's houses, our parents could look over, or up, or down, or even beyond, in the woods, and find us.

I loved being outside, scurrying through the forest with my neighbours, or in my own multi-level garden. Sometimes, I'd journey with my dad to the compost pile where the bugs lived, other times I'd scamper after my mum to the flower bed she'd created on the one flat patch and admire the strawberry plant that tumbled out of an old ceramic sink. But mostly I played there alone, gazing up into the leaves of the holly tree or searching for treasures like an empty snail shell or an acorn still with its cap. From the very top of the garden, I could look down at the roof of our house, or past the house to the surrounding patchwork countryside and the tiny criss-cross villages, or further beyond to the huge grey mountains lying like sleeping dragons in the distance. But mostly what I saw was sky. The top of the garden at the top of the hill was higher than the villages, higher than the town, higher even than the moon (which for most of the year hid behind the mountain, below and beyond us). And my favourite of all was to lie on the sloping grass and stare straight up into the many-hued sky itself, when it swirled around me and the heavy clouds swooped so low they might reach down and nudge my nose.

Wales was all I knew. My memories of London extended to a flowery sofa and a black cat. At four, I was a cheerful, smiley kid, with an extensive range of floral leggings and thick dark hair in the quintessential 90s kid fringe-and-bob combination.[2] My weeks consisted of school, Sylvanian Families, and trying not to get mud on my socks and trainers (or more accurately, trying not to let Mum see when I did). I hated wearing skirts, I was pretty sure we had fairies in the garden and I was best friends with the girls in my year (Amy, Mena, Ffion and Nia). And of course, like any self-respecting kid in 1994, I had a favourite Disney character: Princess Jasmine, from the film *Aladdin*. And she was EVERYTHING.

Princess Jasmine was gutsy heroine and beautiful princess and dream big sister, all rolled into one. I worshipped her. Princess Jasmine had been in my life as long as I could remember, and not just in the film but *everywhere*: Saturday morning cartoons, kids' magazines, boxes of cereal and McDonald's Happy Meals. And we had the video! I could go back and watch Jasmine talk to her tiger or go to the busy market, over and over, endlessly rewinding the hallowed copy until I could chime in with every scene, line and lyric (at least until the film in the tape started to knacker) and my arms became dented in strange patterns from lying on the carpet. Repeat viewings of Disney films marked them indelibly into my consciousness, like nursery rhymes or bedtime stories. I carried Jasmine with me at all times.

And what a story was *Aladdin*! As far as I was concerned, *Aladdin* had everything. The classic plot (adventure and pluck and derring-do!), the charming characters, the unforgettable songs ('Prince Ali', an absolute banger), the stunning animation

---

2. We have the overexposed Kodak memories to prove it.

(who could forget the chase through the crumbling cave?), the genre-breaking humour from Robin Williams' Genie (I was too young to understand the impressions, but I knew it was funny). And even more than the dancing and the elephants and the rapid-fire Genie voices, what I loved was Princess Jasmine. Even at the age of four, I could see she was clearly the best Disney princess. She had gold earrings, a beautiful singing voice, the longest ponytail I'd ever seen and *trousers*. How cool was that? Princess Jasmine was cut from a different cloth to the other princesses, all meek ballads and flowy *skirts*. Jasmine was strong and brave. She took charge of things and made plans. No friendly woodland creatures or cutesy talking fish – Jasmine had a *tiger*. Other princesses sang songs about seeking independence and wanting more, but Jasmine simply threw on a disguise and went right out and found it. No song of wishing, no montage of desire. Just shut the front door and off to market – *literally*.

Four-year-old me, in my small grey village and my routine rural life, adored Jasmine. She was glorious. I watched the songs and twirled around on the carpet, pretending I, too, had hair down to my knees and sparkly golden earrings. The film alone wasn't enough for me, so I cut her image out of magazines and drew pictures of her to stick on my walls, trying to bring as much of her as possible into my own small world. My world was cosy and fun, sure, but it wasn't thrilling in the same way that Jasmine's was. She was somewhere else entirely, somewhere *magical*. When the *Aladdin* TV show came out, I was given a Jasmine video – a collection of Jasmine-focused episodes of the show! It came with a Jasmine-esque bracelet! Shiny gold with a dangling purple lamp! It was the most enchanting thing I'd ever seen, I wore it carefully around the house, never out – it was too precious.

Jasmine was the first brown character I'd seen on screen. I identified with her in ways I had never identified with anyone. In the film, Jasmine lives in a wholly brown-hued world where everyone is the same colour, but outside of the film and in surrounding media – the Disney princesses lined up together in my magazines or my VHS collection spread out on the floor – Jasmine was clearly a different colour to the other princesses. I didn't understand what that meant, but I *did* understand that I matched her, and that was wonderful. She was a girl with me-coloured skin! *I* was a girl with Jasmine-coloured skin! She had black hair in a ponytail! *I* had black hair in a ponytail (at least, when Mum tied it up)! I imagined Jasmine coming to my school, becoming my best friend and running around in my day-to-day life like a long-lost twin. We could pretend to be *sisters!*

This meant a lot to me, because outside of Jasmine not many people looked like me. I didn't look like my mum. I didn't look like my dad. I didn't look like my neighbours or my friends. I just existed in my own little lane of looking a certain way, a certain *Jasmine-esque* way, and without anyone else to look like, I clung on to the comforting idea that I was like Jasmine and she was like me. Apart from my dad and my brother in London, everyone I knew in real life was the same colour as my mum. In books and on TV, most people were the same default pale colour as well. It was confusing, because I often saw depictions of places that looked like my world – I just wasn't in it. A lot of the cartoons and kids' shows we watched were American imports, where other people of colour were sometimes shown to exist, but none of them were me-coloured. Sometimes, books and cartoons would bring in a character of a different colour whose otherness was the key storyline for a one-off special; other times there might be a featured cultural event in which a supporting character became the focus for a single episode.[3] The stories always followed a similar pattern: outline what made the character *different*, explain an aspect connected to their beliefs or culture, show the regular characters learning about this and finish by having everyone connect despite their differences. End of story, resolution reached, credits roll.

This always sat oddly with me. The character was often a plot device to educate the in-show characters (and, by proxy, the audience) and rarely a fully formed character in their own right. And, because they weren't a main protagonist, by the next episode they'd mostly be out of the show again. Background characters retreated to from whence they came: cast returned to status quo. This sucked – how were you supposed to know how they fit into the big picture, you know, outside of whatever *different*-ness they'd introduced us to? Also, the plots seemed to set me up to be educated. The audience was positioned by default to be the 'typical' to whatever the 'atypical' was, and so learned about the new culture from the 'atypical' character. From the point of view of wanting to learn, I was with the wrong group. How did the different kids learn about being different?

---

3. Such as 'A Rugrats Passover' on *Rugrats* or 'Harold's Bar Mitzvah' on *Hey Arnold!*

Still, when shows like *Rugrats* and *Sesame Street* included a Black character or a character of East Asian heritage, I latched on to them as somebody other than 'default', like me. I knew I wasn't really like those characters, but I stuck with them regardless because I didn't have anyone else.

Without thinking, I kept a list in my head of all the people who looked like me (easy – just Jasmine) and all the people who were different from the normal, even if they weren't like me and Jasmine. All the characters were American, because the British cartoons didn't have anyone that looked different from the default at all. And they rarely even featured *people* – *The Poddington Peas*, about anthropomorphic peas, *The Shoe People*, about anthropomorphic shoes, and *The Raggy Dolls*, about (funnily enough) anthropomorphic dolls.

Live-action TV had white shows and Black shows, and not much crossover or anything in between. Shows like *Moesha*, *The Fresh Prince of Bel-Air* and *Sister, Sister* were clearly aimed at Black American audiences. I felt closer to those shows than the ones filled with white people, but when I watched them, it was more of a window into somebody else's world than a mirror for my own.

Outside of TV and books, I kept a running list of anybody me-coloured (or sort of me-coloured). Me. My dad. My brother in London. Our family doctors, Dr Mukharjee and her husband Dr Mukharjee, who worked at the General Practice in the nearby town. We saw them a lot as I often caught colds. I'd sit on a rubbery green chair in Dr Mukharjee's office and say 'aah' whilst she put a wooden stick on my tongue that tasted like sand. They both had brown skin, lighter than my dad but darker than me, and female Dr Mukharjee had long, wavy dark hair in a ponytail (not dissimilar to Jasmine's). I asked Dad about this, and he said *she is from India*. India! Wow.

I kept a close tally on people and characters that looked like me because I was trying to prove to myself that I existed. When my arms went warm in the sun or I accidentally scratched my knee on a rock and saw a stinging slash of scarlet, I felt *real*. But I needed something tangible to prove I was not a mistake and was a person *purposefully* in the *world*. Having a list of people I could identify myself as being 'similar to' shaped my understanding of where I fit. My 'elusive crayon' episode was about more than it merely being unavailable; as I stretched my arms across the waxy paper it caused ripples in my understanding of myself. Because the colour wasn't lost. The colour *didn't* exist.

Why? Didn't things that colour exist? In my still forming four-year-old brain, everything existed in polar opposites and clearly defined categories, like 'big' and 'small', or 'fast' and 'slow'. I was learning without words there was no category for me and my skin colour, and no single category for me and my parents. I'd managed to draw pink crayon Mum with blue eyes and yellow hair, and black crayon Dad with black crayon hair, and I understood that they formed opposing labels of the same category. They made sense in the binary way we understand things as children. Mum was light and Dad was dark. Mum was this and Dad was that. But what about *me*? Where did I go? It was troubling in ways I couldn't process, and without an explicit explanation of *how this worked* and *where I fit*, I didn't know how to ask. I was learning to define myself not by what I was, but by what I was not.

Even then, I think I had some idea the problem went beyond crayons. When school got a restock of supplies and we suddenly had turquoise, magenta, white, grey and dark-or-angey-apparently-*brown* crayons, it didn't change what I was grappling with. Everyone else in my class – so, my year and the whole of the year above – could draw themselves, so I recognised it was my problem. Mine was the one brown hand in the ring in the playground, the one brown leg in the circle to pick who was 'It'. When we discussed important things during break time and at lunch, like whether or not there was, categorically, a Santa Claus (if yes, he had the same handwriting as my mum) and where babies come from (inside a mum, who either pooped the baby out or – according to one unverified account from a boy in the year below – coughed the baby up), we never discussed why there was no Laila crayon. It was only an issue for me, which meant somehow, subconsciously, though I could not articulate this until many years later, *I* was the issue.

Days passed with the unassuming monotony of the very young. Big developments, like the thrill of your feet touching the end of your shoe and knowing you'd gone up a size, went alongside smaller ones, like figuring out how to colour in the page without leaving a kaleidoscope pattern of felt-tip down the side of your hand.

Dad swapped where he was living and went back to London to work, Wales becoming the place he visited every few weeks and London the place where he lived, but time trundled on reliably, with the same soil smell in the cellar and same sourceless roar at the back of the house. The only real difference for me was that I was now one brown person down on my internal list. Mum and I effectively became a single parent family with cameo appearances from Dad. When he was around, the two of us went for walks in the abandoned mines and I studied the ground carefully, taking big steps to place my feet directly on the space where his had been. It was easier, then – I was closer to the ground. Dad showed me how to climb the stiles without ripping my leggings on the wire, and near the old quarry I could root around finding crystals – chunks of rock with thrilling sparkly lines or jagged clumps of gold poking out. Dad told me their names, and I'd line them up, early attempts at cleromancy. We took them home where they glittered knowingly by the door.

Sometimes when Dad left I'd go up to the top of the garden to watch his car pass down the hill. I would lie there and examine the waxy yellow buttercups and the fluffy purple clovers, grass tickling my nose and an occasional insect scuttling across my arm. I was so small and so hazy that it seemed like I could be the soil or the shoots or a swallow in the sky. And I'd wonder at the words the wind whispered in my ear, words that seemed to say, *you are special, you belong here, you are part of this world and we know, because we know you, because we've always known you,* and it was always nice to have confirmation of belonging; nice to have a friend, even if it was only the wind.

By the time I was six, I spent most of my time making up elaborate games based in faraway lands or playing with my neighbours. I began dance and piano lessons during the week, both of which I loved. I became an avid reader and read every book in our tiny school library and as many as possible from the big library in town. I was allowed to borrow five books each week and it was always an agonising decision, which would make it home (short-looking books would be speed-read in the queue to avoid taking up one of my precious slots).

Kids' books usually depicted suburban stories of parents and siblings and pets, clearly shown in full-colour illustrations; I'd already learned I didn't belong in those settings and reading them made me feel uneasy and suspicious. Life wasn't *really* like that, was it? My tastes tended towards the abstract fantasy end – I had a big book of stories about fairies who lived in flowers, like in our garden, and another book about Greek myths, which detailed the constellations – stories I could see in the stars above my very own house. This was much more exciting than tales of Topsy and Tim going to the dentist and Alfie feeding ducks. Though, even in fantasy, the princesses were *golden of hair* and *pale of hue*, and they didn't live in old stone houses or in the forests up the mountains – that was where beasts roamed and heroes vanquished. The only ones who lived there were the witches.

One of my favourite books was *A Necklace of Raindrops*, in which the drawings were silhouettes of people against multicoloured fantastical backgrounds. In the absence of people like me in other books, this was one of the only stories where the characters in my head could all look like me. Something about the stories felt familiar, too, the same way books of myths did – stories of travelling the globe, conversing with the winds and appealing to the ancient might of the elements. Reading on the Welsh hillside in the garden, seat damp from grass and surrounded by the low murmur of the trees, I'd project the images onto the lavender-hued sky around me, between the bats darting in and out of the tangled trees like flecks of light off a sparkler. Up there, where time didn't know clocks and sky unfolded forever, it seemed feasible that the dormant mountains in the distance might wake into monsters, that the many flowers might flutter into fairies once midnight fell, that the glistening dew in the morning was a remnant of some celestial spell, that the world knew things and had simply decided to wait.

Fairy tales began in the woods and the villages before journeying far away across the kingdom – and I felt like I could do that, too. I could start off here on a hill, and then go somewhere exciting to have magical adventures when I was bigger. Up there, in the mountains by the sky, I felt like I could do *anything*; I might step onto the path and walk down to the house, or I might step off the mountain and walk up to the clouds. In contrast, the 'normal' everyday stories alienated me, starting and ending in a version of home that was nothing like mine. It was far easier to imagine myself in a kingdom of magic and might and curious creatures than it was to imagine being part of a four-person family who ate dinner together round the table.

Beyond all these stories, I still had Jasmine. Years were passing, but my list of me-coloured people wasn't getting any bigger, and in the absence of anybody new to identify with I did what any lonely kid would do pre-internet: I went further in, analysing Jasmine, studying magazine clippings, comic books, taped cartoons off the TV, watching *Aladdin* for the fiftieth time. And it was somewhere around the fifty-first re-watch of *Aladdin* that I had to ask myself: was Jasmine like me?

Analysing Jasmine was like finger-painting at school: the more involved I was, the more messy things became. Jasmine certainly looked like me, but she wasn't in a world I recognised. I mean, really, none of the princesses were – there was a distinct lack of T-shirts and mums cooking dinner living in rural France or ancient England or even quite literally under the sea.[4] But regardless of location, they at least had things I recognised like books, friends and music lessons.

Jasmine didn't have any of that. She existed somewhere far away, in a world wholly unlike mine. I'd never seen a palm tree, I'd only seen a tiger at the zoo and though I'd been to the town market, it was nothing like Jasmine's. Her market had sword-wielding guards and travelling merchants: ours was a mixture of extension plugs, knock-off Lonsdale and back-of-a-van Tupperware. The more I thought about it, the more I realised actually nothing was familiar in Jasmine's world.

Jasmine was the only person I could identify as 'looks-like-me' in the whole wide world. But in her world she wasn't an exception to the rule like I was in mine – she was one of hundreds. In fact, the only people who *weren't* Jasmine's colour were the characters who weren't *people*: Genie, the tiger, the carpet, the parrot. I'd daydreamed about Jasmine joining me and sharing the mutual loneliness of being a colour nobody else was. But now I was older, and when I really thought about it, I could see that Jasmine wouldn't need to come over and pretend to be my sister, because she could pass for the sister of basically any other character in the whole entire film. They probably only made coppery brown skin-colour crayons in Jasmine's world.

---

4. Which, by the way, doesn't make sense – surely they are in the sea? Because if they're *under* the sea, isn't that like the core of the earth or something?

Maybe I should have been *there*, in Jasmine's world, all along. Maybe I was somehow stuck in the wrong place. If I figured out *where* Jasmine was, then I could go and be among *people that looked like me* and I'd be the default. I'd be able to see myself in books and on TV and to see people in everyday life who looked like me. I'd fit.

I had a few reasons to believe this was the case. First, because even if Jasmine's world was a far cry from my own, I looked like her and every other person there, and I didn't look like anyone here (GPs notwithstanding, and, anyway, they *were* from somewhere else, Dad had said so). Second, there wasn't a crayon for me. If I was *supposed* to be here and colouring with the same crayons as everyone else, I would have had the right tools, surely. Third, nobody had the same name as me. Nobody had ever even heard of my name and it was rarely pronounced correctly. I never found my name on bookmarks, or puffy velvet headbands, or novelty key rings at service stations. Realising this, my parents bought me a custom bedroom door sign and make-your-own bracelets that spelled my name out, clearly and correctly – but this made me feel worse. Nobody else's parents had to get them *custom* items. Anyway, I didn't specifically want named items, I just wanted to be included, like everybody else. I just wanted the *choice*. If I was in the right place, I'd be accommodated the way others were.

But the biggest reason to believe I was stuck in the wrong place was because when I *did* see my life reflected, I was never there in it. Aged four, this was an issue; by six, an internalised fact. I clearly did not exist. I just didn't see anyone that looked like me in all the many stories that did, in other important ways, mirror my life. Everything else was there, present and correct, but *I* was missing. When I wrote stories, I made all the characters white – usually blonde and blue-eyed, with clearly English names. When I drew pictures of my house and my garden and school, I left them devoid of people, struggling to place myself into the scene despite literally drawing the world in which I lived. When I tried to include a portrait of myself, the image just felt *wrong*, like I genuinely didn't believe I belonged. When I drew myself, I was either absent of context – floating on a plain white A4 background – or somewhere else, some magical glade I'd never visited, or perched on some cliffs I'd never seen. Not here, where I actually was.

Because everyone else fit and I was the problem, I never discussed any of this with anybody. With a mostly absent dad, everyone around me was the same colour as my mum. Endless cartoon kids on TV had a mum like mine, taking them to school and doing the laundry and so on. Even Mum's vaguely American accent matched up with the TV mums. She wasn't the problem – I was.

It was strange. I was content, but either I wasn't supposed to be here (concerning) or I was not supposed to exist (terrifying). Whenever I thought the latter, I became very frightened, there was a loud whooshing noise in my ears and a quickness in my chest, like my heart was trembling, and I would frantically try to divert my thoughts elsewhere instead. I needed to *fit*, and my best bet for fitting in was Jasmine country, wherever that was. One time when Dad was up, I asked if we could go to Agrabah[5] on holiday. Dad thought I meant Euro Disney, where

---

5. You know, where *Aladdin* is set.

you could meet the characters, and I explained, no, not France, I didn't want to meet Jasmine so much as go to where she lived, like in the film (I mean, if we bumped into her that was a bonus). Dad was bemused, but eventually said we couldn't go, because Agrabah wasn't a real place, so nobody could go.

What?! No! How could it not *exist*? Nearly all of the other Disney films were set in real-life places like France, America, England and so on, in what were, I was sure, extremely realistic and factually correct depictions. Agrabah *had* to be real! We could go to the places where other princesses lived, why couldn't we go to Jasmine's? All I took from this was that a place made up of entirely me-coloured people did not exist.

Were there not other me-coloured people? Did we only exist in mythical, made-up places?! The ramifications were terrible – I went straight back to the VCR to further investigate, positioning myself on the rug so fast I almost got a carpet burn. Right at the start of *Aladdin*, a random introductory character (known as The Peddler) explains the strange nowhere land in which the story is set by singing a song about Agrabah. He mentions sand, heat, camels[6] – memorably, this place is 'barbaric, but hey, it's home'. Except how was it home if it wasn't real? Euro Disney this was not. The song was called 'Arabian Nights' – okay, so could we go to Arabia? No, because that was also not a country. I changed gear. Instead of trying to figure out where was Agrabah, I now revisited the film to sleuth out clues to understand *what* was Agrabah.

---

6. Incidentally, the original song was considered to be so racist that Disney agreed to change some of the offensive lyrics, though not all of them.

So what makes a place like Agrabah? I didn't know then that *Aladdin* was one of the first animated Disney films to take place outside of a Western setting in a completely fictional location, or that the original tale was added in to *The Book of One Thousand and One Nights* by a white Frenchman, who (scholars believe) set the story erroneously in China. The story has no factual Arabic text source, and was based on a story Antoine Galland (the French publisher) heard from a Syrian storyteller, Hanna Diyab, who was not mentioned or acknowledged in any way in the publication of the stories.[7]

Disney's story only augments this confused and problematic source material. Revisiting Agrabah now I can see the cringe-worthy jumble of stereotypes: scimitar-wielding henchmen, gold ornaments, sexy harem girls, bedouin tents, silhouetted palm trees, toothless beggars and bearded men smoking hookahs. I learned later that the scenery inspiration included Arabic calligraphy, Iranian mosaics and Turkish carpets (including the character Carpet), and the location design drew on Iraq, Marrakesh, the Sahara Desert and Machu Picchu. Animals range from a Bengal tiger (found in India), capuchin monkey and a scarlet macaw (both native to Central and South America). Few of these influences belong together in reality. *Aladdin* is not an assembly of different historically Arabian cultures; it's

---

7. Hanna Diyab's autobiography was found and translated in 2015, and subsequent reflections on his life and work mean scholars have posited him as the real author of the Aladdin story (and others), rather than it being a folk tale as presented by Galland. So, props to you Hanna Diyab! Let your contributions be known!

generic 'exotic', by way of North Africa, South America, the Arab world and South Asia.

Aged six, I had no way of knowing how or if these things belonged together, or what they referenced in the real world. I just accepted what I was shown and took this mixed bag to mean 'Agrabah' and, by extension, 'Where The-Laila-Coloured-People are'. Most films took place somewhere real, so even if Agrabah did not exist, somewhere that contained all those things (and, crucially, people that looked like me) did. Surely. Because why would *Aladdin* be any different from literally all the other princess films?

I spent many long, lonely hours watching our tape and trying to glean information, as if *Aladdin* were a travel documentary or a manual for self-mastery. Those characters were pretty much all I had, so they had to represent SO much more than any one film or character could. In my case, the ninety minutes of *Aladdin* were a de facto stand-in for an entire community I hadn't found and a link to a whole hypothetical culture I could be part of. I didn't have anywhere else to look – I had tried, in both the school library and the one in town, as well as every kids' show on TV. If you were after a white princess in a white world, you could choose a bookish one in a small town, a cheerful one in a leafy forest, or a graceful one in a complicated family, but if you were my colour, you just had Jasmine.

Years dawdled by, endless springs that stretched yawningly from February to July (summer was a few short days at best) and marked by clamorous winters that tore branches from trees and stole clanking slates from roofs. On snowy mornings we'd wait tensely for the phone to ring confirming yes, school was cancelled, and then we'd dash outside and play all day, avoiding winds that tried to snatch your cheeks and chasing snowballs and sledges down the mountain. We graduated from Class 1 to Class 2 and from McDonald's birthdays to Charlie Chalks. Martin and Kayleigh got a climbing frame and a dog. Lisa, Dawn and Jake got a paddling pool and the very first PlayStation. I got glasses and a desk in my room for drawing, and when I brushed my teeth I was now tall enough to see the top of my head in the mirror above the sink.

I became more aware of having Dad around or not. Novelties like a third plate on the counter for dinner or the stone once again hosting Dad's keys, and perks such as Dad being more likely to give in to my needling and buy Frosties instead of regular cornflakes. Things felt more solid with Dad: he said something, like, *I'm going out now*, and then did. When it was just me and Mum, life felt looser; days had a hazy dreamlike quality, like peering through fog, time passing strangely and activities occurring at random, like, *Laila, it's dinnertime*, or, *We have to go to piano*.

When Dad was away, Mum and I were more likely to be approached by strangers. Like the man who approached us in the library and asked Mum where I was from, and the woman at the post office who'd picked up a bit of my hair and then told Mum how soft it was, and the lady in a queue who thought Mum was my childminder, or the cashier at Sainsbury's who said I had 'exotic eyes'. One time, I was in a cafe with Mena and our mums when two older ladies stopped next to us and literally stroked my hair like I was a cat whilst saying I was a 'lovely little thing'. I didn't like this at all. It never happened to any of my friends, so it underlined that I wasn't supposed to be here and maybe wasn't supposed to exist. But I didn't know how to prevent it. I thought maybe they'd stop as I got older, but they didn't.

When Dad was around we had different food; he brought home Bombay mix or samosas (my all-time favourite), and fruits like mango and lychees. We went out for Indian food at a restaurant with menus and napkins (later in life I was shocked to discover restaurants serving other types of cuisine). The only time Mum and I went out for dinner was when we got fish and chips from the chippy on rattling cold nights. Dad listened to Radio 4, which had *no songs*, and he didn't watch any of the same TV shows as us. We watched shows involving vets and sick pets, or home designs and water features, or programs about going on holiday. Dad watched *Channel 4 News* – the long one – and documentaries with hard-sounding words about things I didn't know. Even the energy was different when Dad was around. He was always asking me questions, wanting to hear about school and my friends and what I had learned that day; or dashing out the front door, with people to meet or places to be or something urgent and undefined to check up on.

In school holidays we went down to stay with him in the flat. London was fun – there were big shops, like the giant Disney Store (they had an entire Princess Jasmine *section*), and a big cinema (they had popcorn *and* ice cream), and a big park with deer and a fountain and lots of good trees for climbing. And my big brother, Hass, was in London too! Hass had a ponytail, and he did martial arts and salsa dancing, and he worked in a restaurant, and he was the coolest person in the whole world. He was smart and funny, and he could do anything. Sometimes he came round to babysit me – we were allowed to get a takeaway and choose a film from the video shop! My brother was the same colour as me, I guessed because he was my big brother, but this wasn't completely clear because he was also only a *sort-of* brother (he had a different mum and dad, and he was *really* my cousin), but it would have been highly offensive to describe him as anything other than my big brother because that's what he had always been. Mum said he was there when I was just a little baby being born, and there was a picture of this: me as a tiny blob baby and Hass as a lanky teenager with thick floppy hair.

But we didn't see Hass that much, so my me-coloured people list stayed small. Back in Wales, with no new me-coloured people on my list, I stuck to revisiting Jasmine until eventually my gilded love for her tarnished like the lamp bracelet I'd gotten years before. Much like the strange green marks around my wrist, several issues became unavoidable. Like: why doesn't Jasmine have a song? Nearly all of the other Disney princesses sing the first and/or last tune of their film, but Aladdin has to lead Jasmine to the world of song when she finally pipes up in the love duet 'A Whole New World'. Jafar gets a song, Genie gets two songs, and Aladdin gets three separate songs. Even an unnamed merchant never seen again gets a song! Why doesn't Jasmine? And why isn't Jasmine in the title? All previous princesses were the headline act (*Snow White, Cinderella, Sleeping Beauty, The Little Mermaid, Beauty and the Beast*[8]). Jasmine was second billing to the boy. I know now that Disney used the name of the source material (as they had done for all others),

---

8. This continued later into the 90s with *Pocahontas* and *Mulan*.

but back then, it just implied that Jasmine was less important than the other princesses. She had less screen time, fewer songs, less acknowledgment in the title. Jasmine just had less to do, it seemed.

Iffy queries − like, say, realising Princess Jasmine wasn't in a real place − became big issues, because I couldn't shrug it off and reinvest in another brown Disney princess. Instead, her lack of real-life location became something I, too, lacked. That single depiction bore the weight of representing a whole community; I hero-worshipped, only to feel crushed, and somehow personally responsible if a character was in any way negated.

Humans are visual; we see the world long before we can ask about it. We observe what others look like long before we know the complexity of their personalities. First impressions count, and we intuitively look for commonalities. Think about how kids will grab on to a character with the same hair colour as them or how owning the same coat as a person on telly can be the difference between who is your favourite and who you simply do not understand. We resonate with the characters that represent some part of us.

Christmas, 1997. I am seven years old. Though I no longer believe in Santa, presents are still the most exciting part of the day. My parents buy me a crayon wheel for Christmas, a plastic turntable that spun around and housed sixty-four − *sixty-four!!* − different colours of crayons. Pastel crayons, shiny crayons, glittery crayons − even one that glowed in the dark! But I went straight for the multiple different shades of brown. *Brown!* Usually the boring crayons that get ground down the slowest, but all I saw when I spun to this section was an endless world of self. For the first time, I was able to sketch the outline of myself, lay my arm down next to it and see the same colour there on the paper. *Raw Sienna. Burnt Umber. Sepia. Tan.* Family portraits became miraculously accurate overnight. After all that wondering, all the confusion and trying to create a colour out of nothing, receiving this gift was like finding some long-lost mythical artefact. I could sense its power and magic, and the paths I could explore now opening up in front of me. Finally, I had the means to draw myself, to prove that I exist.

And then I remember a small shred of baffled frustration sneaking in, thinking: *this is it?* This is all it took to add myself in? None of the animators in the world ever got a Crayola colour wheel for Christmas?

Chapter Two

LAST OF THE DRAGON'S BLOOD

We didn't have a family motto, but we *did* have two ringing catchphrases that people chanted at us wherever we went: *Where are you from?* and *How do you spell that?* The latter was easy, I heard my mum and dad perform the spelling down the phone and out in public[1] several times a day, like it was our own personal radio jingle. But the first question was a mystery. Where *were* we from? It was easy enough to think of myself as Welsh: I belonged here in the gardens and the woods, among the trees and stars. Technically, I knew Mum had dual British and US citizenship, and that she was born in Uganda and grew up moving around East Africa, but it was easier to think of her as a one-dimensional thing: American. Everyone knew America[2]; America was *cool* – Hollywood and hamburgers, corndogs and Clintons, Sunny Delight and *Saved by the Bell*. Mum had

---

1. They went for the rhythmic approach, 'double-you, double-oh, zed-double-ee-are', which I initially copied before switching to 'double vowels, single consonants' later, once the digital era dawned.
2. At the time people said 'America' when what they were really referring to was just the country of the United States of America, aka, the USA.

29

the accent and the passport; she made American-style pancakes (thick, with butter and maple syrup) and American-style cookies (large, with huge chunks of chocolate, legendary at school bake sales). She called break time 'recess', rubbish 'trash', and the cellar the 'basement'; oh boy, she was American alright, neat-o, gee whizz! Besides, everyone else saw her as American. People asked, 'Is your mum American?' And I'd go, 'Yep!' And they'd happily reply, 'Yeah, I guessed from the voice!' Like, case closed, nice and easy! I never mentioned her schooling in Nigeria or Mum's rogue Scottish parent, because that didn't fit in with 'America'. It was easier to just go along with what people wanted to think.

Dad, on the other hand, was from Mauritius: somewhere nobody knew anything about, least of all me, and so Dad was the *properly* foreign parent: dark skin, weird name, unplaceable accent and unknowable country. Mum was just *American*: familiar, less of a threat. Dad spoke another language and ate different foods that weren't easily available. If you wanted American cuisine, you just went to McDonald's. Aside from being raised on a diet of largely American culture, my house held a collection of Mum's old American school textbooks, which I would pore over, familiarising myself with their stateside quirks: kids in grades, measurements in pounds and ounces, music in half and quarter notes. My relatives in the US (aunts and great-aunts) regularly sent gifts featuring what I thought of as 'American' situations: stickers of raccoons and beavers, cards printed with Thanksgiving scenes, and books like *Little House on the Prairie* and the American Girl series[3]. I knew nothing of general Brit-

---

3. Shout-out to the OG Kirsten Larson.

ish history – we lacked feasible plucky heroines – but the Welsh myths we learned at school sat side by side with images of log cabins and horses of the American Wild West in my head; my two threads of known history. This neatly discounted my dad from the proceedings because I didn't understand where he was from; but he wasn't around much anyway, so that was that.

Aside from the deluge of American-based news, films and TV, there was a magnet on the fridge that said 'Oregon', which, according to Mum, was the specific place where her family were. You could learn a lot from a magnet. It was green, with a pattern of trees and mountains. I'd asked why, and Mum had said, 'That's what Oregon is like. Forests and mountains and huge trees.' I asked more and received accordingly: *Oregon had deer and moose, and beavers and groundhogs, and chipmunks – you know, like Chip and Dale!* Somewhere in my mind, I pictured Mum in this context: watched her walking through a dense forest (for some reason she was dressed in brown and wearing a raccoon hat) and heard the wind whistling through the leaves and the frantic scuffle of a chipmunk dashing through a tree (did they dash up trees or was that just squirrels?); saw her suddenly turn at a cracking sound from something larger moving in the woods – a stalking coyote or maybe a moose, antlers rustling the boughs, or a grizzly bear stealthily crossing a ridge. I didn't describe this scene to my mum, and it wasn't rooted to anything she said – it just occurred in my head – yet I filed it away under 'Mum's childhood' and 'America' without any corroboration and referred back to it for years. Either way, it was a magnet more than I had for Mauritius.

Mostly, *I* felt Welsh. I knew *Wales*, felt *Welsh* in some way: surrounded by verdant Welsh valleys and more myths than mountains. I learned Welsh culture and Welsh songs and even the actual Welsh language at school. In my room, I had a felt daffodil from last year's St David's Day, a Cymru flag we'd made at school and a handcrafted Welsh Dragon bookmark – y Ddraig Goch – that Mum got me when I sang at the Llangollen Eisteddfod[4]. Though my accent was different to those of my parents, it was the same sing-songy vaguely northern/ vaguely Welsh accent as everyone else around me, peppered with 'oh aye' and 'fair do's' – proper Wrexham, like. I *knew* the world around me and it was familiar and safe; I had a sense of place here, a sense of belonging. Even though we weren't actually Welsh and just lived here, it didn't matter to me, because it was home.

As I grew older, I began to resent our constant back and forth trips in the car, my backpack crammed around my feet for hours and the grumbly sound of the motorway for the eternity it took to reach London. Sure, Dad was in London, but he was sometimes here, and even the best things in London (like the video shop and the park with deer) paled in comparison to being in Wales. I wanted to stay *home* in half term and play with my friends and go into town, not head away from all my stuff to where everything was different. Even the skies were different in London: only grey or blue, with a sometimes moon but never stars (Dad said it was light pollution, but I knew the truth, they told me: they just didn't like moving from the mountains). The only areas of my life that were consistent were the parts that connected it: the car and the roads. Endless

---

4. It's a wonder I didn't spontaneously burst into a rendition of 'Men of Harlech' at any given moment.

steadfast motorways as we trundled between different editions of our lives. When we drove at night, I'd sleep in the back seat with my head cradled by the seatbelt, watched by the unending rhythm of the car lights catching the cat's eyes like reflections in a river, streetlights passing above me like they'd tried to copy the stars, and failed.

In the mid-90s, my maternal grandparents retired to a small house in the middle of the Welsh coast, a few hours' drive from us. We visited them during school holidays when we weren't off to see Dad in London. I was used to long drives by now – I knew how many books I could read on the journey and which tapes of nursery rhymes were most fun to listen to on repeat when we drove out of radio reception range.[5] Grandma was short and round with a grey bob and wore printed cotton dresses; Grandad was tall and angular, like a wooden ruler in a cardigan and cap. Sometimes my aunt was there too, my mum's youngest sister; all chipper smiles and ginger hair. Mum told me that Grandma had always wanted to come and live in Wales, where her mother was from. Wait – what? Nobody had mentioned this before. I thought Grandma was American – you know, like my American mum and all my other relatives in America – and that Grandad was Scottish, which conjured up images of moody cows and tartan. So Grandma was . . . half-*Welsh*? Amazing – I was, in fact, actually Welsh through heritage (although what this meant for the American side of things, I had no idea).

---

5. Shout out to my mum for putting up with The Smurfs Christmas Party on a loop during the 1997 summer holidays.

Nearly all my memories of my maternal grandparents are to do with their belongings and not them as people. My grandparents' house, for instance: old and vaguely creepy; the smell of cork and talcum powder; all cold hard floors and oppressive furniture. You were never properly warm and there was something faintly sinister about the damp spare room where we stayed on a sofa bed – it was crammed full of boxes that hadn't been unpacked, with thick, heavy curtains and so much lace netting that natural light was obscured. The house was laden with stuff everywhere: pictures and clocks and mirrors on the walls, framed photos and knick-knacks lining every surface, and shelves crammed with dusty, wedged-in books and fragile ornaments. Even something as simple as the arm of a chair would house a blanket and a glove and a coaster and a mug and a hankie and a bible and a glasses case and a sewing project and a pocket diary and a copy of *Reader's Digest*. When I was older, we'd sometimes visit so that Mum could help them sort out all this stuff. They had all manner of curious possessions, such as heavy bolts of mothball-scented cloth and ancient leather-bound books. Once my mum and auntie were liberating another box of stuff and uncovered some solid brass candlesticks shaped like snakes: Mum and her siblings all found them creepy, and wanted to give them to charity, but I loved them, the cool, solid feel of them; the etching of scales and the way they gently caught the light and glittered. So, I asked Mum, if nobody wants them then can I have them? She didn't say yes exactly – they were an ancient heirloom and not a toy; they weren't passing my grandparents' things down to us kids yet; I absolutely could not have candles or indeed any kind of open flames in my room – but she did relent and take them out of the charity shop bag. I didn't know who ended up with them, but I liked to imagine them slithering companionably round the house, twinkly and golden. My grandparents didn't have any Disney videos, just ones about Jesus or TV dramas from the 1970s, and their vast collection of kids' books was even older (Enid Blyton was the contemporary option). They had lots of awkward rules I didn't understand – napkins in rings, grace before eating and an explicit requirement to go to church on Sundays, which was not just incredibly boring but also required wearing smart (aka uncomfortable) clothes. Though my grandparents were always welcoming, between the poky wooden chairs and too-firm sofa bed, it never felt cosy to be there (aside from my aunt's room, which was tiny and had a big quilt and a cat). Later in life, Mum would tell me it was Grandma's lifelong dream to have the whole family to stay and I'd uncharitably wonder why they'd chosen somewhere not just off-putting but also so incredibly far from literally every other relative.

Still, I liked the days we went to the Ceredigion coast and I could run around the windy, whippy Welsh waves – rolling up to the cobbled shore like a single sheet of shivering sea – and I liked to clamber the jagged black rocks looking for seaweed and crabs and sparkling chunks of shell. I liked the small shop in the village, which sold felt-tips and puzzle books and homemade cake, and there were two truly mesmeric things about my grandparents' house: the friendly horse who lived in the field next door (if you gave him a carrot he would let you pat his nose!) and my grandmother's piano. Her piano was larger than our one at home, with a curious triple-jointed lid that required a certain steady hand to open properly: ours opened in one fluid, easy movement, but this piano required you to earn its respect through gentle coaxing before it let you play (it would have been easier to give it a carrot). It had a coppery, nostalgic sound, faintly jangly, like it had once lived in an old-timey saloon or been played at a county fair (or, at least, that's what I imagined those things sounded like). Who's to say I wasn't projecting my family hopes onto the one thing I felt I could link to (bar the horse, of course) and really it didn't sound like any of those things. Many years later, after they moved off the coast of England and my grandma was in a nursing home, I played that piano again, now sat in my grandad's small living room, and I just thought it sounded tired and in need of a tune.

Getting to know my grandparents totally upended my ideas on who I thought they were. Grandma spoke no Welsh, Grandad had an English accent (not Scottish) and their collective stories told me nothing about the countries I wanted to associate them with. They had spent over forty years in Africa, most of their adult lives, and this was reflected not just in their house décor (carved jungle animals and wicker baskets) but in their stories: tales of hippos in the river and chameleons in the garden, and a wild shrieking at night that sounded from the plains beyond the yard. Their *Americanness* was mostly confined to the piano. I didn't mind too much, as I was starting to know them as real people instead of abstract connections. My grandma had a big smile and loved having fresh flowers around the house; my grandad had a fondness for peppermint and telling elaborate riddles. And the sound of my grandma's laugh! Somehow childish and faintly mischievous, like she had the most delicious joke to tell if you were game enough to hear it.

But I didn't see how I linked with them; it was more like we were visiting Mum's friends and I had just tagged along. Visiting my grandparents helped me understand Mum better. When she talked about growing up in and moving around Africa, it felt isolating and bizarre to me; both as an experience she had lived through and something to understand about who she was. It wasn't something anyone else's mum had done or in fact anyone else I knew, full stop – but she and her parents were connected by this. I felt more connected to the other people in my grandparents' village – local Welsh people. Most were Welsh speakers – some only spoke Welsh – and were thrilled by me and my tiny attempts to share what I'd learned at school. A tentative bore da and da iawn diolch went a long way, even if I couldn't carry a conversation, and they'd pass on phrases and new words to me, dyfal donc a dyr y garreg and a book all in Welsh called *Taith Y Pererin*. Anyway, it was more Welsh than anyone else in my family could speak. And it made sense somehow; Mum and her parents, peas in a pod, American by way of growing up in Africa; and me, a tag-along separate entity, Welsh, kin of valleys and dragons, of pride and music.

It's weird to think I was bonding with some neighbour down the way whilst three actual living members of my family were in the front room; like, *hello*, go and hang out with your relatives! But there were many reasons I felt like they were Mum's relatives and not mine. The most obvious one is they were white: she looked like them; I didn't. She understood the unfamiliar structure of their house – the grace and the church and the napkin rings – in ways I didn't. Also, Dad was never present with my mum and me at their house, ostensibly because he was working – although it also felt like this wasn't

Dad territory: he was absent from the row of framed photos that showed me and my aunties and uncles and cousins. And as my mum and I shared a sofa bed in the cramped spare room, there was literally nowhere he could have fit.

In the same way that my mum's parents only connected to her, my dad's family only connected to him, largely because only he knew about them and only he could speak to them. I hadn't met them or seen pictures of them, apart from one picture of my dad's mum, which was on a very high shelf in the living room, out of view to me.[6] Like extended relatives on my mum's side, they sent cards in the post, and I understood they existed in theory, but to all intents and purposes they were hypothetical. During my early childhood, Dad's relatives were even more unknown to me than Mum's, who at least hovered into the periphery of our lives from time to time. There was a set of cousins of Dad's who lived in Birmingham – they had a pretty house and always served tasty food. But apart from them, Dad's relatives were either foreign voices on the other end of the phone or dead.

Two distinct and separate families, each belonging to one parent. Neither one of those sides felt related to me and my little life in Wales. It sounds sad, writing it down, but it was comforting: Mum was American, and she had her people on the phone and her relatives off somewhere in the world; Dad was Mauritian, and he had his people on the phone and his relatives off somewhere in the world. And I was Welsh, safe

---

6. Later in life, fully grown, I was shocked to discover this shelf was not eight feet up but waist height.

in local solace. I had my friends and my neighbours and my school and my dance classes; I had the myths and the music and the mountains and the trees. I had the reliability of rain and the mighty righteous dragons.

Except how much of this was true? Because none of that was really the case, was it? It was all fine to tell myself this was how me and my parents fit, a neat triangle diagram to soothe myself with, but it didn't hold up to any scrutiny. It was fine telling my classmates that my mum was American – but she lived in Wales. I'd ask Mum about 'homecoming' to fact-check – you know, because she was the authentic American one and all – but her years moving around Africa rendered her as clueless as me when it came to the details of high school life. In her final year of high school alone, she'd gone to two new schools: she had no idea about letterman jackets because she'd been too busy trying to keep on top of where she actually was. Many years later, she'd tell me the UK was the first place she'd truly lived and felt a sense of home. I'd try asking, *Mum, does the boy always get the girl a corsage for prom?* And instead of a definite answer or neat anecdote, she'd frown and say, *That sounds about right, sure.* Or suggest I ask my cousins (who I'd never met) who were more au fait with the local culture. Surely you were either American or you weren't?

Even Mum seemed confused. A layer of fog over everything that I peered through curiously. Mum's accent changed when she was on the phone to her US-based siblings, becoming more American, speech patterns shifting into something more rounded and bouncy. She sometimes hesitated between describing herself as a British or American citizen, like neither was truly correct. On cards she signed her name to me as Love

Mum/Mom, covering both the British and American bases – but also suggesting she was quite literally two different people.

Did I have a *mum* or a *mom*? Who was the other one and what was the difference? (Family lore says that one Christmas I got annoyed with this and asked her to stop and stick with Mum, which she did.) It's only as an adult I realised she probably saw herself as Mom, whilst to me she was always Mum.

And how much of this was true on my dad's side? Dad often told me in no uncertain terms that he was British. This did not fit at all with the internal set-up I was working to. People regularly thought he was Jamaican, so he didn't *look* British. How could he be British if nobody else thought so? Even more confusing, Dad also told me I was British. So, why were we so different from everyone else we knew? I'd ask him, *Where am I from? Where are we from? What about Mauritius?* And he'd look a bit confused and reply, *I'm British, why do you ask?* Or, *What do you want to know about Mauritius? We're here now.* This is what's happening now, so let's focus on that. Alternatively, the immigrant parent classic: *You're British. Why are you asking about being from somewhere else?* I could see this was frustrating for Dad, like he was repeatedly telling me that the sky was blue and I just wasn't getting it, but I didn't know where to go to find answers.

At one point, aged seven, Dad sat down with me at the kitchen table, my children's atlas between us. In theory, I'd learned about all the countries when I'd stuck each flag sticker next to its allotted country, but in reality the allure of *over a hundred stickers* had proved a major distraction, and the only flag I could easily recall was Nepal (it was a cool shape).

'Okay. So, I'm from Mauritius. Your cousins live there. You've been there once, when you were a baby.' I sat across from Dad as he spoke, following along, swinging my legs around as I couldn't yet reach the floor.

'Where's Mauritius?' I asked. There was no Mauritius sticker.

'It's next to another island called Madagascar. And next to *that* is Africa.' Dad reached over and tried to find the appropriate page. 'It's here.' He pointed unconvincingly at a patch of space as I tapped my feet together.

'It's that big one?'

'No, that's Africa. And this is Madagascar.' He pointed at a small island; a tiny mark on the page to the right of the big shape of Africa. 'You can't see Mauritius very well, it's too small. It's here though,' he continued, coaxingly. I stared at the entirely blue square searching for a dot even smaller than the Madagascar one, but saw nothing. Mauritius didn't appear to exist. I looked at Dad. Surely he could see this. Maybe he was trying to persuade even himself. 'Okay then.' A weak smile. No questions, okay, that's that, it's clear now! And then Mum came back in and started to cook dinner and that really was that.

All I took from this was that Mauritius was insignificant: not a place to be noticed and not something to be proud of. Maybe even something to be ashamed of. I had never heard of Mauritius on TV, in books, in films, on the news, *anywhere* – quite unlike America, my other country. Maybe Mauritius wasn't a proper country. I mean, what kind of country doesn't even get featured in the atlas book – how small did you have to *be*? I imagined an area the size of the school hall, floating around in the sea, or the desert islands cartoon characters ended up on with a single palm tree and a deck chair. People said the UK was small, but the UK was clearly visible on a map – it had a shape and a capital city and everything. Mum's country – the

USA – had two whole pages in the atlas! Mauritius must be *tiny*.

And that was the sum total of my feelings on Mauritius – until the summer holidays, when three of the most marvellous weeks took place, and we went all the way to see Mauritius. I was as excited about spending this length of time with both parents as I was about meeting Dad's family. Everyone said Mauritius was a small island like the UK – so I guessed it would be the same, plus sunshine. But the moment we left the plane we were hit with a bright warmth, the railings on the stairs blazing hot, the air smelling of sugar and smoke, and we were still in the airport disembarking when it became clear, no, we were somewhere entirely *new*. Jubilant music was playing – drums and happy voices – and there were elaborate painted murals on the walls, brightly coloured wooden dioramas of fish and jungles and oceans and sky. Even the car journey from the airport was thrilling; tiny rainbow-coloured buildings and glowing glass-cased shrines dotted the sides of the roads, huge purple mountains and dark swathes of jungle in the distance, and the sky above a clear shimmery blue, like a tumbled gem. Mauritius was sand and ocean and mountains and jungle and city; practically every type of location I'd ever seen, *simultaneously*, like some wild mash-up level in a game, except it was real.

Dad pointed out the fields filled with huge, towering green sticks far taller than I was.

'Laila, do you know what this is?' I didn't, but it looked intriguing – a jungle of long tendrils and leaves waving merrily at us in the breeze. 'It's sugar cane. That's where sugar comes from.'

I thought of sugar: small white granules in hard paper packets. I'd never thought of sugar being organic matter, as something that *grows*. I thought Dad meant some other thing called sugar, but he said no, it was the *same thing*, the sugar in the packets started out as these towering plants jostling for slices of sun by the motorway. How could something as pedestrian as sugar start off so majestic and vibrant as this sprawling thicket next to us, it was magic! 'Next time we get a packet, we can see if it came from Mauritius.'

The marvels were just beginning. We saw monkeys in the trees, geckos on the ceilings and huge bats that flew around the peach-yellow evenings by the mangroves. The smell of grilled fruit and rum filled the air against the sound of waves lapping and birds cooing. There was a shy plant that curled up when you touched it, and another plant that looked fluffy but was sticky and only grew on trees but sometimes jumped over to your clothes if you walked too near. 'Oops, it thought you were a tree,' said Dad, picking the plant off and returning it to the trunk. Wow! The *plant* thought I was a *tree*! We went to the sea, which was hot and smelled of seaweed and suntan lotion, and ranged from bright blue to dark green to murky turquoise to fuzzy navy to jet black to regal mauve to twinkly lilac (the prettiest one), depending on which part of the long loopy beach you stood on, colours too bright for me to colour. The sand was smooth and warm to run along – no pebbles or jagged edges, just soft shimmery sand like angel dust. At one corner of the sand, waves came in from three different directions and overlapped at curious angles. The water was shot through with thin silver threads that *moved* – Dad said they were actually tiny fishes. I placed my feet between the separate parts of the sea as it changed direction at will, touching three seas at once. The sea buried my legs in wet sand the same colour as my skin, like my feet disappeared into the sand and I had grown right there out of the sea.

Dad said all life had actually started in the ocean, that nobody was on the lands – nobody at all – until the fish walked out of the sea and grew into humans.[7] A *fish* that walked! A fish that kept on growing until it was a *human*! The Welsh sea washed up stringy black knots and occasional rocks; here we found pearly pink conches, a huge starfish bigger than my hand, giant squiggles of plasticky red and purple seaweed, and one day a spiky brown plant – except when I showed it to Dad he said, 'Be very careful, Laila, don't step on it,' because it wasn't a plant, it was an urchin, an animal. It was a living creature, like me and Dad!

Every day, I learned about dozens of new things I had no idea existed. One day, we went to buy food at the market – it was bustling with people, hot and noisy, with all sorts of scents wafting over to us like fresh chapatis and salted lassi and grilled fruit and fried noodles. I'd had a good look around Sainsbury's and could name every vegetable in the aisle, but at the market with Dad I saw dozens of new things: huge clattery coconuts, giant ridgy jackfruit and tangy yellow star fruit. There were peppers, like the red and green ones at home but here they were orange, pink, white, purple and striped. Stallholders sold dragon fruit that was a deep bright pink like if you'd held a

---

7. I'll clarify that I was too young to grasp the hundreds of millions of years of evolution that happened in between.

felt-tip in the same place too long, soft mangos with pastel green and red skins, and perfectly ripe papayas that, cut open, looked like the flesh of the sun. We chopped the coconuts and drank the sweet water inside – the taste of clear skies and seashells – and Dad carved the mango and gave me slices to eat, small fingers scrabbling to hold it by the skin, sticky and yellow and dripping onto my knees; it tasted like wide smiles and treats.

'Can you taste that, Laila?' he asked. 'It's fresh. You couldn't get it this fresh in the UK.'

We kept seeing the image of one particular bird, a funny round bird with a friendly face and a curved beak. The dodo. Mauritius's national bird, since shortly after the first humans arrived. Despite becoming extinct over three hundred years ago, we saw dodos *everywhere*: in shops, on signs, used in advertising, even on money and the passport stamp. And we saw dogs; I'd thought it was the same dog – sandy brown with warm brown eyes and one floppy ear and one straight – smiling and following us everywhere, but then we saw two! Twins! Amazing, like the dog had just split into two. And then one day, a whole pack of them by the bins! Dozens of identical grinning dogs, like they had all come from the same place, one large pack of the exact same dog over and over. Dad said they were stray and they lived all together like that. I asked what kind of dog they were and why they all looked the same.

'They're mongrel dogs; they're a mixture of lots of things.'

Wow – like me! Dad said they were likely all related and that's why they looked the same. I pressed my face against the back window of the rented car, looking at my street dog siblings, happily scavenging for scraps and grinning at each other.

I loved the dusty ground, spackled with something sparkly. And I loved the heat – it wasn't just 'warm', like British summer sometimes was, it was hot like the weather wanted to prove a point; the sun walloping you in the face whenever you left an air-conditioned car in the afternoon. I was always cold in Wales, but here my small body felt literally warmed with joy; nourished by the burning sky. Mum told me to stay in the shade, but I stuck my arms out defiantly to feel the sun's embrace, or wobbled my feet free of my jelly sandals to feel the scorching ground underneath; and when I twiddled my hair as I went to sleep it still felt hot, holding on to remnants of sunshine.

I'd read so many stories about faraway places and now I was in one. Everything was vibrantly alive and even the names of animals sounded out of a storybook: red-whiskered bulbuls, zebra doves, red fodies, silver moonfish and Mauritian flying foxes – not actually foxes but bats, and not bats like in Wales but *megabats*. Not only were we in this fantastical *actual real* place, but Dad was from here. *I* was from here! Surely nobody could descend from this magical place without having a little bit of magic left over.

And among all these myriad wonders was the best part: *family*! My family were in Port Louis: the bustling, crowded capital of Mauritius, a ramshackle jumble of brightly painted homes and ornate buildings lining worn, lived-in roads. My auntie's house had a large yard, which had an earthy smell of damp clay and a seemingly permanent faint rustling in the trees. There were cooing chickens in the yard, stray kittens who meowed at the doorstep and (supposedly) the occasional flash of mongoose over the wall. I'd never even heard of a mongoose, and they weren't geese at all, but small furry things a bit like a weasel and a ferret and a kitten all combined. I never actually saw one but they were there, Dad said so, and every time I sat up by the window and eagerly scanned the hedges Dad said they were probably watching me back, too shy to say hello.

My Mauritian family began with my auntie (my dad's older sister) and uncle, and my two adult cousins, Iqbal and Ameena, and extended to more cousins and relatives, and all the way out to friends of my father and old neighbours. We'd spend afternoons in the living room where the always open front door welcomed a constant parade of cheerful visitors hugging my dad and bearing gifts. People who knew us! Dad himself was different: happier, speaking Creole, which sounded warmer, more laidback and less awkward than English. Even his name was different – nobody called him Rowf like in the UK, it was Rah-oov instead; softer, gentler. *My* name sounded different. Both 'Laila' and 'Woozeer' were heavy, pointed syllables in the UK. *Lay-ler.* Thunk thunk. *Woo-zeer.* Bong bong. Here they jumped around a bit more; Laila had an uptick in the middle and sounded like a mystical chorus instead of a doorbell. Here, Dad was not just Dad; he was a brother, an uncle, a close family friend. He existed here in ways I never saw at home. I wondered if I could belong somewhere like that; easily, innately, unquestionably.

Dinner with my family was a heaving table crammed with unusual looking foods on a pristine cotton cloth; pungent briyani, thick rougaille, smoky gateau piment, soft warm breads and sharp coarse pickles. I didn't share my auntie's language but I could tell how much she loved me, because she quickly learned which foods I liked best and cooked them specially for me (we're talking homemade samosas here, people; *HOME-MADE. SAMOSAS.*), pinching my shoulder affectionately and ruffling my hair. I'd hold an oily, hot samosa on a paper napkin (Dad sent me into the yard in case of spills) and bite off a crisp corner, almost burning my tongue, too eager to wait for it to cool. Iqbal fetched fresh bread and extra napolitaines in the mornings because he knew I liked them – the bread was light and fluffy, and the napolitaines were delightfully bright pink, tasting of princess dreams and promises kept.

Every morning began with the call to prayer and the chickens crowing and the smell of spices and chai wafting upstairs, and I would wake up knowing I had family – family who *claimed* me, who *cared* for me, who knew *about* me. People, *tons* of people who knew me and looked like me and loved me. Pink cake for breakfast! I could hardly believe my luck. Is this the treatment everyone else got when they stayed the night at Grandma's, when they popped down for a weekly tea with their aunt? I'd been waiting my whole life to be here.

I had the same eyes as my auntie and Ameena, and my cousins and I shared similar dark hair in thick curls and waves. My family ranged in hue from my dad and auntie, the darkest, all the way to me, the lightest, although I'd gone much darker seemingly in transit, catching up to my cousins within days of arriving. Previously, I was all the same colour, but over the three weeks my skin patterned with pale patches untouched by the sun, darker patches that were always exposed, and various shades of warm chestnut brown everywhere else (some parts stayed like this; the random light square on my right thigh, which remained until my late teens, and the dark splodge on my left elbow which is still there now).

Compared to everyone else, Mum wasn't just white but devoid of colour, so pale people looked twice. Dad joked about this to me whilst we made sandcastles on the beach, whilst Mum lurked indoors, doused in factor 50 and sporting a floppy hat.

'Here she goes again, with her sun cream!' he'd say conspiratorially to me anytime Mum cracked out the Ambre Solaire. 'She can't handle the heat, can she?' Me and my dad may have been different colours to each other, but we were the same in the context of Mum: she was white, and we were not. This never worked the other way round. I'd known on some level we had this in common; but it was an important point to have clarity on, that Dad and I were a team in a way that Mum wasn't.

At my auntie's house I met a group of neighbourhood girls around my age. My cousin Ameena helped us over the language barrier and we spent all day, every day, playing in my cousins' yard; joyful hours with the cool, musty smell and the chickens burbling away, journeying in for warm gateaux piments and juice in the middle of the day when the sun grew strongest. I fit right in. Tanned forearms the same shade as mine covered in identical soft downy hair; long tangly ponytails of black ringlets; big brown eyes. When the Mauritian girls and I crossed our legs over each other for Stuck In The Mud, or stuck our hands in a ring to draw straws, our limbs blurred into one flesh-toned mass. We lined up facing the wall for Granny's Footsteps and became a row of matching dark-haired heads. I had no idea I looked the same as *anyone*, and I'd never in my life played with *four* people who looked like me *simultaneously*. It was magic. Nobody said anything back home, but they didn't need to: I saw it. We all did. I was *different*. And in Mauritius, for the first time in my life, I was experiencing being the same.

Chapter Three

WE THROW THE BURNED ONES OUT

By the age of nine, all I really understood about myself was that I was *weird*. The lack of understanding over who I was and where I fit got correspondingly bigger as I did: it was fine to run around confused as a small child but as a Big Kid, I should be able to assert some solid facts on how I connected to the wider scheme of things. As I grew older, the conflict over where I should *be*, and more than that, where I *belonged*, intensified. I resented going to London. I missed Mauritius. I didn't understand family in the US. Different lives with different Lailas didn't fit together, they just created jarringly discordant and multiple existences. Was I a Mauritian girl somehow in Wales, or a Welsh girl visiting London, or London-born part-American, part-Welsh and supposed to be in Mauritius? I had no common threads between any of these Lailas. Even small things were different, like common phrases ('dead mint' and 'tidy' in Wrexham became 'awesome' in London, and in Mauritius the equivalent could be in Creole, Hindi or Urdu) or the same games having different names ('tick' in Wrexham and 'tiggy' in London and 'ka' in Mauritius). Even that one solid bedrock of my life, *TV*, was different (admittedly this was just because Mauritius TV was playing cartoons that had already ended[1] and Dad's house in London had cable[2], but still . . .). Each version of me was an abandoned outline on a page and none of them fit together to present a finished picture.

I had places that felt like home but weren't, and places I was supposed to belong but didn't. Welsh has a word, hiraeth, that describes a particular longing for a place you can't return to, a time that has ended, or maybe never truly was – a homesickness for a home that is no longer known. There's a grief-filled regret, and a mournful sorrow of incompleteness that sits in your soul alongside the knowledge that what was missing is lost. This is how it was for me. I was yearning for a time where I fit and a place where I made sense, like I could remember the warm secure way this made me feel – even though I had not experienced it. It was a feeling that was older than me and surrounded me, in the sacred spirit of the ancient stones of my home and the hiraeth of the hills; the nebulous connectedness I felt when I lay at the top of the mountain, listening to the roar of the Welsh wind that carried the echoes of the dragons; the way the quartz grew on the rocks, which grew out of the ground, and the way that everything around me had a place and a path and a purpose. That poised network of existence into which everything fit, everything that came before and after and around me and slotted together at precise intersections

---

1. French-dubbed Gummi Bears anyone?
2. Hellooooooo Cartoon Network!

of ever unfolding geometry, of beginnings and endings, of *belonging*. I felt that all around me, but wanted to feel it within, to hold instead of seek, and to know inherently I was home.

It became harder to avoid my *differences* as I got older; 'quirks' that had been tolerated when I was younger hardened into 'faults' that made me somehow abnormal. And the list mounted daily. There were the Big Things (not being the same colour, not being from anywhere, potentially not existing) sure, but I had a lot of smaller life quirks that also contributed to the overall sense that something was off. Home was off – I could see this from going to other people's houses – because we ate strange foods and had a long list of things we did not eat. We had a bizarre family set-up and didn't watch normal things like *The Simpsons* or *EastEnders* – I wasn't even *allowed* to watch those things. I didn't have siblings, or pets, or a regular *around* Dad; there was a noticeable (maybe even suspicious) lack of life in the house (unless you counted the spiders in the corners and the mice who sometimes pooped chocolate vermicelli under the sofas). My family was either spread out overseas or nearby but not very familyish, like my grandparents who lacked the approachability and familiarity of everyone else's nain and taids. And *I* was weird. I didn't understand the same slang as other kids or get the same references (presumably picked up from TV shows I wasn't allowed to watch or overheard from siblings I didn't have). Questions racked up. Why didn't I have cousins who came round like everyone else? Why did I have a name nobody had heard of? Why did Mum have an American accent if she wasn't really American? Who were we?

With Dad absent, I turned to Mum to make sense of things. Mum frequently seemed taken aback by my questions. She'd blink, then stare at me blankly before answering, or give a slight frown, like I was enquiring about something obscure that she had known only briefly a long time ago. This annoyed me. I wasn't asking about ancient history – this was our life! She was The Parent, and parents were supposed to have The Answers. Besides, I didn't have anyone else to ask. But she didn't have answers, or at least not ones I wanted.

Why don't we eat sausages or burgers? 'We don't eat pork.' But *why* don't we eat it, when everyone else does? 'We just don't.' Why doesn't Dad live with us? 'He has to work.' Why doesn't he work here? 'You'll see him soon.' Why are my cousins so far away and why haven't I met them? 'They live in America.' Why are we here then? 'We live here.' But *why*?!

Her answers didn't fulfil what I was looking for. I knew *where* my cousins were, but I wanted to know *why*: what event precisely had caused this chasm of distance that left the family spread across the globe? I *knew* Dad was working but I didn't understand what was so important about a job in London that he had to be there – Sainsbury's were hiring, he could work there and live with us. Mum's replies were sufficient only for a short time, and once they expired I went back in for more.

I discovered that if I repeated questions, Mum changed her answers. It was like uncovering different layers of the truth – or maybe parts of one big truth, and if I just asked the right questions I could excavate the full picture. Why don't we eat sausages or burgers? 'It's not good to eat too much of those foods.' But why don't we eat *any*? 'We can have jacket potatoes for supper.' Why don't we eat sausages or burgers? 'They're expensive.' But why can't I eat them at other people's houses? 'Because we don't eat them.'[3]

Sometimes I'd retire questions if I didn't find anything that helped me. Other times, I'd phrase them differently in case it uncovered new evidence. On and on we circled these query roundabouts. Nothing made sense; creating a contradictory maze of things I still didn't understand. *Can* we eat a burger? 'Yes, there's chicken burgers in the freezer, we can have them for tea.'

Mum likely heard anxiety in my questions and sought to soothe (most answers included variations of *don't worry* or *you'll see*) and as an adult with years of teaching experience, I know it can throw you when a child looks for answers you're not prepared for and don't necessarily have. And I was surely annoying as all hell, interrupting *Changing Rooms* for the seventeenth time to ask about beef. But as a child, Mum's non-explanations didn't just affect me at home, or in my understanding of myself: it affected me socially. A kid at school might ask where my dad was. Not having a dad was normal by the mid-90s; some kids had divorced parents, others had a dad who had left or was in prison, and some kids had never had a dad in the first place. No dad – no big deal. But I would stubbornly maintain that I *did* have a dad, he just wasn't there, and that particular scenario was pretty much unheard of.

'How come you don't have a dad, Laila?'

'I do have a dad. He's in London.' Confused looks. People didn't have dads in *London* unless the dad had moved out.

---

3. Birthday parties were a minefield of beef burgers, ham butties and mini sausage rolls.

'So your parents split up, like? What's he doing there?'

'He's working. No, they're not split up; he's in our house sometimes.'

'So, what, he's like a ghost? He doesn't live with you, does he. You sort of have a dad but you don't *really* have—'

'I DO have a dad! He's real! He just isn't here sometimes!'

It wasn't just Dad I was asked about but *everything*; the food and the telly and the name and the skin and all the rest of it. Though I had misgivings with Mum's paltry answers, I found myself not just repeating them but doubling down on them in defence; an early lesson in bald-faced hypocrisy. What other answers did I have? The truth was: I didn't know. It didn't make sense to anyone else and it didn't make sense to me.

The things I understood about myself were outside of home and family, and instead connected to the community. I knew the layout of my neighbours' houses and I knew the drive to school through the mountains. I knew the way the fire crackled in the middle of winter and the piercing acidic smell of the quarry when it rained. I knew the classmates I'd grown up with since we were toddlers, and I knew in many ways I was like everyone else at school. How we all preferred Fruit Salads to Blackjacks (even if they did make your tongue go a weird colour), how none of us were especially religious (apart from one boy in nursery who wasn't allowed to be in the Nativity or go to the doctor's), and how we all supported Wrexham in the footie even if the Red Dragons didn't win much and most people also supported somebody else. It didn't matter. We all came together to unanimously hate our archrivals, Chester City FC, aka the poshos over the border, in England.

But how local I myself felt was miles away from how we as a family were perceived. Nobody assumed I was local and people tended to ask, *Is your mum American?* or, *Is your dad Caribbean?* The Welshness I felt didn't extend to my parents – I'd learned what I knew about being Welsh at school, so it all ended the moment the bell rang. I could see I was sort of Welsh, but not quite as Welsh as everyone else; and I wasn't sure what else I was supposed to be. It ended up feeling like I was just less of a person.

My parents were raising me in a country they had no experience of growing up in. Why would they have known what constitutes a classic British dinner for kids? This enterprise would have been hard enough to figure out as a unit, but my parents did not share a background. If you are immigrants together, you at least share common ground with the other person, even if the new culture and society is a mystery: you may not know what other people's houses are serving for dinner, but you can at least serve the food you both remember eating as a child. My mum and dad are from two totally different backgrounds: different countries, societies, cultures, classes, races. Nothing from their experiences was shared prior to meeting, and they had no shared experiences with me. They weren't exactly new immigrants in the mid-90s – they'd both been here many years – but knowing what it was like to grow up in rural North Wales was a mystery to them. Add in the usual intergenerational differences between us, plus continually needing to catch up with one third of the family who was commuting to and fro, and you had, frankly, a lot of potential for a bit of a mess.

Increasingly, I could be found seeking solace round my neighbours' houses down the road. Kayleigh was into horses now and Martin introduced me to *South Park* and Man City. At Lisa, Dawn and Jake's house I basically became a fourth live-in kid. Things were aggressively normal over there, a slice of classic British life. They watched *normal* telly, like *Coronation Street* and *Catchphrase*; they did *normal* things in half term, like go to the pictures or saunter round town; they had *normal* food for tea, like chicken nuggets for mains and Penguin bars for afters (scarfed down whilst we endlessly reran the four levels of *Sonic 2*). Jake and I ate tea in the front room off of Backstreet Boys dinner trays (previously his sisters'), watching MTV with Lisa and Dawn, who were cool teenagers now and knew all the words to the Vengaboys' songs and Eiffel 65's 'Blue (Da Ba Dee)'. My house lacked the predictability of theirs. You could live a routine life at that house: no stray parents popping by once a month; no other languages spoken on the phone; no lonely afternoons wondering where Jasmine was and staring at the clouds.

Other people's houses had more people and, consequently, more going on. I laughed more, talked more, played more, *felt* more at my friends' and neighbours' houses, and key parts of myself were discovered at other people's houses. When other people were around, I liked making them laugh. I enjoyed playing with pets and animals. I loved video games (especially when those games were *GoldenEye 007* and *Need for Speed: II*). My existence started to be defined by escaping my actual reality. It was easier to fit in at other people's houses; the different parts fit together in ways they never could at mine, like my house was a jigsaw puzzle with half the pieces missing.

By nine, I had long known that people who looked like me did not belong in what I knew as 'everyday life'. I wasn't angry or frustrated about this, I just accepted it in the same way I accepted that Christmas wasn't in July. It was just one of those things. What can you do?

Well, you can fervently search for people who look like you and places you do belong. What had begun as me assembling a list of people that looked like me in my early years had become a constant need to track down any and all characters I could even slightly relate to. It was too much to hope for somebody like me (i.e. a brown girl in Wales or a character called Laila), so I latched on to any character that had dark hair, brown skin or a 'weird' name: assets I understood as the hallmarks of *me*. Even with these vague parameters, it was slim pickings. I was so starved of connection that even two out of three was enough.

How do you find yourself? Pre-Google[4] this was mostly through TV and books. Luckily, those worlds were broadening. Dad's house got upgraded cable, meaning I could now access Cartoon Network, Nickelodeon *and* Fox Kids (the thinker's choice). I trained the VCR to record late-night hours of obscure 'kids' TV programming at Dad's house (you know – *cable*) in case I was missing a sort-of-like-me character on some random cartoon nobody had ever heard of (cut to an awestruck young me watching the finale of *Neon Genesis Evangelion* with zero context). On regular TV, the success of Pokémon arriving

---

4. Well, technically, Google had launched by then but 'searching the internet' may as well have been 'translate classical Latin' for all I knew about it.

on *SM:TV Live* meant a slew of other Japanese kids' shows came on air (usually horrendously dubbed and shown in totally random orders destroying any logical arc – but who cared) and I was old enough to not cling to Mum in shops, now allowed to rifle independently through the kids' sections of old books and comics in charity shops or plumb the depths of the big kids' section at the library. I scouted every available outlet for people that looked like me with the same zeal as I scanned booster packs for a shiny Charizard.

All of my searching led me to incredible treasures. Delving deep into charity shop kids' sections, I found old girls' annuals from the 60s, 70s and 80s and promptly fell in love. They usually contained two kinds of stories: either wholesome accounts of cute girls baking and playing with kittens, or alluring tales of older girls in terrific outfits who flounced around dramatically and wept over boys. One day, in an old *Twinkle* annual, I found an unexpected *third* story: the tale of Soraya. Soraya had dark hair and an unusual name (like me!), and she lived with her pet lion (!) in a faraway desert land, complete with sultans, princes, treasures and palm trees. Her story was nothing like the series of adorable cupcakes or anguished heartbreak, just action, adventure and heroics – and she was like me. I longed for more Soraya stories (or, in truth, more Sorayas) but I found these annuals by chance. If another edition featured Soraya, I never found it – still, Soraya was one more to add to my collection.

Discovering the limited offering of anime shown on British terrestrial TV led me to entrancing films that were somehow both poignant and whimsical, like *Only Yesterday*, and TV shows with multi-arc, interwoven plotlines, sprawling lore and huge casts of characters who roamed complex worlds – complex in a way that called to me. My favourite was Sailor Moon, about a group of teenage girls with magical powers and killer wardrobes who fight intergalactic crime. Watching it was an absolute mission (almost on a par with fighting intergalactic crime); it was on at random, unadvertised times on Fox Kids who aired episodes from the first three story arcs in non-chronological order. I would videotape episodes whenever I was at Dad's then watch the sacred tapes endlessly back in Wales; they were usually scrappily recorded and missing scenes, almost always on the tape in a bizarre order. It basically required a full-length investigation to ascertain the actual story – I'd scribble down notes and names of characters to try and ascertain the plot. But it was worth it. I was *obsessed* – the style and the humour and the romance and the friendships and the endlessly enthralling mythology; crystals and kingdoms and time travel and space. I was insatiable in my quest for more *Sailor Moon* (this eventually led me to haunting comic book stores in my teens), going to a cultural festival celebrating Japan in London with Mum and nagging Dad to find comic book, aka 'nerd', shops that sold manga via the Yellow Pages. My favourite characters were tall and dark-haired Sailor Jupiter, a formidable fighter and tough tomboy; moody fortune-telling Sailor Mars, with her pet crows and long black hair; and Sailor Pluto, a glossy-haired darker-skinned woman whose powers related to time and the underworld. Wow! They went straight on the list.

And one fateful day at Jake's house began one of my greatest love affairs, which has endured through every major phase of my life since and I am sure will continue for decades more.

Nothing about the everyday setting – perched on the end of Jake's Pikachu bedspread with a PlayStation controller in hand, two glasses of Asda orange squash precariously sat on the desk next to Jake's Pikachu N64 – heralded this arrival as we spent hours crouched around the small square TV on his desk. Suddenly, there, in the default character roster for *Tekken 3*, I found her. Ling Xiaoyu, a chirpy sixteen-year-old martial arts champion who had a pet giant panda, *iconic* pigtails and outfits to die for. According to the in-game storyline, she had entered the fighting tournament because she wanted to build a theme park with the prize money – instantly fabulous, as the other characters had gritty entry backstories of vengeance and curses – and, even more iconic, the theme of the theme park was *her*: XIAOYULAND (I'll take an annual pass). I didn't know where she was from[5] but dark hair plus a name I had never heard of meant I was *immediately* a die-hard fan, learning every one of her moves religiously until I could have cartwheeled into the dojo and fought alongside her.

All of the characters I connected with were hard-earned – retrieved from obscure pockets of pop culture – and when I found one, I wanted to immerse myself in their worlds, revisiting their stories and constantly looking for something new I could connect with, memorising every scene, moment or line that I could. I wanted to know them, understand them, befriend them, *become* them. I didn't often share these favourites with school friends and finding related merch or media was

---

5. China. She is very clearly from China. I feel I should state that this is actually made very clear in the game booklet (which we never read) and all surrounding media (which we weren't aware of) but for whatever reason I didn't clock this until years later when she came back in Tekken 4.

impossible, but I carried them around in my head like a gang – like Xiaoyu and Sailor Mars and Soraya and I could all team up as some high-powered super squad. None of the characters on my list existed to teach the audience about their culture before disappearing, or to be a counterpoint to a different (and less relatable) main character. My characters were all active parts of their stories. And despite being from wildly different sources (video games, anime, vintage comics), they had several things in common apart from the obvious one of being incredibly hard to find. Heroic adventures. Top-notch fighting skills. Uncommon strength and immense (usually magical) power. Big dreams and storylines of might and majesty. Excellent wardrobes. Exotic pet animals. And above all, the biggest feature that they all shared, that underlined everything I knew and understood about myself, that solidified something I'd known a very long time: not one of them was *in the UK*. Each one was explicitly somewhere else, somewhere far away. I didn't need to question why anymore. My only question was how I could go, too.

In the meantime, how could I fit into the society I was in? There must be something for people who felt Welsh but also sort of didn't. I needed an example of how I should exist where I was. I started to look for anything that could explain my situation and help me make sense of things. At one point, I read a book in the library about something called 'adoption'. One page featured the headline 'Are You Adopted?', followed by a list of statements for you to tick off and deduce if you were adopted. I remember the following statements:

There are no pictures of your mother pregnant or you as
   a baby.
You don't look like either of your parents.
You don't look like your siblings or you don't have any
   siblings.
You feel disconnected from your family in some way.

I mean, it was a full house. Bingo! All of those statements applied to me. I must be adopted! That was the reason for looking
different, feeling distant . . . I dashed over to Mum.

'Mum . . . Am I . . . adopted?' I asked, stumbling over the
word I had first read a few minutes ago. She stared at me.

'What? No! Why would you ask that?' I showed her the list
in the book.

'I match all these things. I'm adopted.'

'No, darling, no. You're not adopted.' This wasn't convincing
enough.

'Are you sure?'

'Yes, Laila, of course I'm sure.' Apparently there were pictures of me as a baby at home, though I wasn't convinced.

Later that evening, my dad sat me down for a 'serious chat'
– except he seemed to think the whole thing was hilarious,
grinning and suppressing a laugh.

'Laila, you're not adopted. Look!' He produced a small,
framed photo of me at a day and a half old. It was unmistakably
me: a shock of dark hair, huge eyes, face scrunched up in an
unimpressed expression. Hmm. I knew somewhere deep down
that this was a picture of me, but this was the first time I'd had
anyone addressing some of my issues. Too much didn't add up,
and even if I wasn't adopted, I wanted an explanation as to why

I didn't fit in – a word or a phrase or anything that could help me understand.

'But what if you adopted me when I was a day and a half old?' I asked. Dad lost it at this, burst out laughing, unable to keep up the serious face. I felt a little ridiculous. We found another photo: late-80s Mum with a dodgy perm, beribboned shirt – and massive tummy.

'That's you! Laila, I don't know what to tell you if you don't believe me. You're our daughter! You do look like us and your cousins. See my mum? In the picture.' He took down from the shelf the one black and white photo we had of my long-deceased grandmother. She had darkish hair in a barely visible ponytail. 'And you have Grandad Woozeer's nose!' my dad continued. 'Right there, in the middle of your face!'

This was news to me. We had no photos of my dad's dad, Grandad Woozeer.

'Really?' I asked.

'Yes!' cried my Dad. 'The exact same nose. That's Grandad Woozeer's nose.' He snatched my nose in his fist, pretending to grab it off my face. 'You better take care of it, you know. Grandad Woozeer might want it back one day!'

Not long after, I found a *word* that *did* apply to me. This momentous occasion happened whilst watching TV with my mum. The Spice Girls – who felt less like a band and more like a life force – were chatting about their lives when Mel B made the comment that her dad was brown and her mum was white, so she was mixed.

WHOA. Mixed. *Brown dad + white mum = MIXED.* Mixed?! Mel B had just described my exact situation and *given it a name.*

I wasn't some unknown, singular aberration; I was MIXED. I had a word of my own! I had a *reason* for all the things that didn't make sense – it was because I was *mixed*.

It was a thrilling, euphoric development: the tectonic plates of my inner world smashed together, forming new ground; comprehension erupted throughout my mind; huge enormous chasms of confusion shifted into alignment. High on epiphany, I turned to my mum.

'Mum! That's like me!' I said.

'What?'

'Brown dad and white mum! That's the same as me! I'm mixed!' I didn't understand why Mum wasn't sharing in my jubilance. She was just watching the show like the world hadn't reformed around us.

'Oh. I see. Well . . . yes, I suppose so,' she said noncommittally, turning back to the TV. I didn't understand her response so I ignored it, because Mel B had given a succinct explanation and any way you looked at it, I had a brown dad and a white mum.

By the age of ten, I was visibly growing, and early issues with my appearance – like weird comments and looks from strangers in the street – were all becoming heightened, seemingly yet another way I wasn't on the same page as everyone else. Mum and I had some strangely tense exchanges, her stage whispering to me concernedly about the tightness of my t-shirts and the way my thighs touched. She was confused why I was standing 'wrong' with my bum out and why my feet were growing so fast and how I was a size six (the same as her) already. Our conversations made me feel embarrassed for reasons I didn't understand and it felt like my fault that she was constantly taken aback. Things were easier at other people's; Lisa and Dawn intermittently gave me hand-me-downs, which I wore on an endless loop, and when I inherited my first 'bra' (i.e. half an elasticated vest) it was tons easier than the jittery discussions at home. Just a simple, *Here you go, pop that under your t-shirt Laila. And tea's ready in ten minutes so let's get a quick run of Emerald Hill Zone first.*

Between the strangers in the street and the weird comments, my appearance in general was an issue. If it wasn't trackie bottoms, t-shirts and oversized jumpers, I didn't want to know: the baggier and looser the better. I looked ridiculous – I've seen the pictures, unfortunately documented in meticulous fashion in my mum's photo albums – and Mum wanted me to have more clothes on rotation but I was still utterly opposed to skirts and dresses, or taking my hair out of its ponytail. Though she asked me why, I didn't know why I was so opposed to these things – or at least not in ways I could articulate. Skirts and dresses attracted attention; comments of 'you're so pretty', which was embarrassing. 'Girly' was an insult, as was pink, frilly, feminine and any form of accessory or ornament: cardinal sins to tomboyish me. Being 'pretty' brought only awkward comments and difficult questions. You know what? I'd rather be ugly, thanks. Pass the shapeless sweater.

How I looked was already a sore subject for totally separate reasons of belonging and identity. Though these comments were objectively meant as compliments, to me, they were vocalisations of difference and I hated them. I didn't want anybody to comment on the way I looked; it highlighted that I was so unbelievably out of place that they *had* to comment on it. I was a walking discussion point. And for me, that was only a bad thing. As I got older, there'd be comments like 'she'll be a heartbreaker when she's older!' or 'she'll be beating them off with a stick'; playful comments that I could have taken as teasing but made me want to run away and hide. When I was out and about, I tried to pull my jumper down over me, or stand nearer walls so I was less likely to be commented on. I can vividly remember scanning public areas for corners and paths around the perimeter to avoid being seen. I didn't care about being 'pretty'. I only cared about my appearance so far as it helped me with my central concern, the still unsolved mystery of who I was: the biggest (and for me, only) compliment I'd received was Dad telling me that I had my grandad Woozeer's nose.

The biggest contention between my mum and me was my hair: ringlety, frizzy, messy. She wanted to brush it every day so it could be 'manageable', and I loathed Sunday mornings, aka Hair Wash Day – an excruciatingly boring and frustrating process that took hours.[6] I hated the hairdresser's (only acquiescing when we went to KFC after) and I hated the daily morning ritual of laboriously brushing my hair into submission, yanking my whole head backwards: a pointless endeavour as my hair re-tangled within hours, like it was acting out a rebellion I hadn't yet got on board with. Luckily, she didn't mind my insistence on having a fringe – but Dad hated it, declaring that my fringe looked 'American' and stating unequivocally that 'Indian girls don't have fringes', which neither Mum nor I

---

6. Once, after I'd learned how to tell the time, I timed the whole enterprise and was shocked to discover it was only forty minutes.

could disprove and was confusing in itself (I wasn't Indian, was I? Would I be more Indian if I didn't have a fringe?). My hair wasn't wavy and fair like my mum's, and it wasn't tight curls like my dad's, so even the daily act of arguing over my hair underlined how dissimilar we all were.

As I spent so much time escaping my home life, I relied on my friends and classmates to learn about pretty much everything important. As I got older, important things included every swearword under the sun – whether 'God' counted as a swear or not prompted an ongoing, lengthy discourse – and whether or not chewing gum was lethal if you swallowed it.[7] I was learning ways to fit in and what that involved. From time to time, classmates took the mick out of me and my weirdness, but I didn't mind because they were my friends. Harder to ignore were the comments at school from a girl in the year above me: Katie. She called me names, started rumours and generally made my life hell at every opportunity – whenever a teacher wasn't looking. Katie was small and skinny, but her presence loomed over me. I don't know when or why she decided she didn't like me, but I frequently felt her large pale eyes searching me during the day. Each class held two year groups, meaning we only shared a classroom every other year; a year of sweet reprieve before re-entering the arena. I often calculated how many terms I'd be stuck with her before I reached Year 6, when she would have left, and I could enjoy bully-free school. Sometimes she mouthed insults at me, other times delivered a

---

7. Yes: a girl in Year 5 had an older brother at another school whose friend of a friend's neighbour had twin cousins who had died that way; one from swallowing Orbit and one Hubba Bubba.

swift kick to the ankles in the corridor, or a chance yank of the hair in assembly.

But her favoured MO was to accost me in the toilets. She seemingly spent every break time skulking around the girls' toilets; rationally, I know this can't be true and a teacher would have sent her outside instead of loitering in the loos, but to my young mind she was perennially waiting for me near the bog, haunting her lair. Around Year 4, her bullying became more specific: I'd go to wash my hands and she'd be hovering nearby, sneering at me and looking at me loathingly by the sinks.

'Ugh! Your skin is the colour of poo. It won't come off if you wash it. You are sooooo disgusting.'

From this one initial slur – that I was poo-coloured – came dozens of spin-offs: I smelled like poo; I was made of poo; I had poo for brains ('poo-brain' became a favourite insult of hers); I was a pile of poo and therefore gross, smelly, waste, disgusting, swarming with flies, a waste of space, a pile of rubbish and so on. Any negative attribute you could assign to poo also applied intrinsically to me, because I was made of poo.

Telling her to shut up or pleading with her to leave me alone only stoked the beast. Comebacks were beyond me and, already so hazy on the particulars of *who I was*, I simply took her words on board. I wanted to say, 'You're the one that's made of poo!' but I didn't have a leg to stand on: she was pale, her hair was blonde (at one point I tried to tell her she was the colour of wee, which even at the time felt weak) and her eyes a translucent blue. I still wasn't even clear on my own colour, but if I'd had to say . . . I'd have said brown. And poo *was* brown. I couldn't argue with that. So as far as I could tell, though it wasn't nice to admit it, I *was* the colour of poo. What was I supposed to say? I couldn't have brought up looking like Princess Jasmine because I'd have sounded like a total baby, and I couldn't have tried to say that poo was purple or something, because I'd have sounded like an absolute wally. The only line of defence I had was to tell her to leave me alone.

Luckily: I had friends. My friends called her out on my behalf, constantly – they would not tolerate one word of her nonsense. If I ever asked, well, *do I smell like poo?* they'd tell me absolutely not, Katie was talking crap and I should tell her to stop being a knob. I'd put off going to the toilet until one of my friends accompanied me.[8] On one occasion, Katie started again on her 'somebody needs to wipe you up and throw you in the bin, where you belong', when Ffion emerged from a cubicle and immediately cornered her. 'Oh, shut up, Katie! You're just jealous of Laila because you're a snidey cow with no mates!' Katie scowled and glowered – but she left the room without saying anything else, scuttling off to the playground.

Ffion managed to hit Katie where it hurt: Katie was not popular and, among the kids whose families were embedded in the community and knew these sorts of things (like Ffion's, but not mine), there were endless rumours going round that she came from a scally family, that one of them was a robber, and all of them had nits. I didn't know if any of this was true, so I never said anything of the kind to her – and it's clear as an adult she likely had some issues that may explain (without excusing) her picking on me. But at the time I didn't really care, either. I

---

8. With apologies to my kidneys.

just knew if my confident and more in-the-know friends could make her leave me alone for a bit then for that I was grateful.

One day I came a cropper at the hands of Katie's younger sister, Kerry. My friends and I were eating lunch in the school hall sat around a big table with some girls from the year below, including Kerry. We were taking it in turns to see how many Pringles we could eat in one go (a classic primary school activity), when Kerry pointed at me and said, 'Ughhh, she eats like an INJUN!'

I didn't catch what she said at first – an engine? Thomas? – but all hell broke loose around me and I realised she'd said 'Indian'. My friends were outraged – exchanging shocked looks and asking me if I was okay. I was incredibly confused. What did that mean? Was it bad?

'What is wrong with you Kerry! You can't say that! That's well offensive!' We were big on offence. A teacher arrived, summoned by the outcry.

'Miss! Kerry was racist! Kerry called Laila an Indian!' The teacher looked at me, alarmed.

'Is this true?'

I didn't get it – why had she called me an Indian? What was that supposed to mean – what was bad about the way Indians ate? Didn't they just eat like us? What if I *was* Indian? Although I had a fringe, so . . .

I can't remember any negative fallout from this; presumably the teacher spoke to me, maybe sent a letter home, but I have no memory beyond feeling confused and embarrassed at the time of the name-calling. In my head, the scene literally dissolves into smoke. A couple of days later, I asked Ffion what 'racist' was. She said she knew, which I believed, but she didn't know how to explain, so Gethin, a clued-in boy in the year above us, described it to me instead:

'It's like, when somebody says something harsh to you, but it's 'cos your skin's brown and that, so it's dead bad. Or you know, like, Chinese and what have you.'

Great, got it – ta very much. I memorised this succinct explanation and clung on to it for years.[9] I don't remember ever hearing about racism from any adults in my life (you know, what it was, what to do if it happened and so on). *I* had realised I was a different colour at a young age, but I came to know the connotations of my colour through my detractors. I understood that if somebody took the mick out of me for being whatever I was, then that was racist. Okay, sure.

Except this didn't always apply. I couldn't work out what the rules were – so, it was racist when Kerry said I ate like an Indian but it was not racist when the boys in the year above me called me Apu, because everyone thought that was funny (I didn't get the reference because Apu was a character on *The Simpsons*, one of the many shows that weren't allowed on at my house, but I'd been filled in that he was some foreign bloke that talked weird). It wasn't racist when Ffion called me Choco Puff and I called her Icing Puff in return, but it was racist if somebody else called me Paki. To me, being picked on just felt like being picked on – generally crap – and whether or not it passed the test of being racist instead of, I don't know, all other normal being picked on, was a totally different set of criteria that I didn't understand.

---

9. Until I was about fourteen and remembered dictionaries existed.

One time, a classmate said they were going to tell a joke they'd heard from their dad but suddenly paused and looked at me. 'Hang on – Laila, if I say this joke it's not at you, like it's just a joke, no offence, right?' I was bewildered but shrugged. Despite the ominous heads-up, I wasn't going to deprive everyone else.

The kid then told a deeply racist joke, which I won't repeat here – but I will say that the punchline involved comparing people of colour, with any kind of non-white skin tone, to burned cookies.

Everyone burst into laughter. I forced a laugh too – but inside, I was horrified. Burned cookies? When Mum and I baked cookies, we threw the burned ones out, scattered them in the garden for the birds to peck at. A burned cookie was a bad cookie, a cookie that couldn't fulfil its function of being edible and yummy. A burned cookie was an unwanted cookie, a failed cookie, a waste of dough. These connotations hit me at lightning speed, and not in those words: it was just one swift moment of registering. What could possibly be funny about identifying with a burned cookie? On some level, this joke didn't apply to me – the kid had said so – but it still made me feel uneasy, because if it hadn't at least been thought to pertain to me in some way, then I wouldn't have been the sole target of the disclaimer.

How upset it made me didn't correlate to how racist it was or if it even was racist (I couldn't at the time work out if it was). What I was clear on is that if something *funny* was presented within a group of white people, then I should put up with it and that if I were to speak out on what was *funny*, I would be seen as Boring and Can't Take A Joke. The cookie joke kid was clear: it's a joke! If you can't take it, that's on you.

I learned that was where to exist in society; that from time to time, I would be the only one in a group of white people and I would need to suspend my feelings, pain and hurt so as not to ruin a good joke for the others. There's an unspoken rule and you'll just have to be a good sport and a fun mate and put up with it, in exchange for being allowed in. This relationship only works one way: against you.

Shortly after I turned eleven, Mum and I filled in the England and Wales 2001 census. The mostly straightforward form contained a riddle: the ethnic group question, which asked you to select one option from:

White: British
White: Irish
White: Any other White background
Mixed: White and Black Caribbean
Mixed: White and Black African
Mixed: White and Asian
Mixed: Any other Mixed background
Asian or Asian British: Indian
Asian or Asian British: Pakistani
Asian or Asian British: Bangladeshi
Asian or Asian British: Any other Asian background
Black or Black British: Caribbean
Black or Black British: African
Black or Black British: Any other Black background
Chinese or other ethnic group: Chinese
Chinese or other ethnic group: Any other

Quite the menu. With hindsight, these categories are hilariously limiting, but at the time it posed a conundrum for my mum and me, attempting to complete the form in earnest.

With no given definitions, you had to decipher the terms for yourself. Mum hovered around 'White British' for a whilst, but eventually chose 'White other' for herself. This still left the problem of me. *I* thought I was Mixed, recalling Mel B, but my mum didn't think I was *what they meant*, not a stance she elaborated on. After much deliberation, she thought maybe 'other' was a better fit – either the 'Mixed other' one, or just 'any other', which was like a last resort option in a category containing only that and Chinese. I asked Mum which category Dad was (he was filling in the census separately in London). More frowns. She wasn't sure – potentially 'Asian Indian'?

'But he's Mauritian?'

'Oh yes . . .' said Mum vaguely, like she wasn't entirely convinced even of that. She scanned the list again, thinking hard, and suggested he might be 'Asian other (non-Chinese)' instead. I considered this.

'Isn't "Asian other" like, Japan and stuff?' I asked. I felt very protective of Japan as I owed Japan a personal debt: Japan was responsible for *Sailor Moon*, chocolate-covered rice balls and *Tekken*.

'Yeah, I guess maybe that's what it's meaning . . .' trailed off Mum, still staring at the mysterious boxes.

At the time, I'd just accepted this confusion as part of the general shadowy business of being me, but even at the age of eleven I was annoyed at the negative connotation of 'other'. Most options had countries or a colour attached or at least a capital letter to denote their importance and standing as a category. 'Other' wasn't even necessarily a human being. I could have been 'other anything': other skin colour, other race, other species, other planet. 'Other' implied *alternative* to the norm. You know, as in *let's use the other plates for dinner* or *we'll take the other route to school*.

That even *Mum* didn't know what category I belonged to tipped confusion into frustration. She was the adult, she had given birth to me: it felt careless to have created a person and not know where to place them on this official-looking government form, and unthinkable that she didn't have a label for me and Mel B, a pop star I had never met, did. If *Mum*, my guardian and creator, didn't know what category I was in, then what hope did *I* have of ever figuring it out?

Who got to decide these ethnic categories anyway? Who looked at that form and thought, *yes, that's the one, send it to print and let's get this into every household in the country*? Seeing all those options laid out on an official, important document implied *these are the total sum of extant ethnic categories and everybody in the world fits into one of these boxes*. And I was the catch-all, *just-in-case* back-up option. *Other* may as well have just been *Whatever Random Thing We Couldn't Think Of. Leftover. Forgotten Erroneous Thing.*

Right at the end of primary school, Mum and I visited the US for a family reunion. The country was massive – you had to *fly* between states, and instead of patchy forest like in Britain, Oregon had huge mountains covered in giant trees with occasional glimpses of waterfalls and rivers, just like in my imagined memory of Mum. We saw chipmunks – like small stripy squirrels! – and another small furry thing I hadn't seen before, pale

and round. I saw it from the car one day, balled up next to a log.
It was a *gopher*. Wow!

We drove around meeting relatives – mostly Mum's cousins
– ahead of the reunion. Some cousins served homemade sher-
bet out on the porch. Some served us peanut butter on bagels
in cool verdant, floral gardens. Some of them lived on a ranch
– like a farm, but more American – Cousin Morgan took us
out to see the cows![10] Standing in the middle of the dusty yard
was overwhelming; you didn't have to look up to see the sky,
because it was straight *ahead*, next to great rolling plains that
extended endlessly beyond the horizon. It all felt authentically
Grade A American to me. I could practically smell the hick-
ory smoke and hear the marching band, whatever those things
might turn out to be. U-S-A!

People had travelled in from all over the States for the reunion, so I had not just my grandparents and my aunts and
uncles, but *Mum's* aunts and uncles, *their* children (my mum's
cousins), and their children (the same generation as me): more
family than I knew what to do with. My uncle explained how
the family hierarchy worked, how we all related and the proper
names for each relative, but it was confusing and nobody could
agree on the rules of what was a third cousin or removed or
whatever. Who cared! I just wanted to meet them!

It all went wrong once we got to the venue – a church.
Immediately, I had the familiar feeling that I was in the wrong
place. Though we'd met relatives for the last couple of weeks,
for whatever reason I hadn't registered what now became glar-
ingly obvious. Every single person was alabaster white; most

---

10. A genuine sentence from my diary entry that day.

with either straw-blonde hair and clear blue eyes or bright auburn hair and freckles. I already knew I didn't look like my mum – now I saw I looked like nobody in the extended family. Unlike in Mauritius where people had streamed through jovially whilst we sat in my cousins' house, at the reunion everyone was just *in* the same place; you just went in and milled around, like fish in a pond. A row of tables was piled high with unusual foods, like macaroni cheese, cornbread, onion rings, chicken sticks, mustard slaw, white rolls and butter, Cobb salad (we couldn't eat this), Caesar salad (or this), Lutheran salad (this we could eat, but it was gross[11]), hot dogs and burgers, butterscotch cookies, chocolate chip cookies, brownies, blondies, snickerdoodles, bowls of candy, bars of chocolate (mostly Hershey's) and hundreds of large buttercream cupcakes topped with icing flowers.[12] People kept lining up for photos in various arrangements – *Just the girls! Now just the farm boys!* – and I used the opportunity to watch them, trying to pick out the people I'd previously met, though collected they seemed interchangeable; a swarm of American accents and bushy hair. There was one other brown person in this entire group – a boy around my age. He was adopted. And then there was me. And that was it.

Concerningly, Christianity was everywhere. My grandparents were Christian, sure, but I'd understood that as a weird hobby rather than a defining personality trait. It was easy enough to ignore the whole religion thing when we visited

---

11. Lutheran salad = lime Jell-O, pineapple, cottage cheese, walnuts, marshmallows or evaporated milk, mayonnaise and a whipped topping. According to the internet you can decorate with maraschino cherries. (!)

12. I'm not sure which relative was in charge of curating the menu but clearly the theme was 'cardiac arrest'.

them (especially if you were hanging out with the horse). But Christianity seemed a fundamental part of the whole reunion – we were literally in a house of God, thanking Him at every turn, singing His praises. Apparently, it was His will that we'd all attended (I was pretty sure Dad had booked our flights, but whatever). God was ostensibly an integral part of the family. I wondered why Mum hadn't mentioned this and if maybe my grandparents weren't the odd ones out but we were. Maybe we were somehow . . . wrong.

People asked constantly about my accent (an accent Mum didn't have) and commented on how different I was (the old, *Hasn't she got unusual hair and Look at those eyes!*). I was upset at getting all the comments I usually tried to avoid and *double* upset to receive this from people who were apparently family. I wanted to know how I belonged to them and where I fit, but increasingly they felt like *Mum's* family, and I a mere tagalong. I wished Dad had come with us – at least then we could have been the odd ones out together. He would have said something funny about all the God stuff, or reminded me about Grandad Woozeer's nose, or said, 'Never mind, Laila, you look like your cousins – remember?' But it was just me and Mum.

Dad's family had felt like *mine* despite our differences, ruffling my hair, deluging me with presents, *knowing* me. They commented on how much I liked the animals and let me feed the kittens, or smiled at how excited I was by the napolitaines – comments that understood me somehow. With Mum's family, all the comments underlined our differences. On the long plane journey home, I watched the clouds and tried to make sense of everything. I'd now met all of my extended family in all of their allotted countries and nowhere had truly felt like home or somewhere I belonged. Mauritius was the closest – but I didn't know the language and that was an integral part of belonging somewhere. Films and books didn't know where I was supposed to go, and neither did my friends or parents. The only place I felt totally secure was in Wales; in the living room with my colouring pencils, at my neighbours' houses with a console controller in my hand, or in the garden with my head in the clouds, held in the warm embrace between soil and sun.

I'd lie in my favourite spot in the garden and try to hold all these disparate versions of myself, but I was too small to contain them. I'd look up at the sky and wonder if that was big enough. In those moments, I wanted to navigate not just versions of me and their potential futures, but much more – more than I knew, more than *anyone* knew. Everything the sky had seen. I wanted to gather up the sum total of everything that had ever been known and hold it all within me in a recognisable human shape. That is what I thought had come before me. That is what I needed to make sense of. And there was too much to hold, like trying to catch a waterfall in a teacup.

My final year of primary school passed in a blur of furry pencil cases, plastic cube hair bobbles and London, where I was taking an endless stream of entrance exams for every grammar school within commuting distance of my dad's place. Despite my frequent vocal protests, my parents had decided it made sense to move the family back together and Dad had moved from his small flat into a big house with a garden, ready for me and my mum to join.

On paper this sounds great – a bedroom with a window? Living with both parents? But I was utterly opposed. After such confusion in my early years, it was shocking to see how quickly and strongly a single thought – NO! – could take over my entire being. The fear of leaving was like a snake in my stomach, a constant pressing threat that made me churn and clench at the very thought of it. I couldn't go, would not go. Suddenly, I knew nothing but resistance. Moving would bring pain and devastation, and I needed to do everything within my power to stay put. Somehow, I *knew* I had to stay in Wales, knew that London would only bring heartbreak and torment, like it was a future I'd already lived through. It wasn't something I thought about and decided against but knowledge I already possessed, a primal reaction that I needed to stay. I could hear the echo of an older version of myself telling me to stay at all costs. *Don't go to London. You belong here. Whatever you do, don't leave.* Wales was home. Moving was a mistake. I begged my parents to reconsider, resolutely denying that I would leave, hatching elaborate plans with my friends on how I could somehow stay behind in Wales. I barely liked going to London in the holidays. Why on earth would I want to live there?

Too soon the end of the year approached. So much was uncertain in my life and losing the only things that felt familiar (our house, our neighbours, my school friends) felt like snuffing out the few little lights in my life for good. I finished Year 6 with the highest SAT results in the school and a Distinction in my piano exam. My teachers were proud of me, and I felt faint notes of something unusual – like I could be worth something, like I could be . . . *good*. But we were leaving. How could I be anything if I didn't belong?

Tragedy dressed as triumph: after failing dozens of entrance exams, (I was smart, but I spent most of the exams zoning out

in terror over the idea of moving rather than writing down the
answers, only acing the exams for Wrexham-adjacent schools),
I finally had a place to start secondary school in Surrey on the
edge of South London in September. People congratulated me
but I was being torn apart against my will. The idea of leaving
this safe space and going somewhere I didn't like, *forever*, was
torturous. My diary entries from this time are long essays of
wondering what I'd done wrong, why I was being punished,
why my parents hated me. I was certain, more certain than I'd
ever been of anything, that I had to stay in Wales, but I couldn't
articulate this, and now I'd failed in the only task that mattered.
And I was heartbroken. I protested every way I could: saving
up pocket money to live by myself and wishing on every star
in the sky.

But stars can be so fickle in that way. I already felt rootless
and now I was leaving my home – the only part of my life to
which I felt firmly tethered. Wales Laila was the most solid,
clearest version of myself. Wales Laila had friends, community, people who cared. The last week of school rolled around.
Usually at school discos, we'd be clad in half of Tammy Girl,
chugging Panda Pops and watching the boys practise skids or
sneak onto the curtained-off apparatus. The Leavers' Disco was
a wake. My friends and I cried and held each other, promising
to write every week and to never forget how much we loved
each other. Some offered to hide me in their houses so that
I could stay in Wales, or told me to move back the minute I
turned sixteen. At home, our neighbours brought farewell gifts
and wished us luck, hugging us in disbelief that we were really
going, asking us to keep in touch, knowing it would never be
the same. After years of hypotheses, it was the end of an era:

the Woozeers, finally going to London. Time trips you up; just when things start to feel safe you are forced to remember that everything can change in one single second.

We had no official moving day, no final ending – just a long trickle of leaving, signing Leavers' shirts and sobbing onto shoulders. Mum consoled me: *We've done this pack-up and journey a thousand times!* But my whole world was ending. I closed my eyes and tracked each inch of the house, committing the number of steps on the stairs and the placement of the light switches to memory, so I could return home in my mind whenever I needed to in the long years to come. I clambered up to the top of the garden alone and looked out at the slumbering mountains in the distance and the familiar clouds above, bidding a silent farewell. Who knew when I'd see these stars again? My whole life was swirling away from me, disappearing like dirty water down a drain. I ran my hand along the amassed rows of rocks and crystals I'd carefully collected over the years, asking them to protect the house; I stared up into the leaves of the holly tree and imprinted the image in my mind, thanking the tree for the shelter; I rested my head on the hill like a littler Laila had, and wished I could sink into the ground and stay there rooted forever, planted in the earth, like the holly tree, like the grass, like the rocks and the quartz and the worms and the inside of the world.

And then we left. One cold, grey night, car numbly packed, motorways memorised, the familiar journey we had done so many times, and the streetlights passing monotonously over as we left the keen gaze of sorry stars.

Chapter Four

Mum Never had a Moustache

London was different with a capital D, in every respect. Take where we lived. Dad's house in London was new and neat, three floors, driveway, painted magnolia and a tidy rectangle of flat grassy garden. Every house on the street had a front door on the same flat level. My bedroom had a window, viewing identical neighbouring houses, no stars, no bats – just the occasional parakeet. If I crouched down and looked beyond the houses, I could almost see the sky; no longer a canvas for my imagination, but a mere backdrop for roofs. In Wales, I'd sensed the creak of previous inhabitants, heard stories hidden in the quirks of the architecture. Now, there was nothing. I was lucky to have a chest of shiny wooden drawers for my clothes at the new house, but I missed the haphazard pile of boxes at the end of my bed in Wales.

Take family. I was living properly with my dad for the first time ever. And *It. Was. Weird*. Previously, Dad was more of a guest star than a main role; more fun than fleshed out. Now, I was afforded close study of him – he was there in the mornings, eating a slice of toast over the sink, and in the evenings, serving a plate of food in the kitchen, and at the weekends, napping on the sofa. But he was mostly at work.

In some ways, Dad was similar to Mum. They were both private people with 101 things to do: Mum's scrap paper lists scattered across windowsills and counters like confetti; Dad regularly exited rooms muttering that he'd forgotten something or had to pop out, leaving a half-finished sentence in his wake. Both had long overseas phone conversations. Dad's were in different languages and took place wherever he happened to be, loudly, whilst Mum snuck up to the bedroom in the attic, muffled and secluded, so far away you had to bellow upwards several times if you needed her. Dad liked to cook, but it was nothing like Mum's cooking. He conjured dishes out of thin air (curry, pickles, *samosas*) and you could literally see the flavours transforming the food: crushed herbs adorning the chicken, turmeric-stained potatoes, seed-studded carrots. Dad had no protocol over life's normal structures. Like, he'd casually shout that there was a tray of samosas in the oven. I'd holler back, 'It's 3pm,' meaning, 'is this lunch or dinner and can I still have a treat afterwards if I have a samosa' – all things Mum would have clarified when telling me about the samosas. Dad did no such thing. He'd just say, 'Okay.' Like he had no inkling of how 3pm linked to samosas and didn't care to find out.

Mum let me bob around unhindered in my small Welsh life whilst she pottered elsewhere. Dad required accountability for *everything*. What had I learned at school? Where was my homework? Had I made friends? It put me on edge – I wasn't used to consolidating my days into conversation. Previously, days just happened, and I along with them. Now, Dad needed a log of every minute. And he didn't just want to know, he wanted to be directly *involved*. Just doing homework wasn't enough, he wanted me to explain it back to him and then he'd offer extra facts or bonus exercises. I did not appreciate this. I'd already completed the homework – couldn't I now go hide in my bedroom? But you had to stay alert. Sometimes he'd shout, 'Laila! Come here!' in a stern bark. I'd drop whatever I was doing, thinking I was in trouble, only to be shown something he found intriguing, like a plant in the conservatory or an animal in a documentary. I didn't understand this was Dad's way of helping me to see what he saw.

My new school was a trek down to neighbouring county Surrey: one of the most affluent white areas of the UK. School was a sprawling campus with a hockey pitch, tennis centre and chapel. I was less a fish out of water and more a fish stranded on the moon. You could have fit in my old school ten times over, and there were at least ten times the number of pupils, spanning right up to sixth form. The oldest pupils were *eighteen* and a different species, practically grown-ups.[1] We weren't in 'Year 7', we were 'first years', which was both unbearably posh (what was this, Chester?) and disheartening, like our previous years counted for nothing.

On our first day, we sat shell-shocked through the assembly in freshly starched grey and maroon blazers[2], necks craning to get a good look at each other. Every class brought with it the need to deliver a keynote on the correct pronunciation and

---

1. They were dressed in suits instead of uniform and blended in with the hundreds of teachers.

2. A colour combination that still, to this day, causes an instant panic in me that I have insufficiently revised for Latin.

spelling of my name; often teachers suggested nicknames like 'Lila', which I declined. Mine was not the only 'ethnic' surname the teachers stumbled over: there were two other brown boys in my class, one with the last name Mukharji, not a million miles away from doctors Mukharjee, the friendly GPs back in North Wales. Maybe they were related? Oh, the things me and my similarly-brown-crayon-coloured classmates could discuss! Were they mixed? Did their parents speak other languages? Did they have any opinions on Princess Jasmine?!

Unfortunately, I never found out. Bullying began that first morning, and it was SO much worse than Katie in the toilets. Instead of just one kid's bolshie name-calling, it was half the class inventing new ways to insult me on the daily. Before I knew it, I was fending off the flaws of being nerdy, tomboyish, introverted, friendless and, most bittersweet of all, *Welsh*. (The cruellest way to finally receive the validation I had so longed for: within hours my accent earned me my first 'sheepshagger'.) Reprises of loser, loner, geek and teacher's pet greeted me at every class. But the brunt of the bullying focused on the way that I looked. Apparently, I was UGLY.

The two biggest crimes were the colour of my skin and the hair that covered it. The hair on my top lip would become a loathed part of my body. First hated by the boys in my class, and later, following their fine example, hated by me, because it made me 'The Man'. Comments buzzed around me like flies round a bin.

'Ugh, there's a strange *Man* in here.'

'The Man is sitting by herself again – oh no, himself.'

Nicknames quickly racked up:

The Man

Monkey Man

Yeti

Bigfoot

Beast

Wolfman

Wolverine

Gorilla

Gorilla Girl

Gremlin

The Thing

Cousin It

Sasquatch

Hairy Maclary

These new ones joined the roster alongside old classics:

Apu

Mowgli

Poppadom

Curry House

'Paki' didn't feature at my new school. They may have been gobby little shits, but they were still middle-class white kids from Surrey: 'Paki' alone crossed the invisible barrier into 'racism'. The bullying wasn't saved for chanced-upon moments (like Katie in the loos), it was a constant onslaught: registration; break time; lunchtime, before and after lessons – even walking out of the building to go home. Routine name-calling became as much a part of school life as the scratchy black jumpers and the brick-like hymn books in assembly. I tried desperately to stay near adults – the only effective protection – but gone were the carefree days of being shepherded around like in primary school. We were Big Kids now, travelling unaccompanied across the vast wilderness of campus. The journey from our form room at the front of school to the humanities block on the back field was effectively the same length as the journey to Mordor and at least twice as traumatic. I quickly learned to spend all non-lesson time cowering in the locker room, skulking round the library or hiding in the toilets playing Snake II on Mum's old Nokia[3]. If I could have crawled into my locker (and some of the shorter boys could) then I would have. Anything to avoid another student.

Less than a week into secondary school, the 9/11 attacks happened, placing 'terrorist' firmly into daily vocabulary. Somewhere in the trickle down of information, nuance was lost (or perhaps never there to begin with) and all we truly understood about 'terrorist' was what they looked like: bearded, brown, foreign, male. Having already been under target for all those attributes it was, predictably, a terrible time for new nicknames. I'd attract phrases like:

'Look, it's Osama and his hairy legs.'
'What's happening, Saddam?'
'Oi, suicide bomber, blown up any buildings recently?'

---

3. I hadn't had a phone before, and technically this was only for 'emergencies' – but I figured hiding essentially was.

The ramifications of bullying were troubling. Obviously, I'd known I was weird, but in Wales I'd had friends – people I'd grown up with who accepted my quirks and cherished me anyway. Here, I had nobody. Tentative relationships were circumstantial – pairing up in PE or dividing into group work, not *friends* like the way I'd had friends in Wales. Nicknames like 'loser' or 'loner' didn't bother me, as I'd heard it before. Plus, now it was basically true: I was alone all the time.

Sometimes I'd try and defend myself. I had friends – they were in Wales! This was met with peals of mocking laughter. *Wales? You reckon you have friends in Wales?! Stop lying, nobody would ever be friends with you, dirty terrorist.* And lo, new nicknames: The Liar, Lie Boy, Porky Pig, Porkpie. These were more annoying than anything – I knew I wasn't lying and *did* have friends. And nicknames like 'Yeti' didn't bother me too much either: it was intended as an insult but a Yeti was a wild thing, strong, mythical and unknowable. It made me think of the forests back in Wales, back *home*. I'd far rather be living in the trees than stuck in double physics with my classmates.

No, the upsetting comments were the most frequent ones: insults about my appearance. I hadn't known I was so horrifically ugly. I'd never really cared how I looked beyond what it meant in terms of family, but if you'd pressed me, I would have said I liked the way I looked, landing somewhere between Jasmine and Sailor Jupiter.[4] I looked like *me* and I liked me, so I liked that. In terms of everyone else, enough people had told me I was pretty that I'd have reasonably assumed that's what

---

4. . . . I'm just going to let my eleven-year-old self have this one.

everyone thought. Not so. The boys in my class let me know I was ugly with a capital UGH.

My instinct was to tell them they were wrong – but worryingly, they were right. As far as I could tell, I *did* have brown skin like the terrorists on TV, I *did* have hair on my arms and legs and, most upsettingly of all, I *did* have a moustache. I'd never examined myself this rigorously, but if I pressed myself up against the mirror and really squinted hard, then I could *clearly* see hairs above my lip. It was like Katie saying I had skin the colour of poo: I wasn't sure if I was being bullied or just receiving particularly aggressive observations.

The brown boys in my class didn't get the insults I did. Maybe because they were semi-friendly with the two main ringleaders of the bullying, but who knows. I'm still not sure why. The only other kid subjected to such ritual abuse was Morris, a boy with a Chinese mum. Morris was followed with endless choruses of '*ching chang chong*' and people giving him orders for spring rolls, and worse stuff that I *didn't* get – boys stole his stuff, chucked his bag out the window, tricked him to fall off his chair and land in the bin. Morris was always scowling.[5] With good reason – I remember him being severely told off for arriving 20 minutes late to a lesson, but the reason he was late was because he was retrieving the contents of his pencil case from whatever flowerbed the boys had dumped it in. We were likely suffering in similar hells. I wanted to ask, but I never spoke to him at all. I never spoke to anyone. I was too busy trying to look less like somebody on the FBI's Most Wanted

---

5. Recalling him now, I think I saw him smile once in the seven years we were at school together.

list. Besides, if I was caught speaking to him it might somehow compound the abuse we shared individually – The Man talking to Hong Kong Phooey? That kind of a crossover episode would be social suicide from which we might never recover. It wasn't just the kids I had problems with. My French teacher gave me detention in the first week for failing our first ever lesson. This was cruel: all my classmates had taken French in primary school. I'd learned Welsh. Dad wrote a letter to explain the situation and ask for understanding whilst I caught up on the four-plus years' head start my classmates had. Except Dad wrote the letter en français, the langue officielle of his home. My teacher – a white Englishman – read the letter, said, 'Ah right, I see', gave me a shifty look, then cracked out a red pen, saying Dad had made a mistake. This, I could not believe. Accepting I was behind and possibly bad in these new subjects, when I'd previously been good at everything we studied? Fine. It was a bitter pill but one I could accept. But this? Something broke, then hardened in me. At eleven, I knew Creole and French were different, but there was no way Dad, the smartest person I knew, could have *confused his mother tongue* in a formal letter he'd checked before printing and parcelling me off with it. Surely this Englishman felt foolish and was copping back. But this changed me. I'd loved school in Wales, loved learning, loved my teachers and trusted them implicitly, loved getting things right and scoring high on tests, loved being the one my friends asked for help. It was a point of pride that I knew the hard spellings and always got poems on the wall. Yet, mere days into big school, I wasn't sure I trusted it anymore.

Well-meaning adults advised me to join clubs or give it time, and I tried to believe this, to just hang in there and be persistent. *Dyfal donc a dyr y garreg.* But as weeks rolled by, settling in became a mythical concept. For starters, it wasn't the odd comment, it was constant. Secondly, though in Wales I'd been creative and kind, now I'd ceased to be anything other than ugly, like I was so ugly there was no space to be anything else. At home, I was too numb to keep up with anything I'd found fun or joyful before. School finished later and as it was so far away I got home practically in the evening only to complete hours of homework and music practice. I'd sit around blankly after finishing, avoiding drawing games and anime, instead using free time to write down every Welsh word I could remember – scared of losing something so important to me (pre-internet 'forgetting' meant 'losing forever') – and writing dozens of letters back home to my friends in Wales. Family friends kept commenting on how much nicer it must be out of the mountains at such a big posh school, but I dreamed of the wild weather and the rattling windows, mourning the things I could have come to know among the grey slate blooming violet in the rain.

My sense of identity, fragile to begin with, started to form along new negative lines. *I am ugly and disgusting. Nobody will ever like me.* With no stance to retaliate from, I focused on downplaying the problem instead: keeping my sleeves down over my hairy arms, avoiding the 'legs out' torture of the PE kit, asking my mum not to put bananas in my lunch box anymore: being Monkey Man and eating a banana was too painful. *I like apples, Mum.*

There were glimmers of hope: I liked my English teacher, who recommended me books, and my form tutor, a Maths teacher who said I had 'fortitude', whatever that was. I liked the poster of the Fibonacci sequence on the wall and the M.C. Escher print in the corridor – all knowing geometry and rational conclusions. I liked our cheerful headmaster, who I'd met doing the entrance exams and who always said hello to me.

I still took piano and clarinet when school asked me to try bassoon – a third instrument I was good at! Outside of school, Mum found me dance, tap and musical theatre classes, like in Wales, and karate, which was new. I cherished these classes. They were near my house (safely distanced from school) and the kids there were *normal* as opposed to the rich kids at school. I only saw them once a week for an hour, but still – maybe we'd be friends.

The first time I found some understanding about who we were came from school. Our English homework was to write about our family histories. What should have been a simple enterprise of writing down names and rulering lines quickly became the opening up of a black hole. I started with Mum.

'So . . . you're American?'

'Well, and British. But I was born in Uganda if you want to write that – might be interesting.' I dutifully wrote this down.

'And your parents are from . . . Scotland and America?'

'Well . . . yes, and Grandma's Welsh. Grandad was born in India. You might want to write that . . . it's kind of interesting.'

'Okay. Apart from India, everything else with Grandad is Scottish? They lived and died in Scotland?'

'Well, his mum was also French. Grandad's dad left Scotland, he's buried in Sri Lanka. In Colombo.' There was a pause: Mum spelled 'Sri Lanka' for me. 'We aren't sure where. I always thought it would be interesting to go one day.' Colombo suddenly called to me, a side-quest from the future. Awesome!

We continued in this vein for some time. Mum's opinion was that it was all mildly interesting, but not especially relevant. We had Native American relatives and links to the Prussian royal family – cool! – but it raised questions, like, what did somebody dead in Sri Lanka mean? We weren't Sri Lankan, so it didn't increase ties there, but it somehow decreased ties to Scotland. The last fully Scottish person in the family had left, never to return. Mum said we had the family tartan – but it felt far away and abstract. If Grandad's dad had spent his adulthood overseas, and Grandad's mum was actually half-*French*, and Grandad grew up in England – well, how Scottish was he actually? How Scottish was Mum, or me? We'd let the Scottish-ness slide.

It was like this with every branch, not just the Scottish. Nobody had stayed put. Relatives sprawled between at least three geographical locations: born somewhere, moved elsewhere, married someone from somewhere else. Finding people who had not dispersed to the four corners of the globe meant mining ancient history: the last fully French relatives dated to the French Revolution. My heritage dissolved into a murky mess, watercolours running into each other. We were really in the weeds now and I could barely keep track. Mum, unfazed, carried on the extended lore, now generations deep into her maternal side.

' . . . and your great-grandmother left Wales when she was twelve, it was very sad.' Join the club. 'She never saw her parents again.'

I noted everything down. 'So, her parents were totally Welsh?'

'Totally . . .? Oh, yes. Her parents were Welsh, born and raised. Welsh speakers. They were both teachers. It was unusual for women to —'

'Wait! And they died there?' I couldn't take in humanising details until I had the hard facts.

'Yes.'

Finally! Five generations away from me, I'd reached a firmly rooted branch of the family. Born there, lived there, died there: 100 per cent Welsh. Cymru am byth! I was at least . . . three . . . sixteenths unquestionably Welsh. Three-sixteenths of me locked into place, a sudden snort of dragon fire and the faint scent of daffodils. Three solid sixteenths! I decided to quit whilst I was ahead and cut Mum off.

Ten minutes later, I was annoying my dad whilst he attempted to watch the evening news. I'd gotten through the fractions on my mum's side, but still had a lot of gaps in my imaginary template. *If Mum is half of me, and I've written down 80 per cent of her heritage, then that's 40 per cent of me . . .*

'Why were you born in India?' I began.

'Well, that's where we were. My dad was working there.' My own dad didn't take his eyes off the TV.

'But your dad was Mauritian?'

'Yes. He snuck away on a boat; actually, when he was a kid he wanted to learn more about music. They were stowaways.' Hold the phone – what?! This was so utterly wild that I had a rush of follow-up questions until Dad reminded me about the homework.

'Oh yeah. Okay. So . . . you were born in India . . . but you're Mauritian?' I asked. 'Full Mauritian?' Dad was still watching TV, but I could tell he was paying more attention now.

'Well, what do you mean? What's "Full Mauritian"? My mother was from India.' Dad looked bemused. God, here we go again, why was everyone in my family so confusing? When we were given the assignment everyone thought it was the easiest homework ever; most people were from no further than Kent.

'So, was she Indian or Mauritian? Because if you're whole Mauritian then I'm *half*-Mauritian on your side and on Mum's side, an eighth American, three-sixteenths Welsh—'

Dad suddenly looked at me and cut me off.

'Well. No. My mum was Indian. She was from Goa.' He was fully concentrating now. 'And my dad was Indian too.' He said this last part into the distance, like he was a philosophising guest on Parky. 'My dad's family went to Mauritius from India – I'm Indian really.' He looked pensively off towards the window.

WHAT?! PLOT TWIST. This was a huge reveal dropped on my life – Indian? Dad was *Indian*? What was all that Mauritius stuff about then?

'You're Indian?! So I'm half-Indian? You're not Mauritian?'

'Well, I am, but I'm Indian too,' he said.

'So, you're 50 per cent Indian? Or 75 if your dad's—' Dad snapped back at me, suddenly impatient.

'Laila, why are you asking me for all these percentages? People aren't maths problems, it doesn't work like that! I've told you: I'm Mauritian.'

'But you just said you're Indian?'

'My mother was from India. Anyway, it doesn't matter – look, *you're* British. It doesn't matter what I am. What more of this do you need for your homework?'

Dad shut me down, eager to get off this confusing trail of semantics and back to the news. He was right, I thought, but I didn't feel British, and nobody else thought I was British. Besides, wasn't I a combination of all these other people? Families weren't chaotic groups of random strangers, families were supposed to be *connected*. I was *supposed* to link back to them. I now knew I was the first person to have been born and raised in the UK for four generations. Surely everything in between counted for something? I didn't want to be some misfit British kid in the sea of all my relatives; I wanted to belong to these people and to have somehow sprung from their stories.

Family had always been me, my mum and my dad. Suddenly, all these stories were swirling in my head: a lost man buried in Sri Lanka; a twelve-year-old packed off to America; a woman leaving India behind; a teenage stowaway crossing continents. My tiny family unit was expanding into something much more vibrant, and this wider version of family felt *alive* – but also overwhelming. I sensed an almighty energy, as though a pulsing heart at the centre created a gravity that tugged through the decades between us all. In my mind's eye, I pictured a globe, suddenly spinning and glowing, threads cascading haphazardly between the countries like ribbons.

The actual homework had gotten totally lost along the line of questioning because my mind was reeling, partly from the rangy anthology of people I was learning about and partly because I genuinely couldn't understand these concepts in the abstract. Trying to hold all these ideas in my head felt like holding a thicket of dust and fireflies in my mind; buzzing and distracting, the globe spinning incomprehensibly. When my dad said he was *both*, I was hearing half and half. Everyone was 50 per cent their mum and 50 per cent their dad – right? How could you be more than 100 per cent person? The fractions had to add up. Yet I seemed to have *more*, like 300 per cent heritage and culture, far more than could be reasonably contained.

I didn't know how to feel about myself. In Wales, I'd had a hazy sense of self at best, mostly tied to my friends, my house and my interests. Without those things to root me, I lost all sense of myself: who I was, who I could be and how I connected to this huge giant web of *family*. Between the questions at home and the constant jibes at school, I spent every moment on high alert. Even my new environment was numb to the true spectrum of experience: London offered flat pavements and uniform roads instead of mountains and winding valleys; rain fell silently against the impermeable new windows and I longed for the solace of a night that never truly fell, a dull glow of streetlamps keeping the stars at bay.

Things were trucking along despondently when in the summer of 2002, something remarkable happened: brown-skinned people became cool. Overnight, depictions of British Asian life appeared everywhere: a whole slew of British Asian representation, which had barely existed before. All things Indian were IN! I devoured everything: *Bend It Like Beckham*, *The Kumars at No. 42*, *Bombay Dreams* and accompanying bop 'Shakalaka Baby', *The Guru* and *Anita and Me*. Where film leads, fashion follows. Saris, gold filigree and tanned midriffs became must-have accessories, whilst everyone tried to do their best belly dancing in their new bedlah-style tops (you know, like Jasmine's). You could buy a six pack of stick-on bindis from

Claire's Accessories or a mandala print boob tube from New Look! It didn't matter if the item was actually authentic Indian, because *clearly* 'Indian' and 'Arabian Nights' were basically the same thing anyway. So, as long as it conjured up an image of a desert temple or a bustling spice market you were good. By the time my second year of school started in September 2002, the 'Indian Summer' was still in full swing. There was an S Club Juniors performance of a song called 'New Direction'[6] on *Top of the Pops* that is etched in my mind because the girls were kitted out with embroidered scarves, bindis and maang tikkas in their hair. The accompanying video featured a Bedouin room set-up and a flying carpet[7].

I'd grown so used to desperately searching out images of anyone who looked similar to me that being able to just *turn on the TV* and see a brown-skinned dark-haired girl was thrilling. I looked up to each and every brown person like a personal mentor – somebody who could induct me into the community and help me understand myself. Finally, I could learn what it meant to be Indian – how did we dress? What did we do? Who *were* we?

This didn't quite pan out: similar to investigating Jasmine years before, not everything held up to increased scrutiny. I recognised some elements of what was being portrayed, like the clothes, the food and the music (known to me from Dad's CD collection), but a lot was *un*familiar. Film and TV Indian people lived in communities of other such people, and had other

---

6. It was no 'One Step Closer', but then, what is?
7. Confusingly, it flew them over a car park and wind farm in the Midlands.

Indian people in their day-to-day lives. I had . . . Dad. Sometimes. When he wasn't working. Many stories emphasised family – ever-present Indian parents and extended relatives milling
around every scene. The only time I'd experienced this was
in Mauritius. Appearance-wise, I looked nothing like Jess (the
protagonist in *Bend It Like Beckham*) or her glamorous sister
Pinky. The fashionable brown women were small and slender,
with glossy wavy or straight hair. In comparison to them I was
big and dumpy, with a coarse mass of frizzy hair.

Initially, I wondered if the reason I didn't look more similar
to them was some side effect of being mixed, but I hit a snag:
Dad, my apparent link to Indian-ness, also didn't seem like any
of the Indian people on screen. He was darker-skinned with
tight curly hair and did not have the ubiquitous comedy Indian accent that every other brown elder had. Maybe we just
lacked the credentials: possibly we didn't even count as properly Indian. Dad hadn't seemed certain on this and at least we
both fit in Mauritius. Still, this wave of brown representation
seemed my one and only chance at belonging to something
in the country where I'd been born and raised. Was the pop
culture Indian love-in related to *strictly* Indian people or could
any vaguely brown person take part – what if you were 'Asian
other (non-Chinese)'?

I'd been waiting a long time to feel less alone – but the
more I compared myself, the more I felt a fraud. It felt the same
as living among white people, that same sideline vibe. Like I
could see it and understand it, maybe even feel familiar with
it, but, somehow, wasn't fully *part* of it. Even trying to join in
with the bits of trendiness my classmates followed led to further problems; Dad furiously told me in no uncertain terms

that I should not wear the free stick-on bindi I'd received from a magazine. I was baffled; wasn't he always telling me to try harder to fit in?

'Why do you want to wear one? They're Hindu. You're not,' Dad stated, a warning flash behind his eyes. He was clearly angry but I needed more of a reason as to what was wrong.

'But they're cool! Everyone's got one!'

'Oh, you're Hindu now?' I had nothing. I tried to explain that I thought it was only a trend and not about being anything, but it only made him angrier.

'It's disrespectful! We are respectful – we show respect to other people!' Dad was so final that I didn't question it further, but I wasn't clear on the issue. Obviously, I didn't want to be disrespectful, but *everyone* was wearing these – girls at school, models in magazines, pop stars in music videos. Were the S Club Juniors Hindu?

My parents and I didn't explicitly follow any religions, but the wider family on both sides was more devout. God was the family patriarch on the white side, most clearly demonstrated by my staunchly Christian grandparents who continually gave Dad Bibles. My Mauritian relatives responded to every call to prayer whilst my parents sat around waiting for secular conversation to resume. At home, we vaguely incorporated bits from both Mum and Dad's upbringing – no alcohol, no red meat, no swears or blasphemy, help others, give to charity – but none of this had ever been explicitly laid out to me as belonging to any specific religion. They were just the unspoken rules of the house. It was probably the only part of either culture I'd just *absorbed* via osmosis. I could see we were the least religious branch on either side of the family tree. If you were going to be as half-hearted with spirituality as we were in our house, was it so bad to adopt other cultural or religious paraphernalia? We were practically picking and choosing already. All the same, the part about being disrespectful worried me – though I admired the detail on that cheap mass-produced bindi, I never wore it.

As I inched towards the melodrama of teenhood, I became thoroughly uninvolved with everything. I no longer felt Welsh and gave up on belonging to a potential Indian community. At home, I was still a problem for my parents, hollow and lonely. At school I still faced daily name-calling, with new names like *Dirty Hippie* and *Tree-hugger* in the mix, now that I'd gone vegetarian and sewn a peace sign on my bag. Everyone within my world despised me, it seemed, yet escape seemed futile as out in the real world nobody like me existed.

And lo, I reached my teenage years, known to all as the least judgmental, calmest period of one's whole life; a time devoid of opinions, dominated by balance and grace. Yeah right! Obviously, the whole thing was hell. No surprises that my first big issue was the way I looked.

During a series of cringy assemblies at school, we were warned about 'puberty' – a vaguely defined time when 'things' might start to 'shift' at sudden rates. These talks were accompanied by grim explicative slideshows detailing the 'things'. Regular-looking girls became ludicrously curvy, Mr Blobby in a carnival mirror, and 'periods' involved what appeared to be murder? Despondent-looking girls submerged in shocking red pools during class, their skirts hideously blood-stained like a scene from a slasher film. The before and after pictures of boys showed them . . . turning into werewolves? It wasn't clear, the

'After' pictures were all abstract hair, spots and rippling muscles, sprouting huge linebacker shoulders like Wolverine with bonus acne.

We'd been separated for the assemblies and weren't supposed to ask the other groups what they'd seen so we had no way to assess any of this. Worse, our *personalities* would be in flux. We'd need to rediscover who we were. I'd never discovered who I was in the first place, so, dear Lord, what more confusion could there possibly be? I thought things got easier as you got older! The only silver lining was that surely at least *some* of the kids at school would gain new personalities. Maybe they'd stop caring how ugly I was – if they left me alone for a bit, it would all be worth it.

But mostly the school's attempts at sex education left me high on fear and doomsday exposition. It seemed feasible to wake up and find I was covered in fur or suddenly eight feet tall. At thirteen, I was not especially tall but nearing Dad's height. My height came from Mum, yet in all other ways we looked less alike than ever. Her hair was a lighter blonde, and I was wider and curvier than my 'runner bean' mum. I knew all about 'runner bean' shapes from magazines the girls left out at school. One time, I frantically scoured one in secret, trying to work out if I was a pear, muffin or an apple. What if you weren't any of the available foodstuffs? Could you be a loaf of bread or a chicken goujon?

Mum struggled to find 'first' bras or school shirts that fit. Whenever the topic came up in conversation, it was desperately awkward: she'd carefully ask what I needed, so we could find a solution to the problem of my body together. What bra size was I? What shirts did other girls wear? But as I never spoke to anybody at school, I had no idea. Besides, I wasn't used to talking to my mum about *anything*, let alone something so intimate. Mum didn't think I could be bigger than a 34C.[8] We went with that. Everything started to fit weirdly. Dad took a different stance, beginning a vocal campaign against me becoming 'fat', using all conversations to further the crusade without any of the averted glances and hushed tones Mum employed.

'Careful, you'll get fat like your cousin. You'll be a lump,' he called out whenever I ventured near the fridge. But I was pretty sure I wasn't fat – and anyway, school had said we were *supposed* to grow. How could I be doing it wrong? I still had several more years of growing to survive!

Meanwhile, my naïve hopes that peers would care less about appearance proved laughable: clearly, I'd never heard of teenagers. In the high stakes world of one-hundred-and-twenty newly-minted adolescents kept in close proximity for eight hours a day, it will be a surprise to nobody (except me at the time) that whether you were fanciable or not became social currency. Overnight, approval became a potent mix of gossip, lust and hair gel (the Gareth Gates years). It didn't matter how entertaining, friendly or charming you were: if you weren't 'hot', you were nothing.

There were daily comparison charts – Top Tens – passed around class that detailed who fancied who, meaning everyone was hyperaware not just of how they looked but how they *compared*. Thinking back, I picture a Piccadilly Circus-style array of screens and infographics in the second year locker room; there

---

8. Narrator voice: I was.

may as well have been a stock market-style graph up showing the most fanciable specimens, detailing who was up or down, and a scrolling bulletin across the bottom with important updates. Even though I didn't talk to anyone, break times were dominated by updates:

'Miranda had Toby at two, Toby had Miranda at one and Opal at two, but now it's OPAL at one and Arabella at two.'

'Well Miranda said she fancies Harry now anyway, I saw her new Top Ten in maths. Toby's her number FOUR.'

Boys outnumbered girls two to one (three to one, in later years), so attention was constant and predatory. Since day one, my peers had identified so many individual issues with me that fitting in seemed pointless. Besides, I'd always been *different*. Why play a losing game? But at the same time, this really seemed to matter. I was thirteen now and had yet to properly belong somewhere. Outside of schoolmates, adults regularly expressed their opinion on where I went wrong: friends of my mum suggesting hairstyles, teachers stating I might try *being like the others*. One of my teachers compared me to a girl she taught in the year below who was always made-up and accessorised: *you should be like Marti, she always puts her best self forward*. Who was I to ignore everyone? And so, begrudgingly, I tried a different tack, one I'd never succumbed to in all of my previous lonely days: Fitting In.

I wasn't aiming to be a supermodel – I was too ugly to ever be 'attractive' – but I figured if I could just lessen the level of attack then school would be more survivable. Like maybe I could get through the day without spending half of it in the bog. Style was strictly segregated: the white look du jour was skinny with prominent curves, poker-straight hair (ideally either peroxide blonde or brown with stripy highlights), glowing orange fake tanned skin with matching lips and eyebrows (if you could foundation-slather your way out of any discernible facial features, you'd got it), and frosted make-up in shimmery pastels[9]. Meanwhile, the brown ideal as seen in films and TV was skinny and slender regardless of height, sleek black hair and bold facial features: dark brown lips, eyeliner, pruned eyebrows and always devoid of erroneous hair.

And so I hit my first hurdle. Though well-meaning adults and kids alike asserted that I could be attractive if I just tried, I didn't know what I was *trying* to get to. Which one was I?! There was no indication on what attractive Mauritian-Welsh-American girls looked like. As far as I knew, there were no other Mauritian-Welsh-American girls full stop. I didn't know any other mixed people so I had no idea what to aim for. Should I mix and match from the white and brown ideals? Sometimes, I'd draw mash-up characters of brown and white celebrities, or self-portraits of me slightly taller: any form of fortune-telling that might illuminate how I'd look when I was older. I couldn't ask my non-existent friends, and I couldn't ask Mum: as a white person with blonde hair she would never have been teased for having a moustache. Besides, she already knew I was friendless and struggling at school. I figured if she could have solved my issues she would have. Like so many things, these were my problems and mine alone.

My major form of guidance was gossip acquired in the low-ceilinged girls' changing rooms; benches lined with Jane

---

9. 2003: the year style died.

Norman bags and bins, lockers slamming, girls screeching, and the constant smell of trainers, piss and *Glow by JLo*. Girls displayed status symbols in their lockers, like a Juicy Couture hoodie or a Paul's Boutique bag, and performed elaborate touch-ups during breaks and after games (ahead of rejoining the boys), reapplying perfume and make-up (I have a distinct memory of one girl applying glitter-flecked moisturiser *onto* her tights[10]). Always everyone was discussing each other's attractiveness, passing judgment and offering tips – even including me, sometimes. I noted down every suggestion that came my way. Unfortunately, most of it was incomprehensible gibberish: foundation, plucking, side partings, chemical relaxer, GHDs, gloss, threading, arm waxing, leg waxing, gels, extensions, highlights, feathering (but not tarring). I had no idea where to learn what any of this meant; the internet wasn't a thing and my house was a magazine-free zone. I'd just have to work it out and hope for the best.

And so began the bizarre operation in which I tried to go against what I rationally understood and instead plunge myself into realms unknown.

First in my quest to conform, I carefully copied the exact way people said certain words, practising my 'normal' (. . . southern) accent at home, thereby dropping the final vestiges of my first twelve years and dodging criticism for being Welsh (conveniently, later in life this would be repurposed as my 'white teaching voice'). One fault down, twenty to go! Next, I copied the standard uniform adjustments: rolled-up skirt,

---

10. She was roundly mocked, but insisted it saved time.

undone top button, trainer socks instead of regulation ankle ones. A girl in my class asked why I didn't shave my legs – I knew how to, right? Armed with new information I snuck off and bought a razor – I didn't know what the process was and ended up leaving weird marks all over my skin, but who cared, now they weren't covered in hair!

Not everything was so easy. By mid-2003, no self-respecting female student would be seen without orange tan tights (aka 'nude') as part of their uniform (under the socks). I requested new tights from my mum instead of the black ones I'd been wearing (they hid the hairy legs better) but the ones she got were lighter than my actual skin and looked like I was suffering from leg-only jaundice. She sourced others; I ended up with three different shades of nude, none of which matched my skin and all of which looked ridiculous (I doggedly wore them for about a term before giving up). Another uniform issue: girls were supposed to wear either white or 'skin tone' bras under their translucent white shirts. I had a white bra but it may as well have been lime green polka dot for all the correlation to my actual skin, a shining beacon under my shirt.

No problem, I'd just wear black tights and socks and a thick jumper year round for the next seven years![11] Next issue was tan. I didn't understand what fake tan was and was revolted to learn it was essentially brown gloop that made you a colour you weren't. Was this . . . legal? Mum said I didn't need it because I was already brown – but everyone else in my year was approaching my colour now, so surely I needed to be darker

11. This is quite literally what ended up happening.

to stay the same distance from them? How did this work – where did it end? Some girls fake-tanned so much they had orange rings on their Von Dutch caps; hardcore girls reapplied before PE lessons, checking each other for streaks; one girl fake tanned with her mum every *week*. The whole thing seemed hellish. What a ludicrous waste of time – I didn't want to spend ten minutes a week for the rest of my life concerned about 'streakage'. I decided to sack off the whole tan thing before bothering to start.

Apparently, for make-up you needed to find your 'shade'. What was a shade and where did you find them? Jesus, it was never-ending. I needed a Lailacentric manual to help me with these problems. People used words like 'caramel', 'mocha' and 'toffee' to describe my skin tone, but this made me think of the synthetic takeaway frappes popular girls brought in as a status symbol, or the translucent sugary syrup inside round silver tins from when I'd baked with Mum as a kid. Those weren't real naturally occurring colours of things, like skin. They were artificial. I wasn't those colours. When I looked at my arms, really looked at the tiny lines of cells and the soft downy hairs, I saw a deep warmth, reddish undertones, lambent copper, the colour of sandstorms in the desert, not the inside of a Taz. I thought I was the colour of unset clay, malleable and still forming, the colour of creation. The colour of young twigs stripped of bark. The colour of thick rivers rich with nutrient; and burrows in mountainsides; and holes within trees: the colour of places of shelter and sleep. I remembered standing in the soft sands in the Mauritius sea, lifting my feet out of the waves, watching the water turn the imprints a deep, dense brown – that was my shade, the colour of sand that meets the sea, the colour of things that existed long before I did, colours that dodos knew, colours the sun had seen for centuries.

Good luck finding that on a swatch in Boots: I spent one terrifying quarter of an hour alone in the make-up section before I scared myself away forever, daubing Maybelline Dream Matte mousse on my forearms in a successive rainbow of not-me colours. Okay, clearly make-up was not for me. I swore off that too, accepting that I was doomed to never get on an even keel with the rest of my classmates.

At home, my body was a constant source of conflict that no side was ever prepared for. At least kids at school were consistent on the things that were wrong with me: Mum and Dad's contradictory statements were disorientating, no one clear takeaway, no single course of action that would have made them both happy. Dad thought I dressed 'weird' – huge flared jeans and a jumper tied around my waist to hide any semblance of shape. Mum encouraged me towards normal clothes (currently clingy floaty-sleeved tops and boho skirts with giant medallion belts: *Pirates of the Caribbean* extra), but was mostly happy for me to wear whatever I wanted (. . .so, not that). She, however, didn't like my still messy hair, encouraging me to brush it into submission – but Dad said if I didn't want to brush it what was the big deal?

Deciding to fit in was tiring enough without the contradictions. Girls at school said if you were tanned, everyone[12]

---

12. 'Everyone' here meaning 'the eighty pubescent boys who made up the rest of our year'.

would be into you. Well, I was tanned and all I got was bullied. I missed the nuance of *fake* tan not *Laila* tan: more *Tango* and less *terrorist*. Another time I read in a magazine that hair with 'volume' was the dream. My hair had more 'volume' than the rest of the girls in my class put together – why did it need to be flat and straight if it was also supposed to have 'volume'? Whatever you had, you needed to be the opposite.

Despite my efforts, nothing helped – I was still weird and there was always something else to pick on. And even though I was trying, my heart wasn't in it. Even then, when I looked in the mirror and tried to see the hideous gargoyle everyone else saw; tried to align the nicknames with the sight of my own face, I just . . . *didn't get it*. I saw the same person I'd always seen: soft, thick hair, occasional freckle, same smudge of a nose I'd always had – my grandad Woozeer's nose! Away from other people's comments, I couldn't help myself – I liked the way I looked. I'd look in the mirror and grin at myself: my crooked teeth that wanted to hug each other, my cheeks that crinkled upwards as if embracing my eyes. Almost every aspect of my life had changed from Wales to now, but I could rely on the notchy way my nose twitched and the way my hair boinged up when I tugged on a coil.

I didn't just appreciate those parts of myself, I *loved* them. They were mine, they'd come with me, they were me. Thinking badly of them would require thinking badly of myself. It was true that I didn't look like any of the peppy white celebrities or the glamorous South Asians but, even so, it was a battle to align the friendly, familiar sight of myself with 'hideous freak', even though I *knew* that's what everyone else saw. It made me feel foolish for not being able to see the ugliness myself. Who was I to ignore what I heard so consistently? Eventually you need to accept what others are trying to tell you.

The decisive moment that changed everything was that hallmark of teenage engagements: a dodgy haircut. The childhood days of fried chicken bribery were over and now aged fourteen, I just had to put up with it. On the day that changed my life forever, I'd asked for the 'in' style: side parting, sleek and straight, zero bounce; visions of Cat Deeley and Rachel Stevens in my mind. *As white and conforming as you can, please.* It quickly became clear this was a thankless endeavour for the hairdresser. He grabbed bits of my hair at random, tutting and shaking his head in bafflement as I sat blankly. With brow furrowed he said out loud, 'I just don't know what we can do with this thickness.' As hours passed, him straightening each part of my hair eight times and colleagues occasionally chiming in with a sympathetic *Still at it?* my humiliation plunged to new depths. There may as well have been a spotlight on me for people to come and gawk at. As he continued sighing and raising his eyebrows on loop, my embarrassment began to tip over into anger. What, precisely, was the issue? What was so *difficult* about hair?!

When he finally offered a chance for escape, I threw money across the counter in a hot blur – insultingly, the same cost as *five comics*, what a waste – and foolishly risked a glance at myself: unfamiliar and seething, and – oh Christ – hair pinned down on one side like flattened roadkill and a – God almighty – bizarre bouffant sprouting out to the other side on the diagonal. The hair from beyond the centre part was clearly non-compliant with the idea of facing the other way and several strands were making a bid for freedom, whilst my fringe had flatly decided not to be absorbed into the main sheath of hair as the guy intended and was already reappearing across my forehead, baby hairs spreading onto the newly exposed areas of my face. What a monumental cock-up.

After running down a nearby alleyway, I tugged on a strand, gripped into submission. Instead of springing back up companionably, the way my hair had always done, it flopped limply onto my shoulder like a dead fish. I stood there by the faint gutter smell of the bins, and in that moment, as I furiously unpinned my hair and felt strands fall lankly down, I knew pure horror. What had I done? Dear God, what did I *look like*?!

Thankfully, we lived so far away from school there was no danger of anyone seeing me and my weird corpse hair. Mum wisely said nothing about the catastrophe on the drive home, and after dashing to the safety of my room I grabbed my mirror and stared at myself. People had commented on my hair for my whole life and I had no idea why. The hairdressers who intimated my hair was bad without explaining why; the strangers who issued comments; the childhood over-my-head conversations with my mum about 'thickness' and 'manageability'; years of Mum's daily wrangling and brush wrenching; and the people around me now who constantly advised me *on myself*, unasked. The whole tedious enterprise seemed suddenly exposed: even the media who only offered one acceptable look per ethnicity and the magazines with endless dull lists of products and the fake advice peddled by ads. These negative realisations collided with how *boring* it all was and became distilled to this one image: me, sullenly staring back at myself. What exactly was so inherently bad about my hair?

And why was I listening? I didn't find hair compelling or exciting. Some of my anger turned into frustration *with myself*, something I had not felt before (or since). Why was I giving so much time and energy to this? I was trying so hard to engage in what I thought people wanted and not only did I still not fit in, I now looked ridiculous into the bargain. Who was it for? I *liked* my hair: as a baby twiddling it to sleep; as a kid boinging the curly bits in amusement; as a scared eleven-year-old crying into it when we left Wales. Just this year my hair had hidden my non-regulation ear piercings at school. My hair was a loyal companion, a built-in comfort blanket, an unwavering ally.

I don't know what it was about this specific day or this specific haircut that caused me to feel all this. 'Angry' wasn't generally in my emotional vocabulary. But as I felt the slippery strands hanging around my shoulders, staring at the strange, straight-haired reflection of myself, a rising rage engulfed all other thoughts like a tsunami. Enough was enough. I didn't want to do this anymore. Forget the nude tights and the straighteners and the trying to care about make-up. Forget the 'tanned is good but not you, Laila, *you're* a suicide bomber', and the 'curvy is great but not you, Laila, *you're* fat'. It was too confusing to try and figure out, too tiring to continually fail. And I simply did not *care*. I was *done*.

It was more than just a fit of teen melodrama. I mean sure, it was a bad haircut (and who hasn't had one of those?) but it was the first time I'd said NO to other people's expectations. Up until then, all I'd been told was that I was different and different was bad. Whether not having a crayon, outright bullying, or simply a hairdresser unfamiliar with my hair type, it all added up to being continually told I was wrong. During adolescence, this was repositioned as my fault. I heard this in teachers offering me an 'easier' version of my name, girls at school suggesting appearance edits, family friends wondering aloud how I could fit in. However well intentioned, the one unifying thread was: *you'd be better if you tried*.

The haircut forced me to reckon with that narrative. Was I really a victim of my own inability to try, and everyone else some kindly saviour? Because actually, I'd stopped being on my own side. As I unravelled these thoughts, twiddling bits of hair in my fingers, I decided maybe I wasn't the one who needed to keep trying. Maybe other people could try to accept that I looked different to them or try to understand me on my own terms. Because when it came down to it, I didn't want to be attractive or popular or pretty. I'd been 'pretty' before and that had changed overnight: it wasn't a very lasting attribute. Why chase it? The only thing I wanted to be was *happy*.

With this realisation came a revolutionary new line of thinking. Maybe *I* am not the problem. Even if nobody else does, *I* like myself. Maybe I could just jack it all in and be my own version of a person! I had no way of knowing what a grown-up Mauritian-Indian-Welsh-Scottish-American person was supposed to look like, but I could just find out – or maybe I could make it up as I went along. Yes! I could *do* things that made me happy! Follow my interests, hang out with myself, have the best time ever! It had to be better than this. And one thing was crystal clear: I would never return to the hairdresser's.

This message of self-empowerment may seem common enough now – clichéd, even – but back then, as a teenage-brown-skinned-girl who had never heard that it was okay to *be myself*, it was huge. What doubled the impact was that this message came from ME. I was leading the charge – and it was thrilling. After locking myself in the bathroom and three furious consecutive hair washes (System of a Down playing on my tinny speakers looped under the door), I grinned at myself in the mirror, shaking my hair like a dog emerging from the ocean, feeling happier than I had for a long time. What a joy it is to be your own best friend! And when I went to bed, I smiled myself to sleep, and the streetlight beamed in with a soft orange glow, and the tree outside the window grew up towards the moon, and the curls tickled my ears companionably, slowly recoiling, turning softly in on themselves, back to where they wanted and were always meant to be.

Chapter Five

REMEMBERING PLUTO

Mauritius, 2004. My Auntie's death had left a palpable gap in the family. It was a comfort that my uncle and cousins lived in the same house, with the same plastic-covered sofas, the same balmy evenings punctuated by the sound of the muezzin, the same chickens (or at least, their descendants) gossiping in the hot dust of the yard.

Despite Dad's contradictions three years before, I still understood myself as 50 per cent him and 50 per cent Mum, which meant 50 per cent *Mauritian*. Dad was my one link to Mauritius but he rarely talked about it – and Mauritius never popped up in films or TV, so I had to make the most of our trip. I took every notebook I owned to document each moment, noting down the particulars of every day like a field researcher even if all we did was drive from the airport to my cousins' in the dark. Pages on pages about my warm jeans sticking to the plasticky faux leather of the seats, the radio crackling in and out of signal, and the lush woodsy smell drifting by.

One day, we visited Dad's cousins who owned a well-stocked general store: loaves of bread, tins of fruit, toys and games, minced beans and sauces, punnets of fresh vegetables and, thrillingly, huge sacks of rice emblazoned with *Laila*[1]. Everything was carefully piled on exposed wooden shelves that went all the way up to the high panelled ceiling like a cave of wonders. The cousins themselves were joyful, cheerfully welcoming us in, joking around with my dad and sneaking me treats. I definitely wasn't biased but it was objectively the best shop I'd ever been in. When we left, laden down with goodies the cousins had refused to let us pay for, Dad commented that if he'd stayed in Mauritius he might have worked in the shop.

'Do you think you would have liked it?' I asked him, thinking that *I'd* have preferred working there over the spreadsheets and errands and meetings that were his job in England.

'It's not about liking it, Laila; you have to earn money to live. We all have to make a living in this world.' He often made statements like this in the UK, and every time we met local people, and it was 'met' rather than 'encountered' because we really did *meet* them. Hotel concierges, cleaners, taxi drivers – Dad would always have a conversation about their life, their family and what their days looked like. Sometimes he swapped details, staying in touch – more than once we had somebody we met on holiday come to stay in the UK with us – other times he'd buy presents for people's kids or pass on extra clandestine tips. Dad made sure to state how this could have been him, and the knowledge that we could have been the ones receiving instead of giving was never far from collective consciousness. For me it

---

1. All those years I'd spent wanting to find my name on something only to learn one of the world's leading food brands had my back.

was a strange thought: Dad, who ran a successful business and read degree-level science for fun, who worked until two in the morning and did hours of admin every day. I couldn't imagine him bagging groceries or arranging fresh towels on a bed.

We met more cousins every day and I couldn't visualise how all these cheerful, welcoming people fit together, sketching a rudimentary family tree in one of my notebooks. Dad's paternal family was enormous, with seven, eight, even ten children on some of the branches. Dad wasn't great with names of relatives and many people had died along the way, so I had a lot of blank spaces and question marks – but every now and then came a link to a real living person. Three siblings over, two generations down, we found our cousins in Birmingham.

'So, they're not proper cousins, are they?' I asked, trying to recall how everyone connected as explained to me at the family reunion in Oregon . . . second branch, once removed . . . carry the one . . . Dad frowned at me.

'I don't know, Laila. I don't really know the "system".'

Dad didn't know the 'system'? Well, I didn't know there was a 'system' – I thought families just were, existing in absolute terms. You weren't a dad in some systems and not a dad in another system, surely? Questioning Dad, 'the system' turned out to be the *Western* system, where the same words were used to diminishing clarity. Naively, I'd assumed all words and titles simply swapped over between languages, one in one out. Here, different relationships had different titles. This explained why Hass, Iqbal and Ameena had different words for 'uncle' when they addressed my dad: different titles conferred the specifics of the relationships. For example, your father's brother was chacha and mother's brother was mamou. And there were even more levels of detail beyond that – sides, age, order, respect. My own uncle in Mauritius was my poupa: my father's sister's husband.

How illuminating! How wonderful and . . . logical. I had a sudden sense of belonging as another branch on the tree, leaves gloriously unfurling – I wasn't just some tagalong, I was somebody's *mother's brother's daughter*, somebody's *wife's brother's child*. The English terms seemed woefully inadequate; a small set of core terms recycled into obscurity, with endless confusing addendums. *My maternal great-great . . . my cousin once removed . . . my second youngest in-law*. Meanwhile, everyone in my Mauritian family had their own individual term; an ingrained way of showing the unique relationship we shared. I had various *uncles* across both sides of the family (and several more if you included obligatory family friend 'uncles'), but I had only one Poupa.

Subconsciously, I'd accepted that the West was the peak of civilisation and everyone else was operating in a lesser system, trying to catch up. This wasn't an opinion I'd formed – just the general attitude I'd inherited from society. This whole exchange with Dad marked the first time I became aware of the Western lens I viewed the world through. But a single Hindi title encompassed a whole sentence of relativity in English. Which was really the lesser system?

Mere days later, Dad introduced another, bigger system to reckon with. We went on a walk further up from my cousins' house. Away from the main roads, Port Louis became a scramble of side alleys and precarious mounds of rubble criss-crossing over the mountain. We continued upwards; homes were packed on top of each other, people's yards defined by rows of stones and the occasional tree. It reminded me of our road in Wales, a road so poorly defined that nobody had bothered with names – except instead of ramshackle cottages, we were surrounded by tenuous-looking constructions of tarp and corrugated iron. Eventually, we stopped at one patch of red, dusty earth by a huge mango tree.

'This is where I grew up. Come and have a look.' He spoke to a lady nearby, then beckoned me over to a small structure made of corrugated iron, held in place by breeze blocks.

'This was your house?' I asked, incredulous. 'You lived here?'

'Yes.'

We wandered inside. The living space was split into two areas via a piece of corrugated iron in the middle, a few meagre belongings placed around the edges. No electricity or running water, no windows, no doors, no floor – just the same dirt ground that was outside the house. It seemed more a temporary relief structure than an adequate home for a family of five.

Dad chatted to the lady in Creole, smiling and laughing, whilst I took in the house, speechless. I was shocked, horrified, upset and confused: I couldn't take in this humble dwelling and pair it with *my actual dad*. Dad had lived *here*? But . . . we lived in a *house* house. This was a shack – I'd seen sheds more ambitious. I'd only seen houses like this on news reports and Comic Relief segments. This was . . . *poverty* . . . was Dad from the *Third World*? Was Mauritius the Third World?!

As we meandered back down the hill, Dad cheerily bade the woman farewell. I thought I might cry. Privilege had drop-kicked me in the face and I was shell-shocked, stinging with shame. I took water and electricity for granted. I had my own room with drawers and a bed. I had never lived in a house that didn't have a door – or a floor. In fact, I could only imagine seeing a house like this in the context of helping poor people: like when school sixth formers went to construct schoolhouses in Mongolia, or in the backdrop of a charity appeal where miserable kids sat glumly in the doorway, waiting for you to send them money. But Dad hadn't come to this house on a gap year. Dad had *lived* here.

We stopped by the large mango tree.

'Come and look at this, Laila. I planted this tree from a mango seed when I was just a kid, too! It's so big now.' He grinned up at the majestic tree as though it were an old friend, sunlight peeking through the branches.

But I was utterly lost, struggling to make sense of what he'd shown me. My understanding of the 'system', of how the world worked, was that we in the West lived in our world, full of cars and shops and Game Boy Colors, and somewhere out there poor people lived in dire poverty reliant on charity, in a different world, literally: the *Third World. We* were two worlds over in the *First World. With your £3 a month these depressed youngsters can be happy kids playing in the sprinkling jets of a water pump instead of a polluted river.* I'd understood that if you were in the Third World, you stayed there: it maybe got easier – schoolbooks instead of hard labour, vaccinations instead of premature death – but you couldn't escape the system. You didn't go from polluted river childhood to a day out at Thorpe Park. That was only a thing in our world.

Dad was inadvertently presenting a totally different version of events. You could start in the Third World and end up completely – comfortably, even – in the First World. It was inconceivable to me that Dad could grow up without electricity or furniture, and then a few years later casually head to the Boxing Day sales or celebrate a birthday at Pizza Express. *In the same lifetime.*

Where were the poignant adverts about that? I'd never heard this message. Dad had done something that you weren't supposed to do, accomplished an impossible feat – like the way you could iron off the water marks from a paintbrush jar on the table; like the way you found MissingNo. for a million Rare Candies; like the way sometimes in a plant pot a random shoot of a different, rogue plant would appear and Mum would say, 'How'd that get there?' Dad had glitched real life, somehow starting on Level One and jumping ahead to Level One Hundred.

As we walked back, I searched for answers that could lead me to comprehension.

'That's where your whole family lived? All of you?'

'Yes.'

'But . . . how did you fit?'

'My parents slept in one room and we slept in the other.'

'But where did you keep your toys and stuff?'

'We didn't have any,' he said, nonchalantly, gently chuckling – it was comforting to hear Dad's familiar bemused tone trickle in. 'We played outside, amuse ourselves, play games, you know.' He nodded back to the mango tree, resplendent in the late afternoon heat, rustling gently. Dad's answers made it sound normal; playing outside and planting fruit pips were things I could relate to. But he had just shown me this house! I kept asking questions. I didn't like how patronising I sounded but I desperately needed to understand. *Where was the toilet? What did you do for water? How did you cook?* What I was really trying to ask was, *Dad, are you from a Third World country? Were white people sending you money? Did a celebrity and a camera crew ever come round and offer to build you a front door?* I was near tears. But Dad laughed good-naturedly.

'Well, that's where we lived! What do you want me to say, Laila? We were poor! You're very lucky to have a house that has all those things.' Dad had told me I was lucky for as long as I could remember. It hit different now – I felt not just lucky but endlessly charmed, plushly living some lavish life of luxury. Emotions swarmed like mosquitos; how neglectful I'd been in taking that life for granted – but also, it was jarring, because in the UK many people *did* take that for granted. People didn't come round and marvel that we had electricity, or fawn over the front door. We weren't considered lucky beyond our wildest dreams, we were just . . . normal.

I sat on the pristine white bed in the hotel room and thought about this chasm, the many differences in what could have been. If Dad had stayed in Mauritius, I would have gone to the local madrasa, spoken Creole; maybe worked in the cousins' shop at the weekends and visited my poupa's house for dinner, helping to prepare the briyani and fetch grain for the chickens. Planted trees. Instead, I went to a gigantic school where I had to suppress everything I liked about myself in order to have any chance of fitting in. I thought of my earlier attempts to find nude tights and understand foundation, and knew disgust charged with deep bitter shame. How horrible. Garish. I needed to seriously consider what kind of life I was trying to live. Because what was I *doing*?

Suddenly, intensely, it returned – looming up against the ceiling, the old sensation that the back of my brain was spilling over, a low growl, like an ocean was flushing out and I was trying to catch it in an envelope. Ideas swarmed my head as I thought about my dad working in the shop in Mauritius and how that was a massive step up from the tiny tin shack house; yet in London, South Asian corner shops were a stereotype and *thank you, come again* was an insult I'd known my whole life; but at the cousins' shop I'd felt so warm and welcomed . . . What if *Dad* had been the one who stayed in Mauritius and we were the ones working in the shop, having rich cousins from elsewhere visiting *us* . . .? What if *we* received the bake sale money instead of being the ones who baked? What if *I'd* been the malnourished kid staring at the camera? The more I thought about it all, the more fractured I felt, stuck at the intersection between loss, guilt, pride and shame, impossibly watching the ocean drain.

Back in the UK, and about to start my fourth year (aka Year 10), I was gearing up for another friendless year of school, too full of ideas, which buzzed around my mind and obscured everything else. At school, I maintained a healthy interest in what was current to keep up with my peers, but privately, I had accepted that the mainstream was not *for* me. For most of my life, stories related to 'real life' excluded me: I recognised the settings but people like me never existed within them. So rarely finding characters became a sense of my own self-lacking. Where was I?! This was true in childhood and true now – teen girls in books and films were preoccupied with boys, snogging and spots. Nobody fancied ugly weirdos, so snogging was off the table, and I had zero concern for spots (ironically, for all of my apparent ugliness, puberty was kind to me with nary a red blotch in sight – I can only assume my body took stock of the situation and decided bringing anything further to the table would be overkill).

As for boys, I had what I assumed were crushes on people ('people' here meaning 'an often-animated range of fictional and non-fictional humanoids of varied species and gender that I greatly admired'), but it was different to what kids talked about at school (namely: who you wanted to snog). Like my list of weird-named dark-haired brown-skinned girls from childhood, I carried my 'crushes' around in my head and didn't know if I wanted to be *with* them, be *like* them, or just *be* the way they were, in a story of my own. Watching teen movies felt like a documentary about some alternate life, all chancy escapades, classroom gossip and awkward flirting. Who the hell were these people and where did they exist? Where were the people wondering if they could learn Creole purely from listening to their dad's side of the conversation on the phone?

Things were pretty dire outside of explicitly adolescent fare. In my mid-teens, the widely derided Ferreira family debuted on *EastEnders*. Panned by critics and audiences alike, how rubbish they were felt personal.[2] In the absence of other brown people they became the representatives for everyone. Popularity of *Little Britain*, the nation's favourite minstrel show, was at a peak, adding to the confusion of what was racist and what was

---

2. In researching this book, I came across several articles on the Ferreiras in which white authors who derided them were flabbergasted to learn members of the British Asian community also didn't like the characters, like because we were starved of representation, we should also be devoid of taste.

acceptable. But worst of all for me was the painful portrayal of Parvati Patil in the *Harry Potter* series.

Harry Potter had been an inescapable presence since primary school, and by 2005 a new film or book release was practically an annual event. As a child, I'd adored the first three books, picturing Harry's world how I wanted, but the release of the films offered a definitive take on everything. The first film (covering Harry's first year of school) was released a term into my own secondary school experience, and (magic aside) looked alarmingly similar: hordes of white people swarming labyrinthine architecture. Parvati – a minor character in Harry's year – was one of a tiny number of non-white faces, like me. In the books, Parvati is giggly, gossipy and snooty (incidentally, all common negative stereotypes of female South Asians[3]), until the fourth volume, where Parvati goes from 'background character' to 'momentary key protagonist' during a scene in which Harry and BFF Ron take Parvati and her even-more-background twin Padma as their dates to a school event. The dates are disastrous and our heroes end up loathing the two girls. This had been painful to read in the books – to the point that I stopped reading them – but the full cruelty of this scene was felt far more keenly on screen: two brown girls outfitted in hideous ill-fitting lehenga-adjacent costumes only to exasperate the main protagonists, played for laughs. The one moment

---

3. Later in the series, Parvati and her twin sister Padma are the only pupils to be literally drawn out of school following a violent attack; overprotective Desi parents, am I right?

in the spotlight for them – for us! For brown girls! – and they'd totally gone and ballsed it up.

Talk about injustice. This was clearly not a story for me. I was an unwelcome fan. I hoped Parvati would have redemption – or maybe a new brown girl would be introduced to play a more crucial role and I'd feel able to be involved. No other cultural phenomenon rivalled *Harry Potter* and it was impossible to avoid as Harry grew with us – and I didn't want to avoid it as I had initially loved it. I just wanted to be included.

Why immerse myself in media that was made by people who had no idea I existed? I backed away from those depictions that upset me, knowing they probably didn't apply to me anyway, because I was half-white. What a horrible hypocritical stance to be stuck in – when I resonated with something, I wasn't able to lay full claim to it, but when something didn't work for me, I backed away. Instead of all the painful pop culture, I started to seek out stories that made me feel affirmed and not ashamed. I knew from my early search for weird-named dark-haired brown-skinned girls that this was no easy task. But I had to try. My identity so far was constructed from negative observations and absences; a colour that could not be crayoned, a name that could *not* be spelled, an ethnicity that did not exist. But you can't become yourself via process of elimination. I needed to see myself in *anything* to know I was valid. Even if I couldn't find somebody that looked like me, I could at least find something that *resonated*.

Life took on two separate strands, like two ribbons twirling around each other. One was a striking fear of some incomprehensible form that had taken over parts of me. Songs I wrote at this time have themes of being hunted or something stalking me, and my diary entries talk about the confusing tangle of threads and ideas I was trying to make sense of. Sometimes after school I would sit blankly in my room, unable to focus. Other times I would cry for hours, not about anything in particular, just silent tears falling down my face like I simply couldn't hold them any longer. I didn't understand why, and it frightened me.

But there was one tiny, precious jewel of a secret. The second strand, dazzling gold: *I believed in myself.* I carried this secret like a talisman in my pocket, and, slowly, the radical line of thought that had begun at the hairdresser's and continued through my self-reckoning in Mauritius now led to a whole journey of self-acceptance; a commencement of self. It wasn't just appreciation for myself but an adoration. I loved myself. I wanted to see myself succeed, take myself elsewhere and be happy. Now that I'd sacked off trying to care about the things other people cared about, I had a lot more free time to unapologetically focus on the things I was interested in. Chiefly, figuring out and understanding my family and heritage, and who I was within that – but also what I wanted to be, what I filled my life with.

And so I set off to seek myself.

Following a map of my own design – the levelled-up version of what child me had done – I ventured out on my quest. First, it was music. Then, books, comics and films. And then it was *everything*: clothes, games, room décor, folklore, history, spirituality and philosophy. Anywhere populated by others was off the table: I knew I wasn't acknowledged in the mainstream and sought places that were obscure or forgotten. I took myself on days out to museums and markets, scoured the TV guide and recorded anything 'unusual' sounding, spent half terms investigating antique fairs and weekends hiding away in the indie record stores in town. I saved photos of various fashion inspirations[4] in a folder of the family computer and used them as shopping lists for my weekly trawl round the charity shops.

Most of my favourite things – across all mediums – had a lot in common: unorthodox form, broad narratives, dense references, complex timelines, magical realism and expansive world-building, all seemingly built on some huge lineage I didn't fully understand. Without knowing any of those terms at the time, I categorised my preferences as 'basically anything that feels like it has *a lot* going on'.[5] I collected my favourite parts, and then made my own things, pinning artwork on every wall next to bolts of cloth from Mauritius and photos of myself, trying to chart my own progression.

---

4. Debbie Harry, Jimi Hendrix, Harajuku street style, vintage circus performers, Sailor Moon screen grabs, Ballets Russes costume designs.
5. Sample artist list taken from my gen one iPod, which miraculously turned on for the first time in thirteen years: Thelonious Monk, Led Zeppelin, Stockhausen, Debussy, Kate Bush, Nick Drake, 1986 Omega Tribe, Wu-Tang Clan, Sérgio Mendes, Radiohead, Asha Bhosle, Oscar Peterson, Tchaikovsky, The Beach Boys, Shostakovich, Piazzolla, Sophie Ellis-Bextor, Ella Fitzgerald, Jimi Hendrix, Amy Winehouse, Antonio Carlos Jobim, The Monkees. Sample work list: books and comics such as *The Passion of New Eve*, *Nana*, *The Master and Margarita*, *Watchmen*, *Candide*, *Chobits*; films such as *Happiness*, *City of God*, *Battle Royale*, *Strictly Ballroom*, *Paprika*, *Reservoir Dogs*, *The Royal Tenenbaums*, *Palindromes*, *Pecker*, *The Red Shoes*, *Orfeu Negro*; series such as *Bleach*, *Monkey Dust*, *Will & Grace*, *Arrested Development*, *The Twilight Zone*, and, of course, still, always, *Sailor Moon*.

Discoveries appeared randomly. A framed photograph in a window led me to Moondog. My brother's flatmate lent me *House of Leaves*. A Comicana display introduced the first volume of *Scott Pilgrim*. Internet mistakes led me to *dozens* of finds. In the mid-noughties, the internet was more of a hobby than an omnipresent layer of reality, and seeking out music and shows online was basically guesswork: searching KaZaA, randomly clicking on a file and hoping for the best. Five hours of downloading later you could find out if it was the song you wanted or not (RIP to our downloads folder).

Sometimes we visited Southall, an area with a large South Asian community, which reminded me a bit of Mauritius – Mum stuck out, instead of Dad and me – yet it was distinctly London: familiar accents and Walkers crisps in the corner shops. We'd visit shops full of fake flowers, framed velvet prints, gold tissue box covers – I wanted *everything*; an opportunity to collage myself a culture. Dad would roll his eyes and laugh – *what do you want these tacky things for, Laila? Your room is going to look like a typical Mauritian home* – but he didn't realise this was the highest compliment he could have paid me. I was drawn to these items not only for the aesthetics but for what they represented.[6]

This might all sound like a needlessly cumbersome way to engage with things – dear God, couldn't I just whack *The OC* on TV like everybody else and be done with it? But it was fun, and it wasn't like I had friends to hang with instead. I'd accepted

---

6. Although you can't go wrong with a chintz toilet roll holder, can you. Timeless.

I was never going to fit in, so I might as well embrace that and choose something else. I'd learned as a child that engaging with things was only possible through a dogged resolve to find characters like me. This teenage process of fervent, rigorous exploration was the logical next step in connecting to myself, the only way I knew how to. This method of *finding* things (instead of just absorbing what was presented) also meant they felt truly mine, like they belonged to me. Not much of what I found was made by or for brown women – most didn't even feature brown women – but it still felt relevant to me because *I had chosen it.* It was lonely, sometimes – both liking these apparently obscure things I couldn't share with anyone and searching them out – but it was bearable, because I had chosen to feel outside of what other people were, rather than *finding* myself in a position of isolation.[7]

There must be few sanctuaries more sacred than that of a teenage girl and her bedroom. Over many late nights, my room became a safe place where I could explore my interests and commit to my quest of finding myself. It was a shrine of self. Lovingly curated playlists sang in my ears, artwork and posters draped from the ceiling, every corner of the space adorned with images of my heroes, links to Mauritius, and words of affirmation scrawled directly onto the walls amid the mirrors and self-portraits. I would mesh together pieces of different things

---

7. I feel I should clarify the obvious here: that a lot of the things I liked were and are HUGELY popular. They felt obscure because they weren't popular in the mainstream at the time, and without forums on the internet or knowledge of fan conventions etc. they didn't feel like it. They felt specific to me.

in my art, like copying my favourite art sketches but making the girls my colour and giving them thick Laila-like fringes, writing songs based on my favourite quotes or adapting clothes to look like the costumes of my heroes. These were the ways I collected everything that I liked and placed it together, into the cauldron-like melting pot of my mind, gently forming a version of myself through love and alchemy.

Sat in my room, admiring my shell chandelier and mirrored cushion covers next to my *Sailor Moon* posters, wearing bizarre mishmash outfits – patterned long-sleeved shirts from Southall layered with lacy waistcoats from charity shops, plastic hairclips and gold earrings from Mauritius, and trailing 'Indian' skirts from Camden Market over flared jeans[8] – I felt safe, and *seen*, even if it was just by myself. Here I was not a deviation from normalcy, I simply was. Somewhere out there must be a place I could go and people I could know, who would share these things with me – somewhere I could be happy. I didn't care what I looked like (which was lucky, seriously, imagine what that looked like), because I was trying to incorporate things my heroes loved with things I believed to be culturally relevant to me, or at least culturally relevant to 'my culture'. Who knew if any of these items were authentically Mauritian – if I was wearing them in the correct way, to the correct events? Could I even be an authentic, correct Mauritian or was I forever marred by my half-whiteness? On some level I knew I wasn't culturally literate with 'my people' (still a lingering doubt if

---

8. Skirts over jeans was genuinely a thing in the mid-00s. I'm shocked too and I was there.

they even were 'my people'). I consoled myself with *this is the best I can do*. My reductive efforts to combine the parts of myself together still felt relevant to me, and, besides, this made me happy during a desperately unhappy time. And it was still unhappy: that persistent strand of sadness that I didn't understand; the free-falling tears from nowhere; the jagged scratches, which stung companionably in the shower; the overflowing muddle of 'who am I' in my head. But I had some solace from all that alone in my room.

Like most teenagers, 'who I was' was a heady mix of who I wanted to be, who I loved most in films and the actual personality traits I possessed. I knew even then that whole thing was extremely 'uncool' – but I'd never been cool, so who cared? I was learning to understand myself via the art and media I consumed, and centre to all of this were – still – the projects I made myself. Making things became a way of processing the bizarre, convoluted circumstances of myself – physically doing the same thing that psychologically I was doing with my own identity.

Later, when I read psychologist Erik Erikson's description of adolescent development as a period in which identity is something 'each youth must forge for himself'[9], becoming the blacksmith of their own identity, I was instantly transported back to my forge: paint smudges on thick peach carpet, walls muffled from layers of cloth and paper, strings of lights and flowers across the ceiling, gold ornaments and train tickets

---

9. Francis L. Gross, Introducing Erik Erikson (Lanham, MD: University Press of America, 1987), 41–9.

lining the windowsill, stacks of books and CDs spattered with ink – and me, not quite done growing, curled in the corner over a guitar, quietly looking for the chords that complete the melody.

It's clear to me now that subconsciously I was drawn to things that reflected the way I saw myself: ill defined, multi-layered, inscrutable, especially in comparison to the flat and simple culture I saw around me. I'd spent my life feeling like I'd never seen myself and consequently I didn't feel like a person, or at least not a person going through life in a routine way. There was just too much going on. The old house in North Wales; the cousins' shop in Mauritius; the huge white Christian family; a long-lost grave in Sri Lanka; my big posh white school in Surrey; Dad's tiny tin shack home; the Prussian royal family; and some Wes Anderson-esque white hippie teenagers in 1970s Nigeria. How did those things fit in the same story, let alone inform one single life: mine? It was easier to consider myself on my own welcoming terms. I would sit there alone and think about how exciting it was to be me: all these stories and countries and moments tied up into one person.

Sometimes, I would lie down to get the view of the tiny scrap of night I could see above the roofs, the way I'd once lain on an old Welsh hill, and, in my mind, I'd scan the map of my ancestry and try to piece it together. Still too much to fit in my head. I couldn't connect to the parts closest to me – Mum, Dad – but if I zoomed out and tried to connect with corners of this complex constellation – to feel something for an abandoned great-grandfather who played piano, or a long-deceased grandmother with dark hair – it felt too bitty to be meaningful;

just one tiny glint of connection. All these existences were so disparate that when I tried to hold the images in my mind, they jostled for space instead of sitting neatly side by side, like trying to store the stars in a box instead of the sky.

But when I focused only on myself, it was easier – I could carefully align things to make sense in terms of me and my one little life. The process of detangling myself from these complex knots of heritage felt like uncovering tiny sparks, like the ones that used to fall out the log fire in Wales, bright glowing freckles on the hearth. Every now and then, under the heavy swarm of heritage, I'd spot one of these glimmers, and I had the sense that it was my task to protect it long enough for it to become something else, like a match or a torch or a lantern.

Nurture these faint flecks into something that could light the way. These tiny sparks gave me a framework to begin understanding myself and my heritage – little lights that offered me a path to follow and keep seeking.

If I could just follow this path for long enough I might find myself. It made the process of searching for things and making new things feel not just fun, but *crucial* – I *needed* to find a sense of self and a way to understand. I *needed* to search out those soft embers and hold them in my hand.

Finally having some handle on who I was had a profound effect on me. Though school was still difficult, I found myself with friends for the first time. People didn't mind that I was always banging on about the environment and animals and random films nobody had heard of because there were occasional things we *did* share. I oscillated between the nerds (we shared *Final Fantasy*, guitar tabs and Flash animations), the emo kids (we wrote lyrics on our Converse and wore Camden Market neckerchiefs), the metal kids (we trod the hems of our Bolts into oblivion at sweaty Astoria gigs) and the girls in my classes (all Juicy Couture and dolly shoes; the cool ones were from Topshop but they were expensive so I had a gold pair Mum got me from Tesco).

As we'd gotten older, the barriers between us all had begun to lessen and at weekends we hung around in large groups, mooching around the leisure centre or hanging around the cinema multiplex. Sometimes we even went into the films. Weekly 'parties' at other people's houses consisted of thirty hormonal teens watching American high school movies and consuming copious amounts of Domino's in somebody's parent-adjacent living room; girls in low-rise Miss Sixtys doused in Impulse body spray; boys with bent necks, flicking their straightened fringes across their face every five minutes, jeans drooping somewhere around mid-thigh.

It was easier to *be* friends with people now – instead of the bolshie popular kids assigning traits, you could now let other people know who you *were* via long essays on your MySpace or the specific font you used on MSN. I was no longer just a collection of other people's insults: I was *Laila who is funny* or *Laila who knows a lot of music*. We spent evenings 'nudging' each other (*heya wubu2? brb afk g2g*), completing 'personality quizzes' to further announce ourselves, or leaving public in-jokes on each other's walls so everyone else knew you were BEST mates (*omg dyu rembr BLUE MUFFIN omgggg tht ws SOOOO random lmao!!! rofl XD!!*). And we had better phones now: texting crushes nightly – if they suddenly stopped re-plying they either didn't fancy you back, had reached their parental enforced phone curfew, or had run out of credit. We'd curate our inboxes to our twenty most-loved messages, and, if you really liked somebody, you'd spend £4.99 to text a page in a magazine and receive a 2D monochrome 'picture message' that would invariably max out the lucky recipient's inbox.

Most of my new friends were boys. By this time boys outnumbered girls three to one in my year at school, but also, being with girls highlighted how I *wasn't* an 'effective' girl as decreed by the standards of the day – uninterested in fashion or make-up and a poor source of both school and celebrity gossip. In the context of boys, I was a misfit by default. I was still painfully aware of being ugly at a time when this mattered, but the desire to change had evaporated, because I liked myself, so that was that. Most people agreed it was the combination of ugly and weird that made me so unfanciable, and I consoled myself that maybe I'd meet somebody similarly ugly sometime and could go out with them. Anyway, pretty seemed pointless – I'd been 'pretty' in childhood and that hadn't been fun either. I wanted to be funny and smart, like my dad. Funny and smart would be longer lasting than pretty anyway, so even though I'd be single forever I hoped maybe when we were all super-old – you know, like forty – I could go out with some fellow ugly loser, because we'd all be ugly by default then, but I'd still be funny. In the meantime, 'weird'? I'd had worse. Bring it on.

Some new friends struck more of a chord than others. One friend, Louis, burned the first two arcs of *Bleach* and *Naruto* onto a DVD for me – thereby introducing me to Mexican-Japanese Yasutora Sado (aka Chad), one of the first explicitly mixed characters I'd ever seen on screen and, incidentally, hotter than hell. I mentioned this to Louis: it turned out he was also mixed race, white dad and Malaysian-Chinese mum. Part of me wanted to talk about this, but I had no idea how. As I was still understanding my own mixedness, I didn't know what to ask – and as we were always in groups of white people the topic didn't exactly come up. Yet every once in a while, there would be a snatched moment of connection. One time, playing video games at mine, we were briefly alone in the living room whilst the others stocked up on pizza. My dad walked in, picked up the phone and started yammering away in loud Creole. Louis looked at me.

'Is that . . . what language is that?'

'Creole.' Louis gave a nod. I ventured a question.

'Is your mum ever on the phone to like . . . relatives and stuff?' Louis nodded.

'Yeah . . . I don't really know who they are exactly . . . it's weird!' We exchanged a brief snort of shared confusion; then one of the others came back in and conversation turned swiftly back to fighting combos.

Another day, three of us were up in central London: me, Louis and our other (white) friend, Paul. We made a pit stop in Chinatown where Louis was collecting something for his mum, following a squiggly hand-drawn map down a dingy side alley (Google Maps was yet to be invented) of looming buildings, where the air was thick with heat, punctuated by an ominous rattle from the dripping fans overhead. Paul and I sat companionably on a metal fire escape as Louis hung around sketchily by an unmarked backdoor.

'Well, this is weird, isn't it? Is Louis picking up drugs?' Paul snorted. I laughed, but I secretly thought it was cool – it reminded me of visiting the Hounslow supermarket with Dad;

he'd exchange a few words and a handshake, then come out laden with a cardboard box of ripe mangos or giant cellophane bags of fresh naan. Did all cultures have their own version of this?

After a few nervous minutes, Louis returned with a GIANT tarpaulin bag.

'What's in that?' asked Paul.

'Oh . . . it's noodles, I think.' Louis looked at us uncertainly.

'Don't you get noodles from the supermarket?' said Paul. I thought of the small cellophane bags and the instant one-meal tubs. This huge bag didn't look like it had seen a Pot Noodle in its life.

'Well . . . it's like . . . special noodles. Like . . . Asian noodles?'[10] said Louis, setting the bag down.

'So, is Malaysian food and Chinese food the same?' I asked. I was wondering if Louis's 'Chinese and Malaysian' bit was similar to my 'Indian and Mauritian' thing. Paul chimed in.

'Yeah, why are we in Chinatown? I thought you were Malaysian!'

Louis looked up, still wrestling special noodles into his rucksack.

'Well, yeah, Malaysian. I mean, I guess, like, Chinese, but in Malaysia.'

We were hardly probing the depths of the mixed-race experience, but I noted these moments in my diary like they were gospels from God. Even these brief interactions reassured me: somebody else who was unable to tick boxes and give

---

10. Louis, when I ran this section by him for proofing, 'Might have been rice . . . nah, I think it was noodles? I kind of can't remember.'

one-word 'I'm BLAH' answers. Somewhere out there must be structures for understanding this, words to describe our experiences and communities who shared them. I couldn't tell where, or when, but at least now I knew with some sense of self I could finally start to figure things out.

And then, not even a year later, those soft flickering lights I'd found and so carefully nurtured were snuffed out for good.

Chapter Six

Across From Ghosts

Calamity began just before sixth form. I'd aimed to leave school and go *somewhere* else for my A-levels, when two weeks before starting, I received a letter saying my chosen college was dropping Music. Music was my main subject, so I'd have to go somewhere that *did* offer Music. Without other options, I wound up back at my secondary school who *were* offering Music – but not the other subjects I'd wanted to take, so I'd have to adapt my other choices to whatever was available and I was allowed to do. This whole sequence of events dulled the hope I'd had of escape.

As First World Problems-y as this sounds – and it is, truly, a mark of my privilege that *higher education* could represent an injustice – my life's dream up to this point was to go elsewhere, and now I was back where I'd always been. People consoled me with *well that's life and welcome to the real world*, but if the Real World was just opportunities falling through and grappling with unplottable pitfalls every day, what was the point?

Dad was previously aggrieved by my Holy Trinity of Point-less GCSE Choices (Music, Art and Drama); the new Trium-virate of Useless, aka my A-level choices, included English Lit-erature and Music, which to Dad represented 'story time' and 'singalongs'. As far as he was concerned, Sixth Form may as well have been an eight-hour-long episode of *Playdays*. My third 'choice' was French. If ever a student should have dropped something at GCSE it was me and French. Dad looked over my appalling grades but declined to get involved, despite being a fluent French speaker – Creole and French were too different he said. Besides, he was busy with work and he'd never done the lengthy exercises I was doing for pernickety French gram-mar.[1] How did he learn it then?

'You don't study it, Laila, you just learn it in Mauritius be-cause it's spoken. You're not Mauritian so you haven't learned it.'

He was stating facts but this landed like a cruel taunt: a hurt-ful reminder of what a poor Mauritian I was despite my accu-mulated efforts.

Meanwhile, Sixth Form was gruelling. There was just one day per week where I finished school before 5.30pm and I was regularly up until one in the morning just trying to complete the work. Gone were the opportunities to listen to music into the small hours and draw pictures by torchlight – within just a few weeks of starting Sixth Form, the idea I'd ever had free time was laughable. Downtime? What was that? The last couple

---

1. Depressingly, my A-Level French teacher was the same white guy who'd pissed me off six years earlier.

of years had been a precarious balance of time by myself – happy time, if you will – and time trying to survive engaging with the rest of the world. And now the rest of the world was about to win.

Somewhere between the stress and anxiety and lack of sleep, the disconcerting, menacing thing that had been stalking me so long caught up with me. It pounced, and I fell. Like being knocked off your axis, plummeting to untold depths where the world became foggy and cold, a distant growling sound and a feeling of being constantly in peril. Life in this colossal tundra was harsh, and I was some small creature lost in the middle of it with a heavy paw pressed on my heart. Everywhere with others became a vast, daunting arena, and everything felt like an attack: a person talking to me, an activity I had to engage in, the act of existing around others. Even sitting down in a class-room I felt hideously overexposed. I tried to find moments I could be alone, and still, and quiet – where I could curl into a ball and just silently wait for danger to pass. Contorting to the wants of human society was too burdensome and risky, and in my small, creature-like state all I knew was the urgent need to be somewhere secure and hidden. To be *safe*.

A third of my year group left after GCSEs, including most of my closest friends. The remnants of the year banded together in ways that hadn't been possible when we were younger, with parties open to everyone – no mincing over invite lists, everything now was just an open Facebook Event. I reverted to the loner tendencies I'd had in my first few years, mooching between groups. As we turned seventeen then eighteen, able to drink, drive and smoke, we had more freedom. Every weekend we'd congregate at somebody's to listen to N.E.R.D, The

Killers and Scouting For Girls[2], swapping bottles of Smirnoff Ice in an overly manicured Surrey garden. Though I was still unpopular, bullying had lessened to simple 'loser' and 'twat' comments in quiet moments. Apparently, I wasn't entirely unattractive anymore – most people still stayed clear of me, but sometimes drunk boys would come up to me and tell me I looked like I'd be 'super-sensual' or 'wild in bed' (I was yet to so much as hold somebody's hand). The one thing keeping me going was dance and theatre. Between my encouraging teachers and the careful friends I'd formed, safely away from school, the rehearsal room was one of the only places I felt truly safe, where it was okay to be frustrated and work out mistakes.

At the start of my school years, the internet had augmented, rather than created, trends and fashion: magazines and TV had told you what was in. By 2007, this was no longer the case: you could discover your own aesthetics via street style blogs and eBay if you didn't like the high street. Fashion trends at this time were wide-ranging but uniformly horrendous: bodycon dress, oversized plaid shirt over jeggings, plimsolls, legwarmers and a trapper hat? Oh, you look great. Footless tights, fishnets, denim rah-rah skirt, a single feather earring and beribboned backcombed hair? Add some glitter then let's head out![3] It was a brave new world: people listened to Hadouken!, Jay-Z, and Calvin Harris in the same ten-minute span. With the breaking down of all established convention, I figured I'd have a chance at fitting somewhere.

---

2. Just kidding – nobody voluntarily listened to Scouting For Girls.
3. 2007: the year fashion died.

I was right: outside of school my new part-time job at a DVD rental store (genuinely a thing that once existed) was a marvel. Most of my co-workers were at least a year older than me – gap year wreckheads and art students from the nearby uni – and they *liked* me. They didn't share my weird tastes exactly, but they appreciated them, and introduced me to the things they liked. We shared film and music, using the digital rental system to leave recommendations for each other and swapping USB sticks of heavily curated playlists. One of them, a boy with green eyes, brown hair, limited edition Converse and a checked shirt for every day of the week, was, like, an actually attractive boy, way more than anyone at school, and he didn't stand around deriding me like boys at school; he thought I was *funny*. During quiet moments (so, most of the shift), we'd sit around taking the piss out of whatever family film was playing on a loop that day, or surreptitiously listen to the five MP3s we had collectively stored on our phones instead of the designated shop playlist, and I'd say something in jest, and he'd laugh at something I said.

He'd *laugh* at something I said. I was Einstein or Newton, upending all known natural order: he was an *actually attractive* white boy, and I was me, and he'd *laugh at something I said*! I wasn't supposed to make him laugh! He wasn't supposed to notice me! Media aimed at teens during this time was predominantly white and heteronormative[4]: white boys fighting over

---

4. TV included: *The OC, One Tree Hill, Gilmore Girls, Gossip Girl*, or films such as *Superbad, Juno, Nick and Norah's Infinite Playlist* (all starring Michael Cera. Seriously, he was in).

white girls; white girls winning over white boys. Even when the film wasn't explicitly romantic or didn't have a completely white cast, the romantic lead was always a straight white man. People of colour were sidekicks, nerds or erotic objects – if they appeared at all, because even those reductive appearances were rare. Girls like me were not romantic interests. We weren't even in the cast. The boy who laughed at my jokes could have been a romantic lead in any twee indie storyline and that alone put him way out of my small, brown, mixed league and yet, clearly he hadn't heard about this, because I'd say something in jest, and he'd *laugh* at something I said.

In the last couple of years, I'd found useful ways to process what I didn't understand. Or at least, get it out of my head in some fashion. Simultaneously, representation around me had changed – series like *Misfits* and *Skins* showed me that other mixed-race people *existed*. I'd seen interracial couples – Will Smith and Eva Mendes in *Hitch*, Miranda dating Robert on *Sex and the City* – and found it *odd* seeing people of two different hues together, even though I was the product of such a partnership. Representation of brown and South Asian people had slightly improved by sixth form with the likable Anwar from *Skins* and the far better received Masood family in *EastEnders* (though I was definitely teased for finding Anwar and Tamwar fit; as they weren't white boys they weren't the designated romantic leads[5]). To my mind, though, the most prominent South

---

5. Though Anwar was played by Dev Patel, and Tamwar was played by Himesh Patel – so who's laughing now?

Asian in national media during the late noughties was non-fictional, real person Shilpa Shetty: the subject of a national conversation about racism after she was targeted with racial abuse on *Celebrity Big Brother*. The series received a record number of complaints related to racism. Comments made towards Shilpa included contestants referring to her as 'the Indian' or 'Shilpa Poppadom' and telling her she needed 'a day in the slums'.

Slowly, I understood that being mixed was one thing and being 'brown' was another. All of my experiences were wrapped up inside of each other; I wasn't so much unravelling the knots as I was realising the knots existed. I was subject to varying degrees of institutional racism, structural bias and postcolonial perspective that – though I didn't understand these terms, I could see these 'things' were 'things' – most people of colour in the UK were subject to. Other problems with being *mixed* had nothing to do with my colour. Having immigrant parents overlapped both with being brown and being mixed, but was somehow also separate. It just resulted in a LOT: navigating two different sets of rules, expectations and cultures; trying to reconcile all the trauma of interracial relations present in my family, alone; lacking any degree of authentic, meaningful representation; having no idea what I was 'supposed' to look like or would grow up to look like.

For the most part, I'd accepted how things were; I was ugly to 99 per cent of people and if I wanted to be liked I had to mercilessly mock my own ethnicity: both lessons that were long ago ingrained as rules of the world. That was just how things were. My first real reckoning with this was on holiday with some girls from my year. The trip was everything you could want from a late-noughties clubbing vacation: warm booze, loud bars, messy people. We traipsed the 'strip' clad in our best 'going-out' garb – anchor print jersey, wedge heels and diamanté strappy tops. One night we met a group who mirrored us perfectly: six sweaty white dudes and a brown guy. Inevitably, members of our amassed parties began drunkenly pairing off. I hung back before realising most of the lads were shouting directly at me. This had happened before. Naturally, I feared the worst, but after a couple of minutes we deciphered the whoops and hollers. Turned out, it wasn't the usual racist bile I'd assumed. Instead, something new: a sudden, urgent motion for me to get off with the other 'ethnic' guy.

'OI! Girls! We need your Asian for our one!'

'You two can have an arranged marriage!'

'Yes! Drinks for the happy couple! Mowgli and Konnie[6]!!!!'

My own friends found this hilarious.

'Oh my *God*, they call him Mowgli, that is *priceless*.'

'Laila, we could call you that!'

'I mean, he is actually kind of fit. You two should get together!'

My immediate reaction was, *Jesus Christ, are we seriously doing this?* but then, I followed my friends' lead; it was all fun and games – just holiday *banter*. This is what happens with white people! I can let my appearance be a punchline, no problem! Have you heard the one about burned cookies? Besides, I didn't have other options: call them out, make a scene, maybe get thrown out? Then what – walk home alone in the dark? After making an enemy out of both the boys – who, come to

---

6. Mowgli from *The Jungle Book*, and Konnie as in Konnie Huq, the ex-Blue Peter presenter.

think of it, were not just plastered but hench, all rippling muscles and pecs – and the girls I was on holiday with? My friends weren't going to back me up, neither would anyone else in the bar. It was one of a thousand moments like this, where taking the wrong cue could land me in trouble. If I cocked this up, I might land on the wrong side of six wankered white dudes. And so, exchanging apologetic glances with this preordained guy I had yet to even speak to, I ventured in.

'Alright boys, but I need to know . . . how many chickens you got in the dowry?'

A couple of hours and many alcoholic units later, 'Mowgli' and I ended up outside on the pavement, away from the blaring noise of the clubs. If you got past the smell of beer and piss, it was almost pleasant; the air was warm (well, muggy), and you could just about hear the sea over sobbing girls ruining their Bad Gal mascara and sunburned lads retching into corners. We perched on an unsullied patch of tarmac, denim-coloured sky fading above, our rowdy mates either somewhere in the club or splintered off in search of kebabs. Without the egging-on of the others, the stream of 'ethnic' jokes seemed bizarre, so I introduced myself, explaining I was from London, and he introduced himself back with a surprise West Country accent. Dom. I hugged my bare arms round my knees and noticed his forearms were brown, maybe slightly paler than mine, and he had thick dark hair – too thick to be white. I was still surprised when he asked if I was mixed. Usually, I jumped into defensive mode when people asked me (it was a variation of *where are you from* and therefore always antagonistic), but he didn't sound accusatory – it seemed safe, like a 'takes one to know one' vibe. Besides, we'd left the white people and it was just us (well, and five hundred overheated strangers stumbling around, but just the two of us chatting). I chanced the backstory of my ancestors, not the answer I gave white people when they asked *where are you from* but the real thing – a pitted version of the truth.

'Thought so,' he said, triumphantly, adding that he was half-Malaysian but, 'from Cheltenham. We all are.' He grinned and nodded back to the obnoxiously loud club. I gave what I'd like to think was a derisive snort (though I've heard myself laughing and it was probably more asthmatic pig).

'Malaysian? So . . . what's the arranged Bollywood marriage thing about?' I asked, laughing but confused, and he looked up with an apologetic expression, hazel eyes catching the sun just starting to rise in the distance.

'Oh, shit . . . they're not . . . you know. They always say that,' he said, kicking a pebble into the road. 'They go hard . . . but they think it's a joke. It's not meant to be, like . . . harsh or anything.' He said this uncertainly, eyes wide. I wondered if he was seeking fellowship or my thoughts, or . . . maybe it was just the effect of the fish bowls.

Maybe they were right to pair us off together because he and I did share something the others didn't. Among friends an unwritten agreement existed that this casual mockery was acceptable – expected, even. I'd learned this a decade earlier. When those lads immediately started mouthing off and giving it all that, I'd initially felt on the spot – but realising they had a brown friend it became a compliment. They weren't *targeting* me, they were *including* me. They saw me as a cool girl (the most mythical of beings), up for the bants and down for the lols. One of them literally said this near the end of the night as I tried to ascertain which friends were coming home.

'Fair play, though, that arranged marriage girl, she is a right laugh – she can take a joke, like.'

I took that poorly phrased compliment from some half-cut West Country stranger and cherished it. I literally wrote it out in my diary because those words, what they meant – it was affirmation that I could be cool, laidback, one of the gang! I could *be included*. I could fit in! All I had to do was relentlessly take the piss out of myself and my ethnicity and allow others the same courtesy! Job done! And I knew all the jokes already – if I was going to be picked on, I'd rather the fault I'd already learned to weaponise. My friends were teased for being flat-chested or having a posh voice; I was just *brown* – tell me something I don't know.

Back in the UK, as formal schooling was coming to a close both parents nursed anxiety over my choices. Mum was concerned about where I'd go and what I'd go to, whilst Dad felt betrayed that I'd 'thrown away opportunities'. I'd been good at Maths and Science, now I'd given them up, he gave me up. He told me he had no idea where he'd gone wrong and asked why I was doing this, seemingly taking my choices as a targeted attack – a weird reversal of when we'd left Wales. I was angry with my mum for not protecting me from Dad's cruel words, but I wasn't angry with him: he seemed genuinely wounded, which upset me, both because I didn't want to be guilty of failing the person I most respected, and because I wanted him to understand why I'd made my choices and how important they were to me. When my AS results were not straight As, Dad was furious – dismissing me from the house and declaring he would no longer pay for extracurriculars, so I picked up extra shifts, plus a teaching job. Luckily, I had a scholarship for school music lessons, but as I tearfully told my dance teacher I couldn't come back – unceremoniously dropping out a year early – she offered me an admin job with the school so I could at least still access one of the only safe spaces in my life. I was now juggling three part-time jobs with music practice and rehearsals on top of full-time school.

Home started to unravel. The harsh, bleak tundra closed in. Dad was tired and stressed from work, and might lash out about anything. Mum was fretful, hanging around the hallway or eavesdropping in doorframes, apparently uncertain how to respond to things or commit to being in an actual room. Often, either Mum or Dad was straight up not there, Dad working in Wales, Mum helping my grandparents move to the Isle of Wight[7], then becoming a de facto carer for my increasingly ill grandma. Mum and I circled each other tensely when Dad was away, not arguing but not fully aligned. I felt like she was distant and shrouded in vagueness, presumably so overwhelmed by me that she just avoided me. When it was just Dad and me sometimes we could speak, openly, on a level that felt honest, but we mostly avoided each other – we both had long hours, and conversations easily became rows where I cried and he stormed out. Even when I was alone in the house, venturing into the kitchen for food felt like trying to cross the ice; me, still the small creature, lost and exposed.

---

7. If you're thinking 'that's far away', yes, everyone tried to convince them to move to Surrey near my mum and aunt, but for reasons only they knew they moved instead to the UK's premier floating retirement home.

School became weirdly disjointed. My dislike of the bitty way we learned stuff only increased in A-levels. For example, in earlier years we'd learned a lot about the Second World War, the Tudors and the Peasants' Revolt. In that order. I had no reference for how these things fit together: there were, like, thousands of countries and civilisations happening yet here we were discussing how ruffs went in and out of fashion for the Georgians. Who cared?[8] What happened before and after and elsewhere? This intensified in Sixth Form from wary suspicion to sullen contempt: I was being mugged off. I made my main French project about Mauritius – I had zero interest in French but saw an opportunity to spend more time thinking about my beloved ancestral home. And this is when things really started to fall apart. So let me tell you the story of Mauritius, as I learned it. The full story, the before and after and elsewhere.

A young island of less than ten million years, with a unique landscape – jungle, beach, mountains, volcanoes – and dozens of unique animals; what had started with fish that walked became geckos that ran up walls, marbled pink snakes that dug the earth, long round snakes that changed colour, and dozens and dozens of birds, all led by the dodos. Cousins to pigeons and makers of worlds across the island, dodos patrolled the forests and planted the trees and perfected the orchards. Over millennia, the trees grew tall and green, the sand turned seven different colours, and the mist rose from the gorges to greet the clouds. The animals grew resilient to the storms and

8. No offence to any historians specialising in Georgian ruffs.

earthquakes, grew so perfectly at home they decided never to leave: the dodos forgot how to fly, the boas buried themselves in the ground, and the bats took over the mangroves, becoming bigger than bats usually do, in fact growing beyond bats into foxes that flew. The duck-sized goose decided to stop swimming, to protect the slow-growing boucle d'oreille; the tortoises grew huge and unusually fast, learning from the dodos how to plant trees; and the eels turned black like the night, for they were shy, only returning to silver when they, in turn, return to the sea.

And so time ambled on peacefully; the creatures were happy on the island and the island was happy to be their home, and the sun was so happy it beamed down on them all, day after day.

After thousands of years of uninterrupted paradise, a ship hit the beach. The island was curious. This had never happened before; a new friend, perhaps? Somebody else to bask in the shoals with the baby starfish? A collective breath as they waited to see what would happen next. And then. Chaos. Ruin. Hell. The Dutch claimed the land, then the Portuguese and the French and the English, all in fast succession, hell-bent on destruction: unleashing ships, sailors, rats, dogs, pigs, deer, slaves, prisoners, devastating the jungle, turning caves into jails, turning forest into firewood, turning dodos into dinner, spreading disease and death and terror, abandoning what they no longer needed in a wretched path of land wounds and corpses and agony, and then, eventually, leaving. And in their wake, the island was left scarred and traumatised, reeling beyond recognition. The fish and the birds – dead. The small flying foxes – dead. The huge giant tortoises – dead. The poor curious dodos, the keepers of the island who had learned to survive the seas and the volcanoes and the earthquakes, so perfectly adapted to their home, so crucial to its environment – dead. Actually, worse: dead and resigned to ridicule. And soon even the boas would be dead.[9]

And though the bloodthirsty invaders left, people remained on the island, people who were not there before. People who had never asked for this, trying to make sense of it all and to heal, like the ravaged island. People who knew cruelty, who were torn from homes of their own and forced into slavery and indenture and rack and ruin, from all colonies and corners of the globe. They built houses on the hills and planted trees, because who else would do it now? The British created the barbaric indentured labour system, to still have workers post-slavery, forcing millions of people – mostly Indians – into inhumane contracts[10], including children five and up. People died on the voyages, endured brutal beatings and gruelling work conditions (with a yearly mortality rate of 12 per cent)

---

9. The dodo survived less than a hundred years after people arrived; the burrowing boa held on to 1975.

10. Designed as a substitute to slavery, five-year contracts, which stipulated they'd earn five rupees a month and work up to fifteen hours a day, six days a week, with 'extra duties' on the seventh day. If you survived your five-year contract – disease, back-breaking labour, appalling living conditions, lack of adequate healthcare or rations, not to mention the inevitable trauma – plus the required sixth year, then you were technically allowed to return home. However, there were numerous barriers to returning home to India, including: no infrastructure to return anyone, convoluted access to the return process, lack of transport, poor conditions on the ship, disease, no resources on returning, forgery, deception, lack of communication. Many died during the process, including multiple accounts of suicide: those that did survive the outbound journey and the subsequent six years usually stayed where they were, resulting in an incredibly large and wide-ranging diaspora of the descendants of the two million plus Indians transported to various colonies under the indenture servitude system.

only for the British to con them further out of their wages and rights. And it went on like this until 1917, with Mauritius finally gaining independence from the British after several years of riots and many lives lost, in 1968.

I sat cross-legged still in my uniform on the chair at Dad's computer in a state of shock, pushing my starchy white sleeves up to my elbows, forty tabs deep in the browser, each one detailing the horror inflicted by the colonisers. I was hot and cold all over, a churning in my stomach like my insides had been sucked out, unable to move. Rage flooded me. That this had *happened*. That people had *done this*. That I hadn't *known*. That we had rituals and memorials all over the shop for different things – 9/11, Remembrance Sunday, Guy Fawkes – and not once in my whole entire life had we had a minute of silence or a poem or an assembly or a Very Special Episode or literally *anything* to remember the people whose lives were brutalised, upended and destroyed by colonialism. Did they not matter or did they just matter less?

I'd been conned by some massive cover-up. I'd learned the sixties was flower power and mini skirts, not bloody revolts in British colonies. 'Colonisation' had conjured up ideas of dusty men in dodgy wigs wielding parchment and stolen coffee; not *Dad*, who, I realised with a lurch, dates and numbers spinning, had left Mauritius *before* the island took itself back from the British.[11] What pain I knew for my ancestors who had suffered at the hand of my other, frightening, hideous ancestors.

---

11. Dad left a week after the Chagossians were brutally and forcibly removed from their home by their British. The British used various means such as deliberately buying Chagos plantations to deprive Chagossians of an income; denying that there were any permanent inhabitants; denying the

I tasted bitter anger – steel and blood in my mouth – for the indentured labourers and ex-slaves, and simultaneously knew aches of guilt and disgust at being descended from both the French and British who had carried out these hideous acts. It was the same dizzying feeling I'd had in my earlier years when I imagined all my ancestors and tried to contain them. It was too abstract, too huge, too *much*, like the raging sea in my head was too big to be held there, trying to fit an ocean between my ears. I wasn't used to anger. I had no idea what to do with this rage. I remember asking a fellow student: did you know about this? They nodded; *oh yeah, colonies right, pretty bad*. I didn't think they fully grasped the situation. *But did you know these figures? The British Empire only just ended? 1997?* And my classmate gave me a weird stare, one I knew well – *here's Laila, going off on one again* – and said, no, not really. *Well, it wasn't on the syllabus.*

I can't explain fully why this angered me, only that it did. I felt the roar of the thousand suns that had borne down on my toiling ancestors in this flippant throwaway comment from a privileged white kid who hadn't considered a single one of those rays (even though this was also me up until now). The syllabus? *The SYLLABUS?!* Fuck the syllabus! Fuck the Georgians and fuck the ruffs. We were supposed to be *learning* – you might hope, about life, the world, everything around us, not how to pass some nonsense set of academic tests, created by a board of white people and localised to this one country. Well, this country had blood on its hands. Would we mop up the mess with an A-level?!

---

residents access to their island; massacring over a thousand animals and pets belonging to the islanders.

As I recall this now, my younger self was like some impressionable teenager who had gone down a conspiracy theory wormhole.[12] I became distrustful of everything – except all this had genuinely happened. Once I'd learned the truth, I couldn't find a way to *un*learn it. It impacted everything. How could I compartmentalise Stravinsky's 1912 importance when meanwhile over in the UK we were busy signing off on ensnaring people via the indentured labour system? How could I consider contemporary audiences at *The Bell Jar*'s publication when I knew that at that exact time Mauritius was under colonial rule? I couldn't rid the images from my mind. How terrible to be British, rich only on the backs of tortured and colonised others. It was possibly the first time I had connected with the whiteness within me – my white guilt, endemic to all whites – though I didn't know this yet. The guilt of the Brits was partially mine – but I was also Mauritian; so that insidious trauma was mine too. Learning about these things uncovered some ancient conflict within me that roared into searing existence, heavy and muscular, digging its claws somewhere deep inside of me.

After the big reveal that School Had Lied, I was not in a particularly willing mood to hop back on board the learning train. I was done. It was over. I could not go on. Life, already close to crumbling, started to disintegrate irreparably. I left the job at the shop. I stopped talking to anyone. I stopped dancing, performing, music. Home remained volatile. Time off and sleep stayed mythical constructs. I stayed awake – but barely awake,

---

12. I mean, I'd read *V for Vendetta* and *Watchmen* just earlier that year – you couldn't trust anyone. (Except Alan Moore.)

and rarely cognisant. And I retreated. I regularly slept just an hour or two at night. Usually, I'd finish work then be unable to sleep, searching for my old friend the moon, but not drawing or creating now, not self-affirming myself into existence, not even crying anymore, merely staring. Sometimes I would creep downstairs and stand pointlessly in the garden, listening to the river, appreciating the muted nighttime colours and a moment of vague, inhuman stillness, but usually I'd just park myself randomly on the floor. I'd lose myself in thoughts of what my ancestors went through and just sit there until it was time to 'wake up' to go to school. Then, I'd go through the motions of a new day (shower, change uniform, pack bag) without any sense of the previous one concluding.

Unsurprisingly, I fell asleep in classes all the time – one of my teachers joked about it with the rest of the class when I zoned out during a video (lights off, warm room and monotonous narration was a strong sleep inducer), and another told me off for slacking when my notes looked liked chicken scratches and I was half-napping on my book. *Get it together, Laila, this is sixth form!* Classmates thought I was a stoner, or weirdly aloof, as I avoided talking to anyone and scarpered the moment the bell rang. Diary entries from this time are sparse and non-linear as reality slipped in and out of focus; often writing is just a series of abstract unintelligible lines on the page.

It's not groundbreaking to say the UK shuns and marginalises people to the point where they look for other places to fit in. I, a British citizen through birth and DNA, born and raised on this scrap of land, found myself repeatedly and systematically shunned from being part of the only society I had ever existed in. Now, having looked deeper, I found my ancestors scrubbed from the page, erased from history in the same way they were casually escorted from their own country so many years ago. I started to feel trapped in some alternate reality, grappling with new anxieties, displaced in the shadowy recess of time.

Days rolled by in the same mutable riddle of torn-up scenes, the same cycle of neither sleeping nor waking, and the whole enterprise of 'life' became a feat of endurance. We were supposed to wear suits in sixth form; I took to wearing my dance shoes and trousers as part of my school uniform as they were softer and quieter when walking. School was a Sisyphean task of trying to stay as hidden as possible. Instead of going to my form room and greeting classmates, I'd sign in late at the register room, a tiny office hidden upstairs, then using the teachers' corridor I'd glide over to the back end of the music department, which was similarly out of the way, only populated by people who had to be there. The back of the department had a spare room with no discernible use that was set for renovation the following year. Our teacher had classified this as the 'sixth form music study room', kept aside for the three of us on the course. I don't think the other two used it much but I hung out there a lot, in the quiet, secluded space, storing my books there instead of the locker room, grappling with eating my lunch, usually taking off my shoes and blazer and curling up in a small ball under a desk in the corner to stare blankly into space like I did at home. I managed to avoid setting foot in the sixth form centre altogether (I found out later many kids thought I'd left after GCSEs). When absolutely required, I ventured out of the safety of this small area to journey two corridors over to the

English wing or French block, both terrifying journeys, the way a mouse might feel crossing an open field, all high panic and vulnerability.

I saw no cause for concern with any of this. School had told us it was a stressful time, so presumably everyone was going through the same thing. School itself became a bizarre ritual to engage with for no discernible reason. I had no idea why I was there every day. Absolutely no part of it made sense. Learning? What were we learning, and why? Exams? For what? If anyone had stopped and asked me what I was doing or how I felt, I would have imploded. I just wanted to find a shelter and curl up for a million years by myself, safe and warm and alone until everything ended. That was all I wanted.

A new challenger entered the arena: applying for university. School assumed we came from families who went to university and didn't explain what it actually was. Well. I was struggling with the concept of what university was (older school?) and didn't know how to ask for help because everyone seemed to know innately (and besides, at this point of whatever I was going through, forming a coherent sentence was essentially impossible). As far as I could tell, uni was a non-optional obstacle course, which involved forms, finishing school, and then moving into a hall to do more school. I'd thought it finished at eighteen. 'Applying to uni' was even more surreal: working out what to do overall in life then translating that into an academic choice at a verifiable institution. It seemed totally inane: *translate being middle-aged into a three course meal or adapt the meaning of juggling swords into a song cycle.* School used vague terms like, 'Uni has a Big Impact on your Future Choice' and we were supposed to take over from there. Talk about an exercise in abstract thought – I could barely visualise my next lesson, let alone my next year. *What did you want from life?* I wanted to sleep, mostly, and not exist the rest of the time. In rare, quiet moments, I recalled sitting in my room and making things. I landed on just one thing: be happy, and then I got stuck, because I didn't know what that meant.

Since leaving Wales, happiness was snatched moments: a forty-five-minute dance rehearsal, a four-minute song break whilst brushing my teeth, a single picture doodled after writing four essays. What brought me joy was the adventure of being myself. Essentially, I'd wanted the same thing since the Jasmine days: I wanted to be somewhere with people *like me* and I wanted to exist somewhere I didn't have to cordon off parts of myself to survive. What I meant by 'happy' was: 'I'd like to live in a world where I feel seen, heard, represented and valued; where I am not labelled diverse but just an equally normal citizen; where I am at peace with my conflicting and wide-ranging heritage; where I can easily see and recognise people like me in the media around me and do not feel shut out of entertainment; where the lives and contributions of my ancestors are acknowledged and celebrated, and where my broad heritage is part of a cohesive identity and not something I feel is constantly scrutinised by insensitive others.' But in the absence of being able to articulate such a goal at the age of eighteen I just went for 'happy'.

My peers talked about the future in clear terms: they wanted six figures a year, jobs in The City and early retirement. Every time I heard people discussing this I was baffled. Where were you exposed to these kinds of ideas? The idea of me having thought about *what house I would live in* was laughable. I'd never had a clear enough handle on myself to even begin thinking about The Future. When I imagined the future it was a dull, steely nothing: like life just capped off. The past was a tumour, the present a fallacy. The *future*? I couldn't consider such a thing. Looking into the future felt like staring down a tunnel with no end, just a dark void, like on the underground. I assumed that every day I continued to survive I crawled further down this tunnel until eventually I . . . wouldn't. I don't mean I thought of anything as macabre as death, just that the end was indiscernible. Days were mostly numb engagements, shot through with a volatile, muscular fear. Presumably it just got worse until it stopped. The idea that *the future* was some positive thing that would fall upon us all seemed wild, a fantastical legend that bore no reality, merely highlighting how absurd all our efforts to 'go to uni' were. I would stare blankly at the interminable UCAS form and hope something would work itself out. If I wanted to . . . play gigs and . . . wear vintage clothes . . . would that be better suited to Keele or Manchester?[13]

Most universities looked interchangeable: degrees in the same boring topics we did at school, red-brick buildings filled with 99 per cent white people. We'd actually visited some, like Oxford, which proved uni was School 2.0. Identical prospectuses were written in a forced cheery tone faintly smacking of desperation, wheeling out national rankings and 'quotes' from photogenic 'students', *pick me, pick me, pick me!* Ugh. Was there no other option? The forms were all listing accolades and

---

13. Manchester, obviously.

playing up strengths, some perpetual push to the top to make a peacock-style presentation of yourself. My school had an alumni programme that kept records of where every previous pupil had gone and read out current students' choices in assemblies. Supposedly, the knowledge that a whole troop of fellow schoolmates had trodden the path before you made it easier. I felt the opposite – that just underlined the connection to school. I wanted to find the university *nobody* had gone to and go there. Safe, alone, away.

I found this mythical establishment on a sepia-toned morning so prophetic it practically had its own soundtrack. Rummaging through the 'uni bookshelf', I found one brochure hidden behind a stack of others on the lowest shelf. When I revisit this moment, I picture sunlight streaming through the roof window and me blowing dust off the hidden tome as I first read the words that revealed my fate, though these are surely Hollywood-style embellishments of my biased memory. What I do know is the front cover was grey: no red-brick building, no assembled Benetton kids, no sequence of stats, no photos. Just grey, with words. The words on the front contained no identikit blurb about how university was going to lead me to lifelong friends and dream jobs and so on. Instead they explained the university was 'about the freedom to experiment, to think differently, to be an individual'. It was a direct message to me, a gift from the gods: it may as well have been read aloud by Morgan Freeman. Something in the tone of the brochure asked, *do you want to be here? Because if you don't, then don't come.* This brochure was not concerned with the perverse popularity contest everywhere else was. This brochure put the accountability on you to know who you were, and not what you'd achieved. And I loved it. The name of this magical place? Goldsmiths. I had never heard anything about it. Not in any of the sixth form assemblies, the UCAS group lectures, the conversations of my peers – nothing. Better yet: nobody had heard of it.[14] No alumni from the school had gone there, no teachers had recommended it to anyone, it was completely off the radar: exactly where I wanted to be. And there it was, finally, somewhere beyond this tundra, the place that I could *go*.

But this radiant morning was a short-lived glimpse of hope in the ongoing maelstrom of life. Dad was livid that I planned to study Music. Each time I continually failed to choose the route of a 'normal' career path he was frustrated all over again, shaking his head, eyes flashing as though lit from within by molten fury.

'Laila, you're spinning me lies! You can't make a living out of this! I've worked so hard for you and you want to go and waste your life on this! You know, sometimes I wonder . . . where did I go wrong?'

Comments like this were both upsetting and infuriating: I'd accepted myself now, weirdness and all, and understood I was poles apart from the rest of humanity, yes – but I didn't think I was fundamentally a bad person. I genuinely felt like Dad was unable to see my essential character in not recognising how important creating was to me – and he was the smartest and most trustworthy person I'd ever met, so if he couldn't see it, maybe that part of myself that I believed to be so essentially, intrinsically me wasn't there. So often we saw the same things

---

14. Well, almost nobody. Dad had heard of it – but Dad had heard of everything. He asked, 'Goldsmiths? Isn't that where Damien Hirst went?'

– but he wasn't seeing this. My dad had, indeed, been working incredibly hard his whole life in order to give me a better start than the one he'd had. What he either hadn't realised or had trouble accepting – like so many parents in a similar position – was that part of building a better life for me meant me having more *freedom*. I didn't have to do the only option that would give me a chance to survive and live, as he'd had to when he'd come to England. I had the luxury of considering my desires and my interests and my skills. I had the privilege of choice.

But try telling that to a stressed out, anxious immigrant dad. Home was a warzone, no telling what could trigger an attack: merely being in the same room could lead to a full-blown row over the person I was trying to become. We were less like separate planets in distant orbits, now something far more chaotic and charged: colliding asteroids or a collapsing black hole. It felt like Dad gave me every reason to believe he hated me – in that language, too, not just 'dislike' or 'didn't align with' but despised me in a combination of shame, regret and fury for reasons I did not understand. Sometimes I'd hear Dad ranting to Mum in the kitchen about what a waste I was, how she too was at fault for enabling my 'bullshit'. Mum could see how important those things were to me, but she was no ally against the constant wrath of Dad, presumably also wondering if one could support oneself by making experimental projects and self-reflective art about identity.[15] She was baffled about my education in general, especially now I was grappling with A-levels.

---

15. Which remains to be seen, so if you enjoy this book please tell a friend and check out the accompanying album, won't you.

'You just do three subjects all the way until the end?[16] Your cousins seemed to have *dozens* of subjects.'

Welcome to the British schooling system, Mum! It was un-believable to me that she didn't know this after twelve previous years of me in the same system. I'd hardly just arrived in the UK, this was the only education system I'd even been involved in – pick up the reins once in a while! For all of Dad's furious bluster, he was, I understood, operating from a place of concern for me. Mum had seemingly checked out years ago, wholly enveloped by some gloom between us and now just observing my life in momentary glimpses. The distance I'd known as a child was now so vast that it felt like I was so far out of her periphery she only occasionally registered me, and even then I wasn't something she was invested in but rather blankly aware of.

We were supposed to be navigating UCAS – like pretty much everything else, I recognised this as a job for me solely. I was reckoning with the confusing system of points and tiers, not just so I could progress through it but also to guide my parents through. *What do you mean you apply through an online form?* I'd spend school breaks copying out lists of what did and did not count towards my eventual UCAS points (dance, yes; karate, no), and when I didn't receive any offers by the end of my first term, I assumed I'd ballsed it up and flunked out of ev-erywhere. Most lessons began with a five-minute catch-up on who had gotten offers from where, encouraged by our eager

---

16. Just a side note that you could, technically, do more than three sub-jects for A-level; but in 2006 it was standard to do five for AS and then drop two.

teachers. I avoided out of embarrassment. It was months later when my mum asked if I'd seen she'd been moving my post into the spare room, and at 1:21am on a random Tuesday I found five invitations, offers from everywhere I'd applied, before going to bed for another night of restless sleep, keeping this to myself. But it was a little lick of light, a feeling I'd long forgotten about, like how I'd felt with my SAT results in Year 6. Like I might actually do something, and maybe, just maybe, be of some worth.

The ember fizzled out quickly in the icy blizzard of life. For my parents, being creative was a hobby they hadn't had access to, little more than a distraction from the main goal of survival. For me, making art was a necessary tool. I didn't know how to process anything without it. Dad found me answering him back and making my own choices to be disrespectful, whilst Mum thought I was independent and self-sufficient. She continued giving me lifts and funding me – able to provide practical support without the emotional parts. As far as she saw, I didn't need that kind of parenting. Dad was then (and is now) serious and intelligent, kind and generous, always helping others. I knew many people viewed him as a bonus dad – something in the wise way he dispensed advice. Similarly, Mum was (and is now) warm and friendly to everyone who ever met her – she always sent a birthday card on time and gave thoughtful gifts. She, too, was a bonus mum for many people – something in the sympathetic way she would always lend an ear. I was the problem: it seemed like my parents were capable of being good parents, just not to me. Dad became daunting and Mum became muted only when the front door closed and they were stuck inside with me.

I was angry at my mum for not doing more to protect me, but with Dad I just held guilt. I could see how hard he was trying to get me to see his point of view, but I was either too unintelligent to understand or too arrogant to concede. I was guilty of being wealthier and better educated than the rest of my family, guilty of holding more privilege but choosing to do something *pointless*. And I was guilty of imagining not having that. I knew I was lucky to have the access I had – piano recitals and poetry anthologies and all the rest of it – but still a sore, tender part of me wondered about life in Mauritius. I could have grown up down the road from my cousins and been a more inherent part of the family, fetching the bread from the market, sweeping the floor, cooking briyani in the summer heat to the sound of prayers and chickens scritch-scratching in the yard. Who would I have been if I'd never known a double reed? Desperate circled my thoughts like vultures.

My understanding of reality became further disjointed, like I was somehow suspended between planes of existence. Avoiding people, not sleeping, blankly staring, slowly ceasing. Months apparently passed in one long blurry illusion. Mum noticed something was up and came into my room at four one morning asking point-blank: are you on drugs? I told her truthfully that I wasn't, and had never tried them. *Then what is it?* I didn't know. I told her it was A-level stress. Later, I'd wonder if I should have lied and said it was drugs – at least that was an explanation, it offered me a branch back to *normalcy*, way less scary than the unknown of whatever was actually happening.

Some cruel curse wove its way through each sinewy fibre of my body leaving not one cell untouched. I started throwing up, randomly, sometimes avoiding too much food so as not to throw it up later. I tried to keep to three meals a day, alarms on my phone, even though everything tasted of grit and steel. Sometimes my stomach would churn regardless, ignoring my efforts to keep it working okay, like it had been bewitched to not work properly.

On several mornings, I came up in unbearably itchy hives or strange red rashes for unknown reasons. I discovered bruises in bizarre places I couldn't remember injuring: just below my ribs, the side of my ankle, dead centre of my calf. Sometimes I saw weird spectral patterns that were not there, or swirling shadows in the corners of my view, or small things crawling, which on closer examination did not exist – but sometimes they did: one time, a spider on my book that a teacher noticed. The high whistling and shuddering rumbles only I could hear, but the strange scrabbling noise in the corner of my room was real (squirrels, in the roof: I found out later). There was a deep shuddering bass in the 'sixth form music study room' that was unexplained until I learned it was the machinery from the kitchen below. Several branches of the tree outside grew directly into my room, brushing my bedposts, even though I thought I had kept the window closed, it wasn't, as reality shattered into jagged fragments. One day at school I ventured from my usual spot, haunting the music department, into the main dining hall, somewhere I'd not been in months. Suddenly, I became overwhelmed by a whirring feeling inside my chest, my heart was racing and bursting, and I found myself weeping and hyperventilating for no reason as I wandered absent-mindedly around the school in the midst of . . . dying, maybe? Leaving this mortal coil? It was years later I'd learn this was a panic attack. Other times I had dizzy spells whilst merely sitting down at a desk, feeling the chair spin around me, repeatedly checking all four feet were on the ground. When the chair was definitely on the floor, but I still felt like I was reeling, I wondered if space was messing with me; the distant sound of my classmates laughing at me became the embodiment of the physical forces playing a trick.

This should have been deeply frightening – but I'd lost the ability to gauge it wasn't normal. It was just how things were now. On my descent into whatever was happening, my usual emotional responses stopped working, like their batteries were run down. I didn't throw up in the school toilets and think, 'Oh my God, what is happening to me?', I just wordlessly did it, then carried on shuffling through the day. I didn't think anything. My mind was blank white noise. I became like a ghost – except less formidable, a passing shadow maybe, or a whisper, something easily lost and forgotten. I had no idea what was going on and no idea who to ask (Web MD didn't exist at this point – although, let's be honest, that's probably for the best). Asking an adult for help was absolutely off the cards – what adults? – and I avoided people I'd once classed as friends, unable to log the specifics of what was happening and scared of questions I couldn't answer. When I'd first got the hives Mum took me to the doctor who said it was either an allergic reaction or a stress rash due to A-level pressure. Exams would be over in a couple of months and I'd probably be fine then. Cool. Thanks. Back to school.

When we'd first moved from Wales, I'd come adrift from the things I knew. Seven years later, that feeling had evolved into something more complex – it was difficult to root myself in anything: school, my family, the world. I wanted to contain the elements within me, but felt like a series of ideas drifting through an unstable glitching realm. Most of the time I was blankly on autopilot – but in the fleeting moments of stillness and solitude when I did manage to find my way back into myself and feel something, it was terrifying; worse than the loneliness, worse than the crying and worse even than the leaving. I felt *nothing*. When people say, 'I felt nothing', what they usually mean is, 'I felt nothing *in response to that*', though they usually feel other things – underwhelmed, let down, confused, bored. When I felt nothing, it was a huge endless void. I felt the absence of *everything*, hope, truth, knowledge, who or where I was. I felt the absence of safety and security, of time and reality.

I had spent my teenage years struggling with two ideas: the first, that I was a whole and worthy person; and the second, that I wasn't. In my final year of school, I succumbed to the latter. It was too exhausting to try and fight my own corner and advocate for myself. I didn't voice my antagonistic opinions. I didn't dress in my mishmash outfits. I didn't search out things I enjoyed, or make space for my interests, or write songs or draw pictures or dream. I couldn't. I felt *nothing*, and in that noxious void of nothing was the full absence of everything I'd ever loved and every hard-won part of me I'd ever found.

Clearly, something was deeply wrong. When I look back at this time of my life, it's a messy part of my memories, like I have knocked a pot of ink over that part of my mind. I know that during my final year of school I did many things: I took three Grade 8 music exams, held down several jobs, played gigs and concerts, went on school trips and attended music courses. I know because I have physical proof of these things, photos and certificates and so on. I have seen a video in which I'm singing at our final assembly with three boys from my year, I own a t-shirt people wrote on, and I'm sure I held conversations with people and maintained some pretence of functioning. But I have no idea *how*. Testament to autopilot, I guess, because all I can remember is staring at books and watching the pages move in and out of focus, trying to take notes and being unable to hold the pen, sitting alone in the spare room at my parents' house, watching the clock move forward unfathomably, wondering how time passed. The only times I remember consciously thinking were when I was quite alone, staring down into the terrifying nothing, the jarringly disconnected moments where life came into focus and I felt a deep primal fear before losing it again.

At some point, I sat exams I have no recollection of, at some other point it was Results Day, which presumably meant school concluded sometime prior, though it would not have been alarming to wake up and discover I'd somehow looped backwards in time and there was still an entire year to go through. That would have been feasible, in fact, distanced as I was from all linear experience and accepted order. I arrived late to Results Day, finding the overwhelming sight of my entire year group rejoicing in the dining hall and assembling in small clumps to chat; our now-ex-teachers grouped around the sides and smiling. A farce. It was disorientating to see such life and joy in one place, to see hope, totally at odds with the cold of my life. The last time I'd been in the dining hall was the day I thought I was dying. I can't recall darting forward to retrieve my own results, but I remember leaving out the fire escape to open them outside, alone. Apparently, I'd passed all three, but hadn't achieved the necessary grade for French, meaning UCAS would have automatically cancelled my place. I'd have to reapply through clearing. I didn't know the clearing process; it was more forms and stuff, and maybe the teachers were there to assist with that, but this would have involved interactions with others and and even more impossibly – re-entering the dining hall. I decided to just directly call Goldsmiths. They asked me to come and play something as I'd not previously auditioned, they'd just offered me the space based on my application form. So, I went home and got my bassoon, and walked to the station. As my former schoolmates lined nearby bars, celebrating and bidding farewell to this part of our lives, I flicked through a pile of hastily grabbed music and walked through a corridor I was not yet familiar with to throw my bassoon together in an overlit practice room, and when I finished playing something I can no longer recall in front of a staff member I never met again, I left.

On the two trains home, I had the vague thought that this was somehow important – that I should go back and update my teachers, or share this with my family, that *something* should mark this moment. But I felt too distanced and sedated, ready to fall into the yawning void, so I just sat blankly on the trains, walked back home, curled up next to my bassoon in the spare room and fell asleep. I woke up hours later, when the sky was dark, when the day was over, when my phone had died some time before. When I turned it on, it was full of updates from the email chain – apparently I was the only member of my class not to attend the pub lunch – and my Facebook feed was a solid block of updates showing everyone else was out for a night to remember, everyone looking bleary, in photos from several hours earlier though presumably some stragglers were still out now. Part of me felt like I'd failed. I should have been partying. I should have been proud. I should have cared. Under the door, Mum had shoved a note saying well done for finishing school and if I wanted some dinner, leftovers were in the fridge. Maybe I should feel sad at this feeble end; but the way it deflated so limply felt more honest than anything. And besides. It was over now. It was done.

I walked once around the dark, empty house, everything still and everyone sleeping. I vaguely recall standing outside but that could have been any other number of these murky, indistinct nights. When we'd left Wales I'd *known* that I was headed to doom and devastation, warned by some desperate voice from the future who urged me, *no, don't go to London, don't go,* like my gilded life in Wales would ebb away into a grim pit of despair. We'd gone, and I'd endured the worst seven years of my life, and that feeling had been proved right a thousand times over. I'd never thought beyond that to what came next because I thought the pit had claimed me and . . . that was it. Things would be terrible until they weren't things. Eventually, everything ends. Even eternities. What comes after the worst? Now, I had no voices whispering anything, no inner feeling from the future, nothing – just the knowledge that it was done. But that was enough. So I went back upstairs to my bedroom, placed my phone on charge, crawled under the duvet, and closed my eyes to the sorrowful past and the nebulous future and the skittish, shaky, present, and

– finally –

slept.

Chapter Seven

NOW COLLECTING ALL THE COLOURS ON THE CANVAS

What started with three strangers in a lacklustre terraced house behind the big Sainsbury's in New Cross Gate (a bin bag full of hastily 'packed' clothes at my feet and just two sets of front door keys between the four of us) became, in just a few short weeks, nothing short of a *miracle*. For so long I'd pined for some faraway light at the end of the tunnel, and now I was here: Goldsmiths. And it was as easy as waking up to find the whole world illuminated. Victory!

Every part of life had changed: the places, the activities, the people – oh, the people! *Friends!* Suddenly, I had a whole ready-made pile of friends: housemates, course mates, friends from societies, friends of other friends, friends you only spoke to during sweaty nights out at the Student Union (but, oh boy, were you the absolute best of friends then). At university, we knew each other first as individuals (*that's Adam, the one who got slaughtered at pre-drinks and missed his own birthday*) and grew collective nicknames later – the inverse of school, where first impressions had remained the whole seven years and we'd become individual only at the end. After eighteen years of varying states of isolation, every part of my life now overlapped at the seams: group timetables, full year seminars, weekly rehearsals, houses on the same road. We shared jokes, lectures, notes, bags, kitchens, clothes, each other. Whether it was the effect of finally leaving school, too much cheap Strongbow (£1 a pint!) or that I was able to sleep through the night now, life awoke all around, springtime in October.

Days were invigorating in ways I didn't know they could be, drenched with stories and projects and passion and momentum. People putting on events and staging shows and organising protests and *making things happen*. There was space for everyone and everything. Opportunities were lurking on bulletin boards, taped on toilet mirrors and falling off of library shelves; a post-rehearsal chat or a flyer on the fridge invited you into somebody's project or launch night party or debut DJ-and-aerial-hoop event. Even empty corridors seemed submerged in ideas – every pinboard festooned with flyers and posters, every door advertising meetups and protests. Everywhere deluged with people *doing* things, and underneath was this constant call to be *part* of it. In some ways I felt returned to childhood; encouraged to play and try things and just be in each effervescent moment, but in other ways I'd fallen into the future.

Is this really what life was? You could dedicate your time to what you enjoyed and work at things that engaged you? I'd had no idea existence could unfold in this way. Goldsmiths (or at least the prospectus) had promised 'contemporary thought' and 'progressive values', fully dedicated to arts and humanities with a politically active student body and large LGBTQ+

community. I wasn't entirely sure what this meant on a day-to-day basis (it conjured up vague images of vinyl listening parties and asymmetric hair)[1] but I'd hoped it would be the opposite of the life I was leaving behind. Back before I'd gone to uni, when I was still working out what I was, my brother had told me that though classes were important, what would *really* matter is what I did outside of those classes; the people I met and groups I worked with, even what projects I signed up for, so I'd kept this in mind.

Still, I wasn't fully prepared for how immediately life transformed. My diary was constantly full: between rehearsals and lectures I said yes to everything that came my way, throwing myself into whatever wacky situation happened that week. I'd be getting changed into a sequin leotard at Angel underground station whilst my friend shielded me with a coat, live soundtracking a piece of immersive theatre in a disused underground station, or engaged in a four-hour stint playing the accordion on a wonky carnival float. Between all of it, some knot of anguish I hadn't realised lurked within me finally came loose.

It's a tricky business, coming undone. Just a couple of years before, I'd felt the total absence of everything, the full blunting knowledge of *nothingness*. At that time I hadn't hoped for understanding or grounding, I hadn't hoped for anything at all. At uni, being somewhere else, I was able to reconstruct myself using all the beloved parts of me I'd forgotten about – the version of me that was watching anime, now in a screening room

---

1. As it turns out, pretty accurate.

with twenty other people[2], or the version of me who tracked down vintage markets alone in snatched weekend hours, now leisurely browsing with friends on a Sunday afternoon. I found myself delighted merely sitting in the kitchen with my house-mates, or fondly gazing at the playground down the road as we wandered home together, dingy orange lights and the dull thud of raindrops on tarmac, just because it meant we'd arrived at *our* street.

Sometimes I felt foolish for finding everything so *meaning-ful* – what kind of overly romantic earnest loser was I? But if I could, I'd tell student Laila not to be embarrassed for finally integrating small parts of my life with the everyday version of myself. Amid the flyers for student club nights, the jumble of battered trainers by the front door and the hastily purchased identikit 'art' (*Pulp Fiction* posters and pop art postcards) ev-eryone Blu-tacked onto bland rented rooms, I slowly began to uncover a real, tangible sense of *belonging*.

During my teens, all sorts of issues had solidified as 'facts': that nobody looked like me, that I had a weird name, that I needed to hide my interests. But this was not the only truth. Now everything was turned on its head, like the groundwork of adolescence had been completely overthrown and we were all starting over from scratch. Like the idea that all my tastes were niche and weird. My new friends at university were im-mediately similar to me in their interests, preferences, sense of humour, sense of *fun*, and the way others perceived me was catching up to how I perceived myself. And it went beyond my friendship group; there was the lecturer who went on a Frank

---

2. Shout out to Goldsmiths Anime Society!

Zappa digression, the *Arrested Development* DVDs on the shared bookshelf and the yellow Beyond Retro bags that were stuffed under the kitchen sink, or how after years of hiding my music tastes my housemate would absent-mindedly sing along to an album I'd put on.

One of my course mates, Danilo, even looked similar to me – dark eyes, thick curly hair – and during Freshers' Week people assumed we were related. When lectures began a week later, it turned out that Danilo (Portuguese born and Catford bred, to Brazilian parents) had his own name-related monologue at the ready for the register. A course mate dropped into conversation that they'd been to an Indian wedding at the weekend, and I realised with a jolt that I'd never talked to anyone else about the Mauritian weddings I had attended – or any aspect of that part of my life.

Many of my new friends were not white, people of colour, and/or mixed. That didn't mean we constantly discussed such things – it would have been weird to start riffing on, say, ancestral belonging, if you were midway through an off-licence run – but even the occasional conversations we did have helped me form social connections I'd barely had before. As we were in white spaces we maintained relationships in the circumstance of whiteness – essentially brushing aside certain parts of yourself and bringing other, whiter parts, to the forefront. This meant we only knew each other through the filter of whiteness and there weren't really opportunities to connect in a more meaningful way as there were always white people around. It wasn't like you could veer off mid-conversation from ranking the Animal Collective discography to suddenly discuss your many grievances of white structures. There was always a white person around who needed inducting into the conversation. This is a conversation I first had in Freshers' Week, but I had dozens of similar conversations as time went by:

'Are you Sri Lankan?' asks a girl with similar colouring to me. We're at a house party clad in half the contents of American Apparel[3]; assembled around the fridge.

'No, I'm mixed, my dad's Mauritian,' I reply.

'Oh okay! My mum is Tamil, so I'm mixed too.' We exchange a friendly smile. The white friend next to us smiles expectantly.

'Well, my dad is from Birmingham and my mum is from Sheffield, so you could say I'm mixed too!' they interjected, at which we laugh but also take the hint: okay, we can't go further into this conversation because there are white people around who need involving. The other common response from a nearby white person was a self-pitying version of this, something like, 'oh, well, I'm just from Colchester, I'm so boring', and it served the same purpose: 'validate me so I don't feel left out'.[4] Any space where bonding might have happened had to exist outside of whiteness. When conversations did happen, they were chanced and rushed – but exhilarating, affirming in a breathless, magical way. Every time I discovered some shared connection with somebody was like plotting an anchor down.

---

3. You definitely remember those capital letter-lowercase letter t-shirts.

4. Of course there were the more obviously racist responses too, like the red-flaggy 'woke guy' response of 'well I would never have noticed, it's not on my radar, I don't notice that kind of thing or see people that way', or the pompous eugenicist reply, 'well, if you want to be accurate you mean RECENTLY mixed because we were all mixed originally'. Like, alright dude, and we were also all fish originally so if YOU want to be accurate maybe you should get in the sea?

We shared an unspoken intimacy and all sorts of quirks in growing up: trying to navigate between home life and typical British life, feeling out of place within both sides of your family, wondering if you were adopted, and so on. I'd barely vocalised some of those thoughts and feelings before, and they'd become almost imaginary – but here were others who'd gone through variants of the same.

Even elements I'd long ago accepted as truth came up for reckoning. For example: being ugly. At eighteen, after seven straight years, I'd long accepted that to everyone else, I was ugly, and I was genuinely fine with that: I knew I dressed weird and looked gross and I'd made my peace. Sure, people had thought otherwise when I was a kid, but whatever, lots of cute kids grow into ugly adults. I cared about being smart (like my dad) and kind (like my mum), but pretty? Keep it. I'd develop a personality, and exist as a loveable munter. I would always be the 'ugly one', and that was A-OK by me.

So you can imagine my surprise when actually, it turned out I wasn't. After the first few weeks where I was not explicitly being told how hideous I looked (already different to school), things tipped even further in the other direction. Shockingly, there were people, real human beings of full faculty, who thought *I* was attractive. Even more shockingly: they were mostly sober. It was nothing short of a miracle. Me? ME?! Of terrorist, man and gorilla fame? Yeah, right.

At one point, my housemate Jason got back from lectures, flung open the front door, threw his bag into his room (a rattling *ker-chunk* sound that became as familiar as my ringtone) and yelled 'Wooz!' with such force I ran out of the room (I can't recall for sure, but likely I had my bassoon strap round my neck and several mugs on the floor). He stood at the bottom of the stairs with a huge grin on his face, door still swinging behind him.

'Mate! Huge news! Guess who's into you?!' he said, spreading his arms wide. I'd sat down at the top of the stairs, agog. What? Somebody was into . . . me? As Jase took off his Converse and hung up his jacket, I barraged him with questions. Was he sure? *My* number? Was it explicitly me – what about our other housemate Claudia who was white, blonde, skinny? She was the pretty one. I was less focused on the *somebody* and more on the *my* number part. Jase shook his head, and gave me an expectant grin. *No, it was your number.*

I wandered slowly down the thinly carpeted stairs: this made no sense. My number . . . was it because I was doing music, surely – or, wait? Was it some unrelated secular thing, like a gig? I said all this out loud as I reached the bottom of the stairs and looked at Jase for answers. He'd fallen silent and stopped grinning, instead looking at me like I'd lost touch with reality. He took my face in his hands and brought it close to his, speaking slowly and deliberately.

'Lails. Tol thinks you're fit. Tolly wants your number because he thinks you're fit.' Oh my days, *what?* Jase gave a big overexaggerated nod. 'Shall I pass it on or not?'

This scenario played out over and over again – sometimes I'd be chatting with somebody and they'd throw in a, *you're so pretty*, and I'd respond with pointed debate. It was just so deeply ingrained that others thought I was ugly. The idea somebody might not only find me physically attractive, but find me attractive when an *alternate and superior option* existed (like Claudia) was at odds with all logic and reason. I had thought I was utterly alone in liking the way I looked. You mean some people saw what I saw? Like I said: miracle.

In classes, opinions were things to be battered about, proudly displayed, or sharpened into tools. People had their opinions wrapped up in other opinions, which could be unpacked and repacked and cross-examined and shared. I didn't really have any opinions like this, and during my first year I felt foolish, because I had a long and lengthy list of things I *liked*, but they were hard to brandish and I struggled to sum up *why* I liked them. I liked *Sailor Moon* without knowing anything of its *critical impact* or *contextual lineage*, and in fact it was less of a factual 'like', and more of a love; tender and gentle, like softly tiptoeing at night so as not to wake the house, or the sound of somebody's heart when you press your ear to their chest. I didn't want to hold that up for examination, to *debate* that in a noisy corridor before a lecture. Yet it seemed childish to connect to things in such a way, and I felt frustratingly naïve in lacking the critical faculty of my peers.

One of my other, more jarring, epiphanies, maybe for the first time, was how my whiteness affected me. I'd spent years wondering what it meant to be *my* colour and examining how my dad and I were similar compared to my mum. As white majority had been the default, and I was always outside of that, I'd rarely considered how this worked in both ways – the privileges that my proximity to whiteness allowed. Subconsciously, I'd learned that an acceptable brown person is one who can instantly adapt – but now I was unlearning that, consciously. I'd been socialised within white contexts, which gave me an understanding and insight *into* white processes. I may not have been fully accepted into them but I could survive within them in ways others couldn't. That, in turn, gave me access to more closed-off parts of society. I was light-skinned and received less confrontation. I possessed social conditioning adjacent to white people. I literally contained whiteness within me – some claim to some aspect of whiteness and the privilege that entails.

Elsewhere, terms like 'PoC' and 'QPoC' (Person of Colour and Queer Person of Colour, respectively) allowed me to iden-tify myself as belonging to something, in a similar way to how 'mixed' had functioned for me when I'd first heard that term a decade before. It helped me see what I was, instead of being limited to what I wasn't. Terms like PoC offered the idea that it didn't necessarily matter if you had the same exact background as somebody, because as people of colour you had broader ex-periences you could connect with. I appreciated this. It wasn't always possible to find people with the same background – half-white, half-brown people – and seemed impossible that I would ever find somebody mixed Scottish.Indian-Mauritian etc.

One day, in a book-lined study that smelled of biscuits, I stood at the edge of a rehearsal room with thirty other peo-ple when one guy, Jaya, asked me what my name was. Laila, I replied. 'Oh, and what's your surname?' he asked. Woozeer, I said. Then something remarkable happened. He grinned, said, 'Ah! Of course,' and replied with his own surname. I was stunned – this was a truly unique response. I'd never in my life given somebody my surname and received an *Ah! Of course.* I usually received confusion, further questions, or *sorry, could you spell that? I didn't catch it.* 'Ah! Of course' was recognition – an acknowledgment of something I didn't know could be acknowledged. It turned out that Jaya was also Mauritian, and within just a couple of minutes of conversation it transpired we both had immigrant Mauritian fathers and British mothers[5] with Scottish grandfathers. Both of our dads had been in the UK for decades; neither of our mums were particularly Scottish to the outside observer; we'd both grown up with a limited understanding of our extended family . . . and on the list went. I couldn't believe it. I'd never met somebody with such a similar background – it was like discovering a long-lost sibling.

Once we had established these shared crossover points, we found all sorts of other connections – an interest in writing, a passion for food, similar tastes in music. We both grew up in countryside-ish areas before ending up in London. We had similarly big social circles and enjoyed partying and entertaining.[6] We even *looked* similar: matching colouring, soft curly hair, wide smiles. It was the first (and to date, only) time I'd met somebody who didn't just have a tangentially similar story to me but shared *actual specific experiences* – we could talk about Mauritian street food, then university modules, then what it was like being the creative black sheep of the family, and then back to rehearsal notes.

How rare to find somebody you share so much with; how enriching to have such a person in your life!

Had my parents known this familiarity with somebody? I thought so. They had circles of people they overlapped with – Mum had a coffee morning group with other American

---

5. Well, British-American by way of Uganda in my case, but I wasn't about to split hairs at that point.
6. Granted, I'm sure we shared that last one with half the student body.

women in the UK, and Dad had a network of Mauritian friends, mostly guys who had emigrated at a similar time to him. Did my friends have Jaya equivalents? For the majority of my white British friends the nearest they had to go to find somebody of similar ethnic and cultural background was their own family; if not, most didn't need to go further than the school register for fellow white British kids. If you're mixed, it's immediately tougher to find somebody with the same heritage as there are *so many* ways to be mixed. You might find people partially the same as you, or with a similar mix of ethnicities, or from a similar region to you. But that was about it. Finding somebody like Jaya felt like a one in a million occurrence.

The first few months of university passed in a heady mix of frantically dashing to 'early' morning lectures (in practice, anything before 2pm), attaching rehearsal schedules to the fridge and getting off with each other's housemates. I picked up a weekend teaching job at my old dance school, which alongside my student loan meant disposable income and financial security. It became easier at home now I had more stability – when I went back to my parents' for parts of the summer, Fridays before work, or occasional bits of reading week, the tense atmosphere of my teens had somehow dissipated, organically, like the passing of a cloud.

I was able to appreciate the things we shared in a different way; like how Dad had retired and found a creative streak, interested in classical music and photography. Living outside of the house gave me a firsthand insight into how other people had grown up; my friends had introduced me to things like *Loose Women*, roast dinners, pasta sauce in a jar. I'd never encountered this at home. Mum had never met a sauce she couldn't cook from scratch, a confused glance when I put one in the basket during a home Sainsbury's shop. Dad was dismayed that I liked English breakfasts, saying they were both stodgy and greasy (he was right, but also – that was kind of the point). But the differences we had felt more like contextual quirks now, rather than personal attacks. My parents had never drunk even a glass of champagne at New Years, arguably leaving them outside one of the cornerstones of British culture, and I'd thought this was just a choice. Turns out pubs were a sin. I once referenced meeting a friend at a pub whilst Dad was driving me back from the train station and we almost had a car accident.

'Pub? You were in a *pub*? Oh God, Laila, you don't go to the pub do you?! That's so horrible. You drank in a *pub*?'

But who didn't go to the pub? We went to the pub after rehearsals with lecturers, after concerts with the audience, on quiet nights with each other just to hang out and chat. It was like Dad thought a pub was an illicit underground brothel, full of depraved drunken savages and seedy dealings, rather than a de facto social environment for most British people. Friends talked about going to the pub with their siblings, their parents – having a local back home and so on. I knew now that it was okay to be part of that blend of British life, that growing up here and existing in British society in a way my parents hadn't didn't mean either party was wrong, just that we would have some differences. We might never quite get to the same page, but simply being able to acknowledge that made it easier to accept.

By the time my second year rolled around in a now familiar blend of slogan tote bags and ironic charity shop knitwear, I'd grown massively in confidence and had a clearer understanding of who I was as a person. I was comfier, able to drop down into life and experience it, instead of skimming over it timidly. I had moved past my old fears and concerns from school so swiftly and thoroughly that it was hard to even acknowledge a trace of them. Had I truly thought I'd be considered ugly forever, that I'd never find another Henry Cow fan, that nobody else had watched *Cowboy Bebop*?

After our lease expired, I changed housing: lodging with a husband and wife who were both musicians – conductor and opera singer – who quickly became surrogate parents, and their teenaged daughter (who stopped by occasionally from boarding school) who was like a bonus sister. Maybe not the average university experience, but it was a golden time for me. I appreciated the familial vibes, expert musical knowledge and combined wisdom of the two of them (especially when they offered to read over my essays).[7] Life at their house was very different to the house I'd grown up in. For starters, their house was smaller, lives constantly on display to each other, which made things feel connected, everyone more intrinsically in-vested in the way your days unfolded. Their house was always full: a constant stream of fellow musicians, rehearsals round the grand piano, fresh coffee brewing in the kitchen and sheet mu-sic spread out over the dining room table. I recall life at the house as somehow suffused with light, at the top of Telegraph Hill, with west-facing windows that let the sun in and the spare

---

7. They appreciated the reliable extra income stream and knowing somebody would be in the house if they were both called out to last-minute gigs in Aldeburgh or Amsterdam.

room painted a warm yellowy colour. Life there was a glorious glimpse into a future I wanted for myself; full of art and joy and music and friends.

Recalling the person I'd been just a couple of years ago – all hazy hopes and nervous shuffles – was bizarre. Nobody teased me for being 'ethnic' – they *knew* me, and teased me far more gratuitously about things directly related to me, like the stance I adopted for playing (*I thought it was a bassoon recital* – not interpretive dance), or my taste in relationships (*Laila's only interested in fictional girls or ugly boys*), or my perennial lateness (*what I do is tell Laila two hours earlier than I actually mean*). I'd come wholly together, fully casting off the curses of school. Now I could really explore.

As I made my way through my reading lists (and overdraft), new perspectives came not just from my setting but directly from class. Our lecturers encouraged us to be critical not just of the subjects we looked at, but the context: the ways that subject was constructed, the societies it existed in, and the power implicit in who gets to decide what is worthy of learning and what's not. Growing up in white society, I'd learned that the white culture around me was complex, established and worthy of celebration. The rest of the world had hardly come up. For me, this had led (at least in part) to jarring meltdowns and huge chasms in my understanding of my heritage: with one part so highly regarded and the other dismissed, apparently non-existent, it made me feel unequal and lacking as a person. Culture and history outside of the UK was lesser – less worthy of study and analysis, less worthy of celebration, less needed. These were issues I'd had at school but had been unable to fully unpack or articulate. Now I was collecting tools for the future; tools to make things and build things, tools to excavate what was helpful and tools to tear down what was not. Sometimes in lectures a point would suddenly spark off a memory of something during my childhood and I'd scribble notes down in the margins to explore in the library later with journals and JSTOR at my disposal. What falsehoods had I internalised as truth?

All manner of life-changing realisations occurred. For example: the 'Other'. I first encountered the concept of the Other in a second-year lecture on ethnomusicology. Traditionally, the idea of the Other refers to the *opposite* of 'Self'. You can think of Self as a default state or perspective. The Self and the Other are linked, because we need the Self in order to know the Other. The Other helps to *prove* the Self: like two sides of the same coin, if you remove one side, it's no longer a coin. Because Self is our default perspective, it is the one we feel personally invested in, and the position we side with. Self is comfortable, known, safe and familiar. Other is the opposite of Self. This means that even when we do not have any other qualities to define what Other is, Other is inherently uncomfortable, unknown, dangerous and strange (because it is the opposite of Self). Self actually controls the Other, because Self defines what Other is.

Learning about Self and Other meant being able to see that the idea of the Self presented to me growing up (the default perspective, the position to identify with) was one that was white, Western, usually male, heterosexual and cisgender. I'd not connected with Self and had been Other. This had only been enforced by a constant stream of comments that – whether compliment or insult – highlighted how different I was. The unending stream of media in which I didn't exist or was Othered also affected other people's views of me: they saw me as unknowable, strange, an outsider. Eventually, I'd become so marooned that my *own* Self was obscure – creating a conundrum of my own understanding of *who I was*. The times I'd felt okay about myself, found some idea of identity and some joy in who I was, had been when I was alone. When there was no default Self and implied Other, but simply: just me. Away from the contrast of anything else, I could find my own version of Self, but whenever there was anyone else, I was straight back to being Other.

But Self and Other don't have to be set in stone. Postmodernism (. . . bear with) argues against the idea of an identity being stable and concrete, instead suggesting identity *changes*, and can be created, edited and curated without needing to align to a central idea of Self and Other. As I scribbled down this statement in my notebook, I added next to it – *be your own version of Self!* – echoes of the words I had found for myself years before (an idea deeply aligned with my own escapades of collaging ideas of myself in my room each night as a teenager).

It was customary that after lectures we would dash to the Goldsmiths caff to nurse our hangovers rather than muse on real-world applicability of whatever we had just learned, but a lot of the concepts left me reeling. They wormed their way into my subconscious and put me into a state of constant questioning, beyond academic considerations of classical music and looming essay deadlines and all the way into my life as I understood it. It was the same feeling I'd had learning about the different family naming traditions – that the accepted system I'd been given was not only lesser, but somehow *obscuring* a different, better system. I'd be lugging back a loan-fuelled shop

from Sainsbury's when I'd suddenly have a breakthrough moment of clarity around the 'where are you from' conversations
I repeatedly found myself in, or idly listening to music on my
bed when I'd trudge through my teenage diaries to ascertain if
I'd ever understood a world beyond whiteness.

In my life, whiteness was the default, the assigned, and the
backdrop for everything. Whiteness created the context for
most of my experiences. When I'd felt left out of the media as
a child, or alienated in conversations as a teen, I'd seen this as a
problem exclusive to me. I'd been told I was picky and seeing
things that weren't there, which led to some deeply stressful
times.

My understanding of myself was unbalanced. Early exploration attempts (mostly disordered burrowing through the internet) were aided with reading lists, professional guidance and
critical discussion, and I filled in the blanks from school. How
the colonial legacy loomed over centuries and across continents, displacing entire populations, affecting their descendants
and their nationally prescribed way of thinking. How the attempts to curtail and sever tradition and communities blunted
the people who lost their cultural languages. How the dom-
inant Self systematically eradicated the Other and positioned
it as worthless and *less*; and how that ingrained itself over lifetimes and years, all the way down to me and my little life as a
speck on a mountain in Wales, holding a crayon, examining my
arms, trying to imagine I existed.

All the heroes we had in popular culture were white men,
part of a tradition stretching back to the earliest foundations of
the West. Sometimes I played a game where I thought through
every white man who had passed through my life, every single

one: people I knew, characters in films and TV, people I'd passed on the street, names in textbooks, lists of classical music composers, superheroes in comics, politicians on TV. Every. Single. One. I'd hold that image in my head and then flip it, so they were all brown women, or queer people of colour, or people in some notable way *like me*.

The representation was patchy at best, rarely anything beyond stereotypical. An overwhelming array of what could have been. Exotic animals as pets, gold accessories, palm trees, ethnic-coded outfits – every portrayal used the same signifiers to *other* brown girls, to show them as something unknowable and fantastical. It turned out that even my beloved Princess Jasmine was voiced by a white actress, and both her and Aladdin were 'drawn' white: their bodies and faces were modelled on white people, converted to brownness via a paint job (notes to the animators were to reserve the ethnic coding of 'hooked noses' and so on for the bad guys).

Representation gave you *things* I couldn't fully appreciate – my friends who grew up without the anguish of searching for themselves seemed to have a better handle on who they *were*. They knew what they were a product of, the kinds of things life might have to offer them and the kinds of things the future might bring. Better representation afforded you something bigger than yourself – belonging, proof of existence, validation. It gave you options for who you could be.

Around this time in 2010, there was more representation for people from the wider South Asian diaspora and mixed people in general, including Mindy Lahiri in *The Mindy Project*, Tom Haverford and Ann Perkins in *Parks and Recreation*, and Raj Koothrappali on *The Big Bang Theory*. Any brown or mixed person was a small reminder that people like me existed. But some struck a chord that others didn't. Take a show like *The Mindy Project*, which was created, written and produced by its star Indian-American Mindy Kaling. The depiction of Mindy's life felt realistic to me – avoiding stereotypes, showing interactions between each other and just generally having people reference aspects of their lives in an organic way, instead of a presentational or educational manner that was clearly intended for a white audience (like the way characters of colour were used on the shows I watched in my youth). It normalised people of colour experiencing their lives rather than explaining everything to some assumed ignorant voyeur. One of the reasons the show succeeded in doing this was because it was the product of somebody creating, based on their own experiences. Kaling had control over storylines, characters and the show, allowing for nuanced and realistic depictions. It wasn't just a case of showing somebody brown on a screen and calling it a day.

On the other hand, a character like Raj in *The Big Bang Theory* was painful to watch. The character relied on stereotypes, racism and other characters' mockery. I watched a decent amount of the first few seasons of this show, because it was thrilling to see a brown person as a regular lead in a show, especially a brown *nerd* – but it was painful because Raj was consistently the butt of a joke. Yes, he was *there*, in the credits, but Raj – and specifically his ethnicity – was a consistent punchline. He was presented as feeble and lesser in counterpart to his white friends (who as a group were already unpopular and awkward to begin with). Raj is self-loathing, repeatedly denouncing his Hindu and Indian heritage; he is weak-willed, indecisive and relies on his white friends' capability and agency to get him through life; he is unsuccessful with women to an extreme degree (played for laughs). At the start of the series, his primary characteristic is being unable to speak in the presence of women; twelve seasons later at the end of the series, Raj is the only lead character to not be in a successful relationship. In one episode, which succinctly sums up everything wrong with this character, Raj's selective mutism prevents him from talking to a woman, so one of his white friends steps in to save him by performing a hideous caricature of an Indian accent down the phone as Raj. It is cruel, racist and reductive.

Behind the scenes, Kunal Nayyar (who played Raj) was reportedly paid 75–80 per cent of what three of his four white co-stars were paid until Season Ten[8] – a decade into the show's existence – and the credited writing and production crew were white by an overwhelming majority. Ostensibly, both shows had a lead Indian character, but the difference in how those characters got there – the reasons for their existence and the people responsible for their portrayal – meant they resonated in totally different ways. It was the difference between a character that felt genuine and a character that felt damaging. Before you portrayed a person you needed to understand their story.

In my earlier years, I'd felt connected to my heritage in a raw and intense way, but now I was able to take a step back. The confusion I harboured over my wide-ranging heritage was easier to navigate now – less 'shaken to my core' fear and more hypothetical and abstract. I don't mean my ancestry had

---

8. White Jewish co-star Simon Helberg also apparently received 75–80 per cent of what the other three leads – Kaley Cuoco, Jim Parsons and Johnny Galecki – received until renegotiating at the same time as Kunal Nayyar.

become smaller – it still felt overwhelmingly vast, an ocean in my head – but *I'd* changed. I'd grown. Now I had more going on I had more to cling on to, able to ride out the waves instead of drowning.

As my third year flew by terrifyingly fast, I had only vague ideas of what to do next. For most of my life, 'creating' was an urgent need – and it had always been an intensely personal act: whether it was clunky felt-tip portraits or elaborate collages, my whole life I'd subconsciously been making things that could help me understand myself. All my projects were one big blur of learning how to fit the pieces together, and became essential to me because I was fulfilling needs that otherwise went unmet: representation issues; a structure to stitch my heritage together; the desperate desire to connect with something, *anything*, that resonated, even if it was just my own stuff.

Entering university, I figured I'd just continue to create things that affirmed myself. But at university projects became whatever the module said they were, with no core obligation to reflect one's innermost identity. Maybe your perspective could function as a starting point or reference, but maybe you didn't use it at all and your inspiration was entirely outside of yourself. One classmate wrote an essay investigating music that related to how people play video games; another composed a piece based on data of how many students entered the library. They were so much more evolved than me, it seemed so sophisticated to be able to treat work as exercises in craft, or opportunities to explore whatever you were mildly interested in. I was uncharacteristically shy when talking about my inspirations because I felt so childish next to them, constantly remaking myself in this endless self-portrait jumble, still a four-year-old stuck at the 'draw your family' stage.

The thing is, I couldn't imagine ever being done with mining my ancestry. Though I no longer felt connected to my heritage in a such a raw and intense way, it still existed as a huge swooping tangle of threads and knots, that I needed to chart, rather than a potential source of inspiration I could casually peruse. It was bigger than me, and far more complex – some pulsing, living thing at the middle of it I'd not yet uncovered and the persistent call to explore. I couldn't see a time when it would be small enough to sprinkle into projects, or put neatly to one side – there was too much of it.

And it also felt like my heritage was so *rich* that making a project about something else – like, basing it on a TV show or a poem – would fall flat. Examining my own creations I felt my personal work came alive in a way that other work didn't, which meant I usually ended up reinterpreting the same topics, and I disliked this. My classmates found philosophical angles to approach their work on any topic under the sun and managed to tack them on to an established canon of discourse – most producing dazzling work regardless of how innocuous or abstract the source material was. I envied this to some degree, because I didn't feel like I could hit the same marks. Them being able to make magic from anything meant they were either smarter, more curious, or more able to juggle abstracts. Possibly they even felt their personal background was so clear it didn't need to be addressed and could remain packed away until later rather than knowing a constant need to process it. Who knew? All I knew is that when I followed the same blueprint

– engaging with something outside of my own personal experience – even though I liked the results, the work lacked the same energy. It was merely ink on a page, whereas whenever I wrestled with that glowing mass of sparks instead, some small speck of firelight might end up in the work.

Though I felt this intrinsic need to use my heritage, it wasn't easy. A big problem was that my heritage was too obscure – it was farcical. I lacked familiarity. Incorporating a traditional American folk song or Mauritian sega rhythm into one of my compositions was ridiculous: I was more familiar with Radiohead. The idea of involving my ancestry in such a direct way veered worryingly towards cultural appropriation of what was logically my own culture. My attachment to my heritage felt weak because it wasn't knowledge I'd accumulated through experience – it was second hand and learned. It needed bolstering. For me, trips to Mauritius had been like field trips, and films with brown people had existed as research documents. I'd had to *construct* my identity in the same way I was now writing my academic essays: digging around for research, taking notes from whatever I could find and forming tangible viewpoints that could be backed up if necessary.

That method of cobbling together information was fine for 'Stravinsky's Approach to Harmony During the Russian Period',[9] but less than desirable when it came to relating to yourself. *Forming* my identity through research and guesswork made it flimsy and haphazard. If I had some nascent cultural knowledge in my DNA, I didn't feel like I'd accessed it – a white kid on my course could have incorporated sega rhythm into their

9. I got a First for that one, thanks very much.

work and it would have had the same amount of authenticity, the same degree of learned and assumed knowledge, the same degree of plagiarism and inspiration.

Okay, so my cultural heritage was not something that would endure interrogation. I wanted to be able to combine the art of my background in a way that felt true to my own experiences. And that's when I realised, though I didn't know any one explicit part of my ethnicity, what I did know was being between it all: I knew all of it, all at once. I understood the dialogue between being all these different things, the inherent plurality of being a sum of parts, the way I'd always been lots of Lailas simultaneously. Most people saw me differently according to the situation – 'Wrexham Laila' or 'in Mauritius Laila' or 'Among White People Laila' – but I never lost the intersections between them.

This could be my way of incorporating authenticity into my work. After all, none of the work I'd made in childhood and adolescence was to understand any one part of my culture, I'd always wanted to make sense of all of it together. The image that I had, of all these different strands of people and stories and journeys all colliding together in one blazing event, felt clear to me. I decided I could use that going forwards to make other things that resonated with me.

Telling stories is an ancient part of all human life; we need windows into the lives of others to be able to empathise with them. If we never look through a window anywhere else, we get stranded with our narrow view. Art can function as that window by allowing us a glimpse into experiences we won't necessarily have. But as much as we need windows into the lives of others, we need mirrors, too. If we're unable to recognise our own image, it's tough to visualise your options, what paths you might follow, who you *are*. If you only have windows into what you don't share with others, you become unclear on what you *do share*, which creates an unstable footing. I'd managed to perform some mind-bending gymnastical feats when I'd aligned myself over and over again with the stories of white men, clearly visualising their paths, whilst utterly unable to imagine a future where somebody like me existed.

Creating your own work is a chance to take control of your own narrative. Growing up, I'd been trying to make both windows and mirrors for myself. Though people of mixed ancestry are rarely mixed in the exact same way, the effects that a lack of representation has on us are universal: alienating, obstructive, and causing periods of deeply felt inadequacy. I'd occasionally imagined myself as short-changed out of an authentic identity, like I had just too much to fit together – but now I was able to see how that one large whole could be just that: *a whole*. Finding commonalities and learning how to share them; presenting my experience of a plural and multi-layered heritage and forming a pathway to connect my experiences together. These are the things I thought about as I neared the end of university and entered my final term.

Days and nights became strangely stitched together as everyone sacrificed a regular sleeping schedule in order to get their final essays and projects handed in. You might find yourself eating a sandwich with your housemates at 2am, forgoing nutrients in lieu of a word count, or leaving the library for a 4pm 'breakfast break' at the cafe over the road. In between the ProPlus restocks and frantic footnote maintenance, we began to flirt with ideas of 'career plans' realised by the alarming prospect of paying full price in Topshop. I'd more than met my previous goal of being 'happy'. I had ideas of *projects*. I wanted to help people in any way I could, take part in things made by other people, continue learning and improving, and find a space for myself so that I, too, could keep creating things. I wanted to find the spaces in which I could thrive now I knew they existed. And I wanted to tell stories that resonated with me and made me feel seen.

Prior to university, I'd thought both stories and life in general didn't happen to people like me. Now I knew better. As I took stock of the options I had for the next chapter of my life – further education, job-hunting, living with friends – I couldn't see a clear path, but I trusted myself to find one. Besides, I could just make it up as I went along, create my own idea of a career!

There was a note of finality in the air as we bade farewell to university; leases expiring, Mucha posters down from the walls, overflowing clothes rails unceremoniously stuffed into binbags. We spent our last few weeks forgetting the student numbers we'd memorised and frantically trying to bleach the bathroom clean in order to get back our full deposit. During huge nights out, friend groups overlapped at the seams and the whole of the student union felt like a mate (especially once you'd drunk enough plastic cups of Carlsberg). Entire days were spent languishing in the Telegraph Hill sun sharing one crumpled bottom-of-the-bag cereal bar between three people. I leapt at every chance I could, trying to squeeze the last few opportunities I could out of a place that was saturated in them. A visiting examiner offered me a scholarship on a course. A lecturer submitted one of my essays for publication. A flyer that landed in my student inbox led me to an audition for an Edinburgh show. With the help of the conductor whose house I was still lodging in, I secured places on three different master's courses. And in those last few weeks of university, of togetherness, of completion, as we packed away the strands of our lives and bade farewell to the corridors that formed us, I had no idea what came next, but I was sure it was *something*.

Chapter Eight

EVERYWHERE BIRDS

Summer rolled over my life like waves to shore; a season of perpetual motion, with opportunities unfurling all at once, like wildflowers, and me chasing each and every one with arms outstretched. Laden with an array of instruments and most of my worldly belongings crammed into a Bag for Life stashed in the back of somebody's car, I contorted into the one square foot of space like a *Tetris* piece. First, to Wales: where it always all began: a performance course in Aberystwyth, nights in the dunes and chips by the sea, salty warm evenings unfolding in a fervent reverie and the sound of woodwind warming up; to Surrey: sun-stained rehearsals, sleepy train stations and other people's sofas; to Edinburgh and auburn skies and the *festival*, Post-it notes on walls and – our show! – a mass of stapled flyers, lanyards round eager necks and progressively sweaty costumes. And this whole simmering summer being always at all times gloriously surrounded by people – new people! – new friends and new contacts and new colleagues and crushes and peers; people who picked you up after gigs and snuck you pints; people who helped you move from one chapter to the next; people who'd plus one you into shows and kiss you on the cheek when you smashed a blurry 1am promo gig, warm forearms in the wings and an ecstatic blur by the bar; people to sing with; people to distract from the daily reshuffling of schedules like, *when can I next do laundry, what day do I need what instrument? and where are my belongings? (phone charger: front of accordion case; floral playsuit: crammed into the pink bag with the* Legally Blonde *score and spare uke strings).* On and on life went like this in a blur of crumpled fivers and squashed peanut butter sandwiches and remembering to save the train tickets for expenses, until October, when it was over, back at my parents' with a dull thud and a sore bank account and a vague sniffly cold, no plan, no purpose, and no people. Just me, my old teenage room and ten weeks of dirty clothes.

What next? I hadn't planned for this kind of a comedown. In spring, with even less of a plan, I'd applied to do a master's (why not?), but after the success of the summer I figured I could cobble a career together via all my new 'contacts' (i.e. people I'd met in quick change areas) and life could just . . . carry on that way until the credits rolled. But what seemed viable in the bleary haze of scrawled email addresses and promises of scratch nights seemed a lot less likely back at my parents' with an empty diary and the clear light of day. So I picked the easy option: I'd stay at my parents' and complete the master's, thereby buying myself some time to *figure things out* before re-entering the fray (and at the very least, getting through my laundry). My last stint at my parents' had been fraught, but now that I was an *adult* with a *degree* and a *career* things would be easier, right?

As anybody who has ever moved back with their parents as an adult knows: no. Freedom was replaced by curfews and car sharing. I may have felt like a brand-new best-yet version of myself post-uni, but to my parents I was the same hapless teenager who'd just . . . gone somewhere else for a bit. Mum and I argued over little things like getting up before 9am, and Dad and I argued over bigger things like *what was I doing for work?* implying that a degree from an arts university represented the culmination of some diversionary chapter before real life began. Shrinking into a smaller version of myself, I tried to explain I was 'forging a path of my own', but knew this sounded like 'faffing about aimlessly' to Dad. Mum was easier to assuage – sitting her down to explain I could wake up unaided[1] – but I was defensive with Dad, not least because his voice echoed my own late-night doubts (was twenty-one too late to jack it all in and retrain as a plumber?).

My diary was full of meetings and auditions, plus endless tasks that seemed required simply for life to continually happen: *schedule promo tweets, collect flyers, buy charger.* I had lots of 'informal chats' with potential collaborators, which usually left me out of pocket (parking, tube fare, a drink) without leading to anything paid. Black-shirted classical gigs paid a flat £20 and required your presence for a whole Saturday of rehearsals, sticky-floored pop gigs paid in drinks tokens for a 6pm sound check and 9.20pm set (great, you can use the redundant three hours to tick off more tedious admin whilst perched on

---

1. 'Unaided' here meaning 'with eighteen different iPhone alarms set at one minute intervals'.

a wobbly bar stool), and black box theatre work paid . . . nothing. Literally nothing. Just the fleeting experience and promise of an interesting night out. I regularly lugged my bassoon ninety minutes one way to the back of beyond (zone four) for a ten-minute performance and the hope of a new contact. This was freelancing, right?

Alongside, I began my master's. At Goldsmiths, I'd shed a lot of my school understandings around the Western canon, and had graduated with the idea that we – meaning *everyone involved in music* – were all on the same page and therefore all collectively working to overcome the trappings of such a view. But my new university was operating on a totally different protocol. It was a jarringly regressive experience; a largely white student body (many Oxbridge rejects) and conservative subject selection. I was reminded forcibly of school – even the ornate brick buildings seemed thematically similar. Pop music? Inclusivity debates? None of that, thanks.

Small unwelcoming incidents stacked up. For example, as a performance student, private tuition on my first study instruments was part of the course. At Goldsmiths, there'd been no first study bassoonists and, consequently, no dedicated bassoon teacher, so they hired a teacher specifically for me once I'd accepted my place. I began lessons when other students did and everything unfolded in the exact same way as the other performance students. My master's had the same situation – no previous bassoonists; no teacher – but instead the university tasked me with finding and organising my lessons, which led to them starting halfway through term and taking place off site instead of within the department. I became the go-between for teacher, finance department and music office – extra work my peers weren't facing. At one point, either I or my teacher forgot to sign off a form (both of us new to the particular departmental system) and a member of the office accused me of lying and fabricating invoices.

In terms of playing, I wanted to incorporate contemporary playing techniques I'd studied at Goldsmiths. One of my performance lecturers was particularly derisive about this, saying point-blank they didn't understand what I was trying to do. They'd frown at my programme, argue with me, tell me I lacked vision, and openly laugh at me in front of my course mates. It felt like a targeted attack – like okay, maybe we didn't have any common ground but what was the need to be so direct? Maybe that lecturer thought ridicule would best impart wisdom, but it didn't inspire me to reconsider my artistic choices – instead it felt hostile.

I began to experience the same nettling discomfort as my teenage years, like I had some unseen target on my back. Luckily, I'd become fast friends with my course mates, and formed a bond with some of my more progressive lecturers. And, unlike in school, I had the knowledge now that I could escape that hunted feeling – it was not a feeling endemic to me, but a product of the environment I was in. If I was going to survive my master's, I *needed* safe places.

Consequently, I decided to start a contemporary music collective: WOLF PACK. WOLF PACK would be a safe space, a collaborative group where we'd create concerts of contemporary music based around a one-word theme, and explore that theme not just via the pieces (spanning the full gamut of 'contemporary'), but with scenes, costumes, lighting, sets, props, physical movement and dance – so that the concerts wound up somewhere between concert, cabaret and gig. I was inspired by the pieces I'd worked on during my time in Goldsmiths, like narrative experiences in disused car parks and game pieces that issued instructive booklets to the audience, as well as ideas we'd studied like Fluxus, performance art, noise music and intermedia. I also wanted to do away with the parts of traditional music performance that I didn't like. Try conveying the majesty of Elgar's *Romance* for bassoon in a starchy white blouse behind a dilapidated music stand on an overlit stage. Tough stuff. The drab garb, dry programme notes and *convention* of the whole thing turned me off, an obstacle to adequately sharing the work. I *loved* music, when I studied pieces, I found colours and stories; I heard questions and sought answers and desired to fit it together and illuminate its spark. We all did, surely, otherwise why did we all love it so much? I wanted to bring all that to the stage to share with audiences the way I experienced it without diluting it down for convention's sake.

This may have sounded ambitious for, essentially, a bunch of students with no budget, but it apparently also sounded intriguing (or at least fun); what began as me and my course mate soon grew to almost thirty eager 'wolves' in our merry band. We were a blazing force right out the gate: staging our first six concerts in three months, performing in nontraditional venues around campus and securing invitations from festivals in London. Programme listings looked like the contents of my iPod circa 2004[2] and we created zines (instead of programmes) that outlined not just the context of the pieces, but who we

---

2. Stockhausen, Kate Bush, Antonio Carlos Jobim, Yoko Ono, Jamiroquai, John Zorn, Frank Zappa, Big Star, Steve Reich. ★★.

were and what we thought of them. I brought in aspects of my own beliefs: we used recyclable or 'waste' materials to make everything (in practice, a lot of hand-painted cardboard props) and donated part of the ticket sales to a theme-relevant charity.[3] WOLF PACK led to some truly unique performing experiences, like HOME, a four-hour immersive show staged in an empty cottage. We decked it out to resemble a family home, with performers taking on roles within the 'family'; the 'teenagers' playing solo in their 'rooms' whilst 'older relatives' invited the audience in. Once in the home, the audience could wander at their leisure, invited to consider what it means to create a home, what it sounds like, what it means to live with another and how you create the sacred intimacy of a home between strangers. Or LOVE, staged in a chapel. The concert began in darkness with performers playing without announcement – the audience gradually catching on and hushing – and then as the performance progressed, lights slowly illuminated performers in wedding gowns, lacy crowns, formal suits. We used the acoustics afforded to us to further punctuate the songs, like performing up the aisle and reaching the song's apex at the altar. The audience received paper flowers we made of leftover photocopies of the music and were given the option to 'object' (their choices informing the next piece), before joining us during the 'reception' as the boundary between audience and

---

3. Here's our 2014 bio: *WOLF PACK are an award-winning collective who create eclectic, cross-disciplinary concerts based on a one-word theme. Fiercely innovative and highly original, we rebel against your average sit-down concert, incorporating off-the-wall inventiveness, theatrical sensibilities and unconventional humour. We feature unique collaborations with actors, dancers, composers and visual artists.*

performers broke. Audiences were always intrinsically involved – a vessel for our ideas, instead of blank observers.

Combined with our black and white costumes and huge WOLF PACK bunting, I'm sure we looked like a start-up cult to the uninitiated. But between devoted hard-working performers and our combined unbridled creativity we got a lot of support. Several of my lecturers suggested pieces and offered helpful connections outside of campus. But we encountered issues from the office – seemingly an extension of the lukewarm reception I'd had. At one point, our posters got taken down from areas where other, more traditional, musical societies – choirs and chambers and so on – had posters. When I asked why, they said I wasn't registered as a musical group, but speaking to the leaders of other groups, not all of them were either. WOLF PACK was provided a ton of admin – when I plonked the sheaf of A4 'registration papers' down on the pub table where the orchestra was hanging post-show, a friend (and student director of one of the choirs) asked, *what the hell's all that?* They'd never seen the registration forms and neither had the former a cappella director behind the bar. Next concert, our flyers were again taken down – they 'didn't have room'. The concert after, they wanted an advertising fee nobody else had ever paid. Another time, they asked me to pay an expensive cleaning invoice, despite students supposedly being able to book out performance venues for free. Yet again, I asked around: none of the other student-led groups had ever been footed with a bill post-concert. (That time a trusted lecturer appealed on my behalf.)

It's tempting to frame the office as villainous authority figures and us as plucky kids trying to take down the establishment

– I've wondered if even they saw it like that. But I wasn't trying to *tear down the establishment*. Sure, we were different, but hardly burning Mozart sonatas or defecating on punters. I just wanted to take my ideas out of my head and put them on a stage. Being new, I'd made a point of sticking to the book – sending clear, direct emails to ask for the rules on booking venues, for example, rather than relying on goodwill and 'stopping by the office for a chat' like many of my peers, or like I myself would have done at Goldsmiths. It didn't help. I soon delegated all departmental communications to other wolves – students better known to the office.

I don't know if it's because they compared WOLF PACK to choir and chamber groups. I don't know if it's because I went somewhere else for my undergrad, because they didn't like my 'by the book' formality, or because I was one of the few PoC in the department (some of the other few PoC were in WOLF PACK). But I strongly had the feeling of being Othered. And to twenty-one-year-old fresh-out-of-Goldsmiths me this smacked of *wrong*. I was being held back and that made me push harder. We were in a university on a creative arts degree – surely a place of challenging convention and expanding horizons, encouraging students in their artistic endeavours. Why weren't they helping?

WOLF PACK was the highlight of my life at this time. I wanted to do it forever. I reached back in time to versions of myself staring up into the sky in Wales or burrowing into my bedroom as a teen and thought: *This was it! I finally found it!* I needed this moment, I needed to facilitate being able to *do this*. It helped me understand a part of myself; *why* I wanted to make things the way I did, and what it meant to me to process. That mass of stars in my head was in some incoherent, vast way how I experienced everything: my life, my identity, my heritage, the world around me and my place in it.

Less than a week after I finished my Masters, life threw me some cheer. Walking home from an Edinburgh Fringe after-party, I'd stopped at the traffic lights as the sun was rising, only to discover as I refreshed emails on my phone (a terrible habit I later quelled), that WOLF PACK had won a grant for creatively led enterprises! We could continue! We were successful! Victory!

After turning twenty-two and finally making my dad happy by passing my driving test, I promptly moved back to London, where, as everyone knows, you will rarely need a car and never find a parking space. Initially, four of us signed the lease on a two-up two-down terraced house, though six lived there and we fluctuated between five and nine housemates in subsequent years (a living room was a luxury nobody could afford). The walls were thin, the carpet was thinner and the bathroom was home to a populous mould colony. The gas was on a meter, which usually cut out midway through cooking (we never topped it up by more than a tenner) and the boiler made a noise like a constipated donkey every time you so much as turned a tap on. But hey, who cared, it was home: I liked the comforting murmur of chit-chat that trickled into my room all hours of the day and wrestling with the hallway bustle of other people's coats, ten deep on a single hook. And we were the party house! Every group's got one: cut to us shoving the beds in the living room up against the wall for weekly gatherings with bonkers themes[4], funnelling forty people onto our tiny patio, the smell of rain and rollies and off-brand cheese puffs in the kitchen.

Our first happy golden years were a fertile time. We worked in theatre, film, music and graphic design – between friends of friends and hand extends we had a built-in black book of talent to call on for all our ambitious self-led projects – plus a ready-made audience to boot: usually 'guest list' rather than paying customers but, still, bums on seats! Nothing like a full house! We organised events, programmed each other and split profits (when they existed), always desperate to get reviewers through the door. I said yes to everything; recording seventeen pages of dialogue for a friend's 'immersive audio play' whilst sat under two duvets in the middle of summer (a makeshift sound booth); stopping off for bagels on Brick Lane dressed in white spandex and giant white wig whilst carrying my accordion home at 1am. It's not where you're at but where you're going. And we were *going places*.

Or so we tried to believe. At the time we did not appreciate any of this: we were chronically broke and e x h a u s t e d. Days were a constant shambles of job applications, existential crises and doing whatever it took to make rent. Sometimes one of us would get a well-paying gig, celebrating with a trip to the 'nice' cinema – but, equally as likely, somebody would have a dodgy month, eBaying their life possessions and scrounging

---

4. Sometimes the party themes were discarded WOLF PACK themes: 'Worst of Netflix', ''Murica!!' and 'Philosophy and Cheese' are just a few that come to mind.

11pm Sainsbury's reductions.[5] Outside of the same all-day Saturday job I'd had since I was seventeen, I went after everything, running WOLF PACK (another grant, this time with office space and mentors, plus a place for me on an entrepreneurship scheme), starting a blog and going to dozens of auditions. We all kept odd hours but often crossed over for a cuppa in the kitchen, wondering aloud if we were making any headway at all. How many times could you tweak your CV in one month? Was anyone even *using* LinkedIn? Would the landlord notice if we were three days late on rent?[6]

Still, it was worth the graft for the jubilant payoffs. Like gigs where I stood precariously with my guitar on carpeted stages, cables poking like cobbles through thin plimsoll soles, looking out into the light feeling perfectly alone, perfectly still, perfectly snug and secure in that moment. Because that moment – just before a string is plucked, just before you open your mouth and let the story fall out – that marvellous moment is when you take all the thoughts you collected and all the ideas you have captured and all the stars in your head and give them back, like bottled sparks. That moment at the beginning is second only to the moment at the *end*, that final gilded moment when you silence the strings, step back and stop. Now the thing is done. Now, that whole attempt is bestowed upon the audience – it's not yours anymore, not when it's finished. That's the moment when it ceases to be your story and becomes their

---

5. If things got really dire, people moved to their parents' and dropped off the face of the earth.

6. Endlessly, but don't bother; definitely not; miraculously . . . no?

experience. *This I know is true. And now you know it too.* That's the part when you know you have taken something as fleeting and intangible and fragile as a *moment*, forged it out of torn-up thoughts and given it away in the truest way you know how. And with all these people to receive it? I'd work my whole life for a handful of those moments, to know a thought completed.

Trying to ingratiate myself in multiple worlds – theatre, classical music, contemporary music – I was subconsciously adjusting to fit in all the time. Adaptations for me included: not sharing my prior experiences or achievements for fear of seeming 'cocky'; not discussing being mixed; not using my surname; speaking in my 'white' voice (perfected years earlier at school); dressing 'white'; keeping my hair tied up and out the way; talking only in terms of the Western canon; highlighting my 'whitest' credentials (my master's); keeping my ideas and contributions connected to works within a Eurocentric canon (everything else was saved for self-led work). And of course, unendingly taking the piss out of my own existence. Nobody was the butt of my jokes more than myself.

Alone I was focused and poised. This would have been intimidating and unapproachable around others, so I allowed them to see me as the vague, daffy one (the same way in high school my withdrawn disassociation had been read as 'sleepy stoner'). How necessary it was to do this, I couldn't work out: I'd just been conditioned to do this over the years. Even projects that explicitly wanted to 'champion diversity' and 'uplift unique voices' – i.e. hire non-white people – required navigation: *highlight culture as your USP, what the culture is doesn't matter, we just care that you have one in case somebody asks about our track record with diversity.* And yet, for all my hard work, issues were everywhere, a constant discomfort like grit in my shoe.

In terms of performing, I went up for anything that included 'ethnic' or 'foreign' in the description. Auditions went precisely nowhere. The old adage of 'acting is *reacting*' was obviously invented by a white person because for everyone else – especially somebody ethnically ambiguous like me – acting is *accenting*. I got accent requests on the weekly: Brazilian, Indian, Spanish, Hawaiian, Cuban, Latina . . . mob boss, drugs lackey, foreign student, terrorist. *Can you sing in an Arab accent?* Maybe, is there a fee?

Teachers said I had the light agile voice best suited to wide-eyed ingénue roles,[7] but I lacked the look. Curvy and dark did not say *pure-hearted innocent princess* the way skinny and blonde did. I was less 'English Rose' and more 'Venus Flytrap'. Instead, I went out for femme fatale and seductress roles, at which I was crap. Casting directors chatted the same 'you look so sensual' shit I'd previously heard from sixteen-year-old boys; feedback contained comments like 'earthy', 'worldly' and 'sturdy' suggesting I would have had better luck playing a wizened tree.[8]

It was easier to find roles in devised pieces through people who knew me personally – eliminating the need to battle stereotypes as they could cast based on who I actually was. Slowly, I discovered I had a second problem resulting from the first: as I'd spent my formative years filling in for 101 ethnicities, I had

---

7. You know: Cinderella, Johanna in *Sweeney Todd*, Maria in *The Sound of Music*, Dorothy in *The Wizard of Oz*, Cosette in *Les Misérables*.

8. FYI I'm available to play any and all Entwives in your *LOTR* spin-offs, just call my agent.

failed to develop more of a sense of what kind of performer I was through, say, trying things out.

Another issue: smaller fringe projects asked us to send Kickstarter links to family, friends and 'patrons' in a bid for them to extend funds our way. Though Dad gave heavily to charity it was usually Médecins Sans Frontières or disaster relief. I couldn't email and ask if he'd forgo those noble causes to pledge fifty quid for our devised physical three-hander with birdsong accompaniment based on 'Pierrot through a Brechtian lens'. *What?!*

I went for a lot of function band auditions – at the time, pop songs with some vague jazz/big band spin were popular and I tried out for many bands made up of identical white guys in suits with names like 'Children of the Horn' and 'Jazz In Your Pants'. The other popular format was Black male musicians with a couple of female singers and possibly a token white guy on keys or baritone sax. These bands were described as 'soul' or 'R&B', functionally shorthand for Black. Unsurprisingly I never got callbacks for any of these bands – and there was never feedback about my playing or experience, just that I 'wasn't quite right'.

Even in teaching I ran into problems. More than once I submitted a teaching application to a school and received a call asking if I could speak English, what my visa situation was, and if I'd taught in the UK before. One time I got asked for a 'brighter' headshot – they ended up editing mine to overexposed black and white, whilst all the white teachers had colour profile photos. Another time, I joined a tutoring site using the name Layla McDonagh (variations of both my name and Mum's maiden name) and, despite having the exact same copied and pasted bio, received significantly more responses on that than my own name. Another time, applying for a peripatetic prep school job, I had an Equal Opportunities form that had clearly been tailored in-house. When I arrived at the ubiquitous Ethnicity question, alongside 'White', 'Black' and the usual, the answers didn't have any Mixed options but instead said 'Split'. *Split?* Split personality? Split the bill? Split, one of the largest cities in Croatia?

Now I can parse these issues into separate incidents – but they didn't exist as individual moments. It wasn't like one week I tackled the voice–look dichotomy, next week pivot to addressing the visa assumption. Struggling under a constant deluge of racist assumptions, microaggressions and whitewashing made it impossible to articulate the issues. Once, aged twenty-three, I applied for a touring job that wanted somebody with a musical theatre background (check), knowledge of folk music (check) and festival experience (check). Bonus attributes were driving licence and more than one instrument (check and check!). With £30 to my name, the £23.30 tickets to the audition in Brighton were a risk, but I literally ticked all the boxes – life was about taking risks and going for it, right? En route to the audition, I checked the map on my phone when a man approached. I weighed up how wary I needed to be – would he try and nick my bassoon?

''Scuse me, you lost? It's just down there. That road,' he said slowly and clearly, pointing down the road. I stared. How did he know where I was going? Was he on drugs? 'The language school? It's down there—'

I cut in, 'No, I'm looking for—'

'Oh!' he said, laughing, surprise on his face. 'You speak English! I thought you were looking for the language school! You know, because . . .' he said, gesturing to my face. I was too shocked to respond, beyond hurt. He'd assumed I was looking for the language school based on *my face* . . . what? Was I understanding this correctly? He slapped me on the arm and walked off chuckling, not noticing I was stood there reeling. *Based on my face?* But . . . I needed to focus on the audition. I put this interaction to the back of my mind, subconsciously registering this was the first time I'd been to Brighton without white accompaniment and not a mistake I'd make again.

At the audition, I was greeted by five white people in a dingy wooden room above a pub; an electrical fan whirring in the corner and the smell of vinegar and mildew. They wanted to do the interview *first*. Okay. Sure. A girl with a brown bob asked had I understood the show was about folk music? Yes, I said, which is one of the things that drew me—

No, she said, *BRITISH folk music*. As in, traditional music of the *British* Isles.

Again, I clarified yes, that's what I meant, and before I could elaborate on children's choirs in the Eisteddfod and a book of Scottish folk tunes that had been my great-grandfather's and the rest of my vast heritage, another girl cut in, a smattering of silver piercings and dyed-black dreadlocks wrapped in a bandana.

Did I realise they were going on tour? 'Yes,' I replied, 'sounds great.' She stayed looking at me judgmentally, and then spoke slowly and deliberately.

'No, like *roughing* it. In tents.'

I didn't respond as quickly. This was one of those white people comments that sounded like a statement but was really a challenge for you to account for yourself. I recognised the almost imperceptible change in atmosphere, the slight rigidity of her gaze, the threat that laced her tone, how two of the others were now looking away. I tried desperately to work out what I was accounting for in this moment as I answered.

'Yes, I understood that – that's another one of the things I liked about the advert,' I stated, realising with a plummeting feeling: I'd been so distracted by the language school guy that I'd forgotten to tie my hair up into its usual audition bun and it was instead freewheelin' around in its natural state, giant ringlets to my waist. *Bollocks.* Sure enough, the dreadlocked girl raised an eyebrow and then did a mock model pose.

'There's no, like, mirrors or hair curlers. It's not a beauty pageant.' Yep, there it was. I looked back at her, explaining that was really fine by me and I was not the stylish sort, whilst internally trying to gauge whether tying my hair up now would help or if the damage was done – but she was scribbling something down on a paper and exchanging a glance with the other girl. I played my piece, thanked them for their time, and left, hoping they'd read my CV and see the things we shared.

I felt suddenly tired, bassoon weighing on my shoulders, feet aching in holey trainers. Five minutes later I received the email saying I hadn't got the job. Did this spur me into a righteous anger? Did I find myself suddenly determined to march back in and prove them wrong? Did I decide to go home and *solve racism* so as to avoid future days like this? No, I did not. None of those thoughts crossed my mind. Instead, I slumped into my bassoon case on the train, got in two hours later and cried on my lumpy single bed, too broke to consider going out and, frankly, too defeated. Later, I wrote a song detailing how utterly useless and insignificant I felt; I played this to a friend who told me it was 'too bleak'.

Mentioning these various injustices to friends brought further injustice: they either didn't believe me *or* didn't think these incidents were anything more than human error or bad luck. At this point, I was mostly working with straight cis white men; invariably the people in charge were an assortment of Tom-Dan-Nick-Chris-Steve-Will-James'. In some respects, this was great – access, contacts, always a spare white man to walk me home – but it was also isolating. Peers thought I was having a 'normal' hard time – everyone struggles initially! People were happy to tell me how hard the industry was without ever having navigated it from the same vantage point.

Raising the issue with friends implied I found an issue *with them.* I had to be careful. If I brought up a band audition where I 'wasn't the aesthetic', odds are somebody I knew *had* got the job. It could come off like I thought I was better, or the person who got it didn't deserve it. People would say, *well I flunked an audition last month, why are you making it about race?* This would jeopardise my position within my existing groups, people thinking I was quick to play the victim card; friends would think twice about recommending me in turn; who wants some whiny conspiracy theorist in their band?

For my white male friends to have acknowledged I was suffering would mean *them* acknowledging that they *weren't* suffering in the same ways. That didn't happen, so I stopped highlighting issues and internalised them instead. Maybe they didn't want to think the world was so unbalanced, or maybe they'd not heard any other reports of this happening (in their largely white male circles), and so to them, my stories genuinely were one-offs. White female friends were more likely to accept what I was saying, but usually brought up their gender to show they understood my point: totally ignoring that I had those issues *as well*.

Either way, conversations diminished larger structural problems into smaller ones that were mine alone. It didn't help that I was too close to fully untangle the issues. I didn't ask 'why are agencies creating function bands of identical people?' or, beyond that, 'why are clients more likely to hire an all-white all-male band?' or, getting really pedantic, 'what bearing should the demographics of the band have on an event?' I just asked why I was never suitable. The system worked, other people got jobs. It wasn't an industry problem but a *Laila* problem.

Within my own work, feedback picked up on my 'winsome and regal' presence, I got comments of 'ethereal', 'effervescent' and 'haunting', like I was a sentient moonbeam or guitar-playing ghoul princess, and always comments about *different* or *unusual*: those comments were better than 'sturdy' but still positioned me as *Other*, outside of established convention. I'd wonder why my work *needed* to fit in a canon, or conversely, why it couldn't? More frustrating was that audiences seemed to feel the same – friends talked about fans who found their work and stuck around, but I was embarrassed that I was constantly starting from scratch, with no crossover between projects. Audiences apparently found my stuff mildly interesting whilst it was there but rarely came back for more. People ostensibly regarded my work as some diversionary interlude that could be appreciated on its own terms for a short time before returning to 'normalcy'; like a tree in full springtime bloom, granted a fortnight of fawning over fluffy pink petals before reality resumes. Pretty and evocative, yet ultimately ineffectual. But my songs were merely lullabies in which I hid my roars.

By 2015, the world was becoming increasingly more hostile. Racism was somehow both everywhere and nowhere: people universally understood that projects needed to be more 'diverse' and 'BAME inclusive', yet no white people had ever directly seen or acknowledged racism in their projects and circles. Schrodinger's Racism: known and unknown, seen and unseen. Two years after future nightmare PM Theresa May's infamous 'Go Home' vans journeyed across the UK – just in case anyone was under the delusion we were a welcoming nation – Cameron was re-elected and the looming Brexit vote heralded in a new era in normalising anti-immigration rhetoric and rewarding xenophobia. In the US Trump launched his campaign by calling Mexicans 'rapists' and it was downhill from there.

In April – mere weeks before the general election – the country reached a new low as the UK's biggest-selling newspaper *The Sun* decided to actually print, using words, IN THE PAPER, an article by noted racist Katie Hopkins entitled 'Rescue boats? I'd use gunships to stop migrants'. In it, she compared migrants to 'cockroaches' and said 'show me bodies floating in the water . . . I still don't care'. Hours after the article was published, a fishing vessel in the Med capsized with an estimated 950 people aboard: only twenty-eight survived. Later in the year, there was global outcry at the death of drowned Syrian toddler Alan Kurdi whose small lifeless body washed up on the shore.

Within films and TV, roles were frequently whitewashed from the source material – taking away characters of colour from audiences and jobs from actors. For non-white roles, white people still appeared in 'brownface', or playing parts different to their ethnicity without the 'ethnic' make-up (still offensive)[9]. The 2015 Grammy Awards featured overwhelmingly white musicians, and the 2015 Academy Awards featured only white people in all lead and supporting acting categories. The hashtag #OscarsSoWhite began trending on social media, and think pieces abounded on the relevancy of the awards and their failure to reflect the community; yet, the following year the top twenty acting awards were again only white people.

In fashion, words like 'tribal', 'ethnic', 'Aztec' and 'Asian' became trends, and outfits and items belonging to specific cultural groups were repurposed for white people (box braids? Hair chandeliers?). Sacred faith and spiritual practices not native to the West were rebranded into 'wellness', which white people profited from: always ready to operate from a place of taking what they wanted, strip it out of context and ignore the rest. People became more emboldened – stroking my hair, or taking it as a fun challenge to correctly guess what mix I was.

---

9. Brownface: Peter Sellers in *The Party* and Fisher Stevens in *Short Circuit 2* are two famous historical brownface roles but this method does still happen. See: Ashton Kutcher in the *Popchips* adverts, Gemma Arterton in *Prince of Persia*, Ben Barnes in *The Big Wedding*, some of the extras in *Aladdin* (2019). Non-brownface but portraying PoC (TV Tropes describes these as subcategories of brownface, 'ethnic get-up' where the performer wears garb to signify their ethnicity but no actual brownface, and 'let's ignore it' where the character's ethnicity is an informed attribute): Mike Myers in *The Guru*, Jake Gyllenhaal in *Prince of Persia*, Emma Stone in *Aloha*.

Sometimes, people would see my dad and ask why I wasn't darker (clearly genetics hadn't received the memo it was a paint chart) or regaled me with the 0.4 per cent 'Other' they possessed courtesy of an online DNA testing kit.[10]

Meanwhile, by my mid-twenties the 'in' look had become tanned skin, thick eyebrows and long dark hair. Because white girls, the Curlys and Candles of this world, achieved this via fake tan, make-up, hair extensions, false eyelashes and cosmetic surgery, it didn't seem to be understood that you could also naturally look this way. Questions came at random, inopportune moments. I'd be exiting a sweaty, overcrowded toilet or avoiding an obstacle course of Pret takeaway bags in a cramped backstage area and I'd hear *where's your falsies from?* directed to my bare eyelashes. Once at a house party, a girl couldn't believe I *didn't* have extensions, asking me to flip my hair over so she could see where it was actually connected to my head, showing others, everyone running their hands along my scalp. Another time I was changing costumes and a white woman looked over at my bare stomach, asking, 'Wow, you're really that same colour all over?' Yes, were others not?

The idea I'd altered my appearance wasn't offensive. What frustrated me was people had so few points of reference for somebody who looked like me due to DNA rather than dollars that they actually *did not believe me* – crudely checking for

---

10. Since then, people have only gotten more obsessed: between the fetishisation of mixed babies and children, the apps that allow you to blend two different ethnicities to 'guess the colour' and the weird, zoo-like spectacle of white people obsessing over the colour of others' hypothetical children.

themselves. Brown women in the media were mostly glamorous models: Priyanka Chopra, Jameela Jamil, Hannah Simone – slender silhouettes and long glossy hair. I was a taller version of my teenage self. At twenty-five, I was still the terrified tomboy who'd fled Boots a decade earlier: my 'style' extended to jewellery that didn't need taking off and charity shop clothes from my teen years with the occasional vintage dress from uni-era shopping trips. Little had changed since I'd sworn off make-up and hairdressers: make-up was limited to flicky eyeliner on gig days, and outside of audition buns, my hair did whatever it felt like (mostly moult). I sat out eyelash glue and bronzer conversations because I had nothing to add – but this was perceived as me being too proud to join in, or too secretive to disclose my beauty secrets.[11] Girls' bathrooms get held up as bastions of sisterly support, but when filled with white women I found them hostile.

Potential suitors (i.e., randoms we met on nights out) threw me nicknames and choice comments; whether it was who I looked like, stereotypes they'd project, or 'assessment' type questions that would not have been out of place on an Equal Opportunities form, people just could *not* rein it in. Too-warm sleeveless people in clubs would yell *Hey Pocahontas*, bravado-fuelled strangers in kebab shop queues called *Oi Tigerlily, I bet you taste of caramel*. Christ. Dating apps were even more of a shitshow: less posturing and more clinical. Microaggressions abounded. The majority of my opening messages were

---

11. The flipside was when people told me I was lucky: quite the take. Let's swap life experiences, then tell me that again!

something like: *hey Laila, can't tell where you're from in your pics or just wondering what colour you actually are coz the first pic is lighter than the second??!!?* Besides, I'd seen my friends automatically swipe off a 'weird name' so I knew what was likely playing out at the other end of my own weird name. It was clear if I wanted to date, I had to put up with a certain amount of this nonsense. People who made *no comments whatsoever* were . . . well, they weren't. It came from white people and PoC. The few people I'd met who were mixed were not so much 'potential romantic liaisons' as 'people I met and connected with in unfortunately fleeting situations' like somebody I met on a plane, or a house-mate's friend who visited one weekend. As finding somebody with no preconceived ideas was impossible, I figured it was a question of what I'd put up with in exchange for love (or at least somebody to split a Netflix account with). The whole thing was an absolute shambles.

I rarely engaged in relationships or even actively 'dated', ostensibly because I was work-focused – those high concept shows won't overly present themselves! Also, even if you did find someone with good chat that didn't look like Bob Durst, who could be arsed with the gradual spiral of giving up that was dating? Instead, I revolved around people who came into my life organically – friends of friends, colleagues from gigs, people at parties (ideal, even I didn't have to leave the house). Dates arrived in my life like piecemeal temp jobs: brief, unful-filling and passed on from people I already knew. People who hadn't met me just had too many preconceived ideas for me to work through. I'd stick with known people who wouldn't project all their weird biases on to me.

Or so I thought. Turns out if they know you, it's worse. Same weird biases, same promises of *I'll be with you forever* after mere weeks, WAY more weird fetish projection. I had a few months of sort-of dates with a white guy from work who initially made comments about me being 'exotic' and 'like a holiday' – nothing new there then – but I figured this would drop off if we got to know each other. Instead, he would detail further how he'd fancied Indian women growing up, how his favourite food was Indian, how he thought Indian women were more sexy – one time eagerly asking if I had any 'costumes' in my wardrobe[12]. He wanted to watch *Slumdog Millionaire*; I turned it off after fifteen minutes due to an excruciating awkwardness I couldn't then articulate. Another time, I made dinner for us – curry, his request – and as we sat down, he disclosed a long-held fantasy he had about getting home from work to an Indian meal cooked by his bashful brown bride, their small and silent brown kids lined up adorably around the table. I was literally still shoving speaker wires off the poky kitchen table when he launched into this spiel, caught off guard. What do you say to that?[13]

Another white guy, a friend's friend with whom I shared an even briefer situationship, told me he had a 'saving people' thing. In his words, 'like Harry Potter, but more Aladdin'. He was ecstatic we might be together, staging increasingly elaborate ways to ask me out: he'd been waiting and now, here I was, just waiting to be rescued! He'd show me the world the way Aladdin does for Jasmine. *You can be my princess and I'll save you.*

---

12. Turns out he did not mean the sequinned Union Jack dress I had from a show.
13. 'Fuck off' would have been a good start.

At the time, the obvious thing was to say yes and just go out with the guy – you know, why not? He liked me, friends were supportive, it was the least problematic thing I'd heard that week. But something stopped me: maybe our mutual friend, or the sacrilegious Jasmine thing (turning my childhood heroine into a come-on? Gross!), or . . . maybe just the optics. He was unemployed, living at home; I was a grant-winning musician. What was he saving me from? He knew the problems I faced in work but – like me – deduced the issues lay with me, rather than the structure: he could save me *from myself*. He couldn't see I'd saved myself a thousand times over already. Both times I sacked it off before anything really happened for reasons I can see clearly now but couldn't verbalise at the time. What's more concerning: that mid-twenties me assumed this was par for the course in a healthy relationship, or that, at the time of writing, both of those men have married South Asian women?

Worse than the racism and microaggressions from the world at large was discovering it in my own family. I had known that my rarely visited, USA-based uncle was pro-gun, right-wing and, in my mum's words, 'not on the same page' as her or her sisters, but he was still family, right? Uncles cared about their nieces; I knew this from Poupa in Mauritius. Not so: my American uncle and I had a blazing argument in which he made it clear, repeatedly, that I was young, Not American, and therefore ignorant. It began with gun control (I was pro, he was not), moved to school shootings (I said they were a problem, he said not), moved on to police brutality and structural racism (I said it existed, he said not), and then – this is what became unforgivable for me – he dismissed the Black Lives Matter movement as *unnecessary*. He was annoyed at the protestors in his area because they had held up traffic. He was frustrated that they were delaying his journey home, as racism was 'only a problem in the South' and therefore, crucially: *not his problem*.

I don't think I have been so angry or let down before or since. I was seething, my insides churning like a molten furnace, my body clenched in fury. I couldn't fathom how this man, a blood relative, had stood in front of me – a *whole mixed-race person of colour* – and said those things so definitively to me. Was he asleep at the wheel? How could he be a generation above me and never have done even the barest minimum of interrogation on how society was structured? And there was *me*. His *sister* had been married to *my dad* for decades; I had been this man's niece for more than two decades and he had seriously never wondered what that meant? I thought back to the family reunion when I was eleven – had he gone home without the barest trace of thought as to how I, one of his two nieces (his only niece in attendance), might have felt being one of the only non-white attendees? It was tough to know my existence had made such a small impact. It shouldn't have taken having me as a family member for him to give a shit – but the fact that he *did* have me as a family member and was still so ignorant was immensely painful.

At the time, I did two things I never do: raised my voice, and left. Storming round the corner I found Mum. Her main concern was to calm me down from this never-before-seen fit of fury. She didn't want things to be *awkward*. She was embarrassed about her relatives but didn't see my disgust. I was clear, saying it was bad enough being half-white but these white people as my *family*? Ugh. She didn't say anything; she seemed pensive, sad. But this wasn't an issue to sit on whilst fog rolled

around – racism was a living, thriving force and needed challenging. We couldn't apologise it out of existence. This was *our*
family: *our* responsibility to tackle. Who else was afforded the
protection of blood? I battered Mum with questions, trying to
hold her accountable. She said things like, *I have no idea where
he got all these out-there views, we were raised to be kind and tolerant*,
or, *well, it bothers me too, but it's just so hard to get through to them*.
This didn't cut it: it echoed other white people who made
comments that essentially dismissed the issue whilst acknowledging it *just* enough so that you couldn't raise the point again.
Let sleeping dogs lie or, *well it's not the end of the world*. But people
were dying! It quite literally *was* the end of the world.

What of everyone else in the family – they didn't share his
views, but had they not challenged them? Why not? Clearly
they didn't feel motivated as members of society, but they also
didn't feel motivated as *direct relatives of a PoC*? I was *livid*. It was
a rare strain of anger for me to feel – pointed and targeted. I
wanted my mum to be better. I wanted the whole family to be
better. I wanted them to care. If they could not be people I was
proud of at least they could be people I didn't have to feel hu-
miliated, disgusted and oppressed by. Did they not understand
how racism tore up a life, cut through to the very soul of a person and shredded even the softest secret parts of you? Of *me*?

From then on, every single time something violent happened in the US – a murder, a shooting, a racist comment
made by a (then) would-be president, I felt a guilty lurch in my
stomach. I was culpable. If I had been a better niece or a more
engaging presence, then maybe my uncle who supported all
this crap would have thought twice. Maybe if I'd been older,
or married to a white guy, or more pious. Maybe if I'd tied my

hair into a bun. If I'd had a smart overnight bag instead of three battered Bags for Life; if I'd studied maths instead of music; if I'd had an American passport; if I'd written better thank-you notes; if I'd spent more time in the living room instead of feeding carrots to the horse.

Guilt pent up in contradictory, foundational ways. Between society, work, family and relationships, it was a lot of rejection to handle. I was guilty at the proximity I had to white spaces but I was also guilty of having all those tools at my disposal, yet *still* failing. I knew what was required and I still couldn't deliver. I was guilty of benefitting from whiteness and guilty of knowing why I wasn't. Imagine standing on a cliff by the sea, breeze flicking your hair, shoulders warmed by the sun, watching person after person dive into the turquoise depths. Happy shouts from below mingle with the salty whip of the wind, and you tread into the crumbly ground beneath you, finally working up the courage to jump in. You take a run up, feel yourself plummet down, pick up speed, a thrilling rush as you hurtle towards the water and the inevitable cold splash and then – you stop. You never hit the water. You are suspended in mid-air, just unnaturally trapped in limbo, caught in between – just, *there*, defying all logic and reason. This is how the guilt was for me. I was guilty of jumping and guilty of not landing.

Away from the guilt, I was *embarrassed*. The flipside of mostly being in self-led work is that nobody else is hiring you: I wasn't good enough. The logical conclusion was that I was not good at making things. I was not a compelling performer. I did not create engaging work. Being creative was one of the few constants from childhood all the way to now, when it turned out, after decades of study and attempts and practising and drafts and *trying*, actually, I wasn't. It was hard to square those two things away – what I believed (that I made things that were good) with what was true (that I didn't). It was tough to part with my idea of myself, and to feel the things I had known to be true slowly diminish. I should just learn to accept this and get on with my life, put my ideas back in my head.

It's not that I thought my works were all next-level master-pieces of unparalleled genius. I was way too much of a per-fectionist to ever think that (hello, classical music?!) but, if art is the attempt to capture a fleeting moment of truth and to preserve that single moment in amber – and I thought it was, or at least for me it was – and maybe not just the moment, but maybe (if you were good enough), everything around it, everything before and after, inside and outside, capturing not just the moment but the *context* of the moment, the *meaning* of it, and the truth of the thing – well, okay, I didn't know if I was doing that exactly. I didn't know if I was even *capable* of doing that – probably missed out on one too many practise sessions in Sixth Form – but I felt like I sometimes got close. You know, like sometimes I made a thing that somewhere along the line had caught *something* close to the truth. And even if that wasn't worth much, even if it wasn't perfect or noble or *art* surely it could have been meaningful in some way, to somebody beyond me, right?

Occasionally, people caught me after shows to say something in my work had illuminated something for *them*, and I gathered up these kind words like a bouquet. I literally *kept* them in folders of screenshots and a notebook in my guitar case filled with sweet comments from after gigs. I desperately wanted to make things that meant something, that when I unearthed a kernel of truth it could go somewhere, be gifted to somebody who received it. Because if my truth found a place then I found a place. And what I wanted more than anything was to belong, to know *you did this, you are here*. But then I had the bad auditions and the failed job applications and the partnerships that went nowhere. Worse was the endless, exhausting job of trying to get people to come and see my shows or subscribe to my blog or *share with a friend if you enjoyed it thanks*. Trying to cut through the noise like a gull calling into a storm.

Doubt stalked me. I became convinced that I was the untalented one in my friend group and everyone was too polite to say so – an insecurity that hadn't existed before. Problems spawned problems of their own. By my mid-twenties, most of my peers were significantly further along in their careers than I was: we'd started around the same level (or at least I assumed we had, I have to believe that much is true), but as I hadn't had the same opportunities to develop my craft and further my progress I was languishing behind. Worse was knowing I'd let down my dad, my grandparents, and all those unknown lost relatives who had nothing and had worked and worked and *worked* until something happened. All of that promise, hope and resilience culminated in me, some talentless loser who had spent years pursuing, what . . . a feeling? a moment? . . . that I couldn't even capture because I wasn't good enough. It was hard to take that much rejection. Eventually you have to believe what others are telling you.

Life finally upended when I came a cropper of that salacious mainstay of mid-twenteens millennial life: Tinder.

'Hey Laila, you don't strike me as English, are you? J Nice pics btw.'

Nothing new here, but for whatever reason I was so wearied that I posted a screenshot to my Facebook. Like, another day, another dickhead. To my shock, most of my friends found it funny. They sent messages like 'lol, classic – pint next week?', and clicked on the 'laughter' reaction. And it was *this* that triggered the turning point. Because an unwanted assumption like the one I'd been volleyed on Tinder was part and parcel of life as a young brown person. I dealt with the irrepressible needling of those 'microaggressions' (they did not feel micro) daily. They were a constant presence, the grit I could not get out of my shoe. That I could deal with. But when my friends found it *funny?* Didn't check in, ask how I was, just thought it was some messy entertainment in their social media feed and moved on – that told me things needed to change. I took the mick out of myself on the understanding that, yes, we could joke about it, but we all knew the horrible truth of what lurks beneath. This interaction showed me that *no we did not*. I'd censored myself in such an apparently effective manner that people saw this as fair game for comic relief.

I decided: No. I am not going to do this anymore. I'm not playing this game, silencing myself on autopilot just to blend in and be a portable punchline. I'm not sitting by and being the one who has to acknowledge all these issues and never say anything about them. I'm not going to go my whole life wondering if the self-deprecating shtick is legitimately part of my personality or just a survival mechanism I can't ever shed. I'm saying SOMETHING. And then I did what any self-respecting blogger would do and wrote eight angry paragraphs about it: *What It's Like Not Being White*. A post in which I described my everyday experiences and the comments I got day in, day out and the many thousands of ways this clawed at me.

I thought I'd maybe get thirty views. A couple hundred would have been good – though it wasn't really about the views, it was about the saying of the things that needed to be said. But by that evening I'd had *thousands* of views, my house-mates and I in the 'garden' sharing Camden Hells under lilac skies, hitting refresh every ten minutes and watching the stats bar zoom to impossible heights, the sound of DJ Fresh next door soundtracking the sunset.

On Day 2 those views had doubled. On the third day of the post's existence, both WordPress and BuzzFeed picked me up and put me on their respective front pages. And as more days went by, and the stats bar soared inexplicably, the post sailed further away from me and across the internet, and the whole time I received comment after comment, message after message, from PoC and mixed people and non-white people the world over, like a million bottles being sent towards shore, with one same idea throughout. Amid the long paragraphs of yearning, the outpouring of accumulated experiences, the words and people and profiles, was one binding message, four words over and over, constant, like a heartbeat I could finally hear: *I feel the same.*

Chapter Nine

THE TREE THAT BLOOMS THE WHOLE YEAR THROUGH

Every glance at my phone yielded glory. Not only was I not alone, I was surrounded, an endless outpouring of people who felt the same as me, collectively held emotions unspooling across my life: people emailing me, writing response blogs, asking if we could go for a coffee, somehow finding themselves realised in my writing in a way they hadn't known they could be. And white people: apologising, falling over themselves, shocked, confused, eyes opened. From August to Autumn it continued, my blog continuing to journey far beyond my usual realms. I'd note five hundred-plus WordPress notifications whilst waiting for the kettle to boil, see an email from a friend of a friend that said, *hey we met one time, I'm mixed too, just wanted to say hi,* or be packing down a gig when somebody approached with an open expression and a, *by the way I read your blog . . .*

It was unexpected but wonderful. How affirming that the simple act of stating your truth could achieve this marvelous *connection.* Even in publishing the post, a part of me had expected to be shut down and dismissed. Instead the huge response validated all the feelings I'd had – the things I'd known were unjust and racist, that nobody had corroborated – and this further illuminated to me how racism operated. Yet another cruelty of white spaces is that though I had long had this yearning to connect, I'd assumed others were uninterested. I'd thought I was the weird one for wanting to bond over shared culture all the time – and it was easy to believe both because the topics rarely came up and because I'd been wearing the 'weird' mantle for quite some time. Now the truth was beaming through. The reason people didn't discuss such things openly wasn't because of disinterest, but for the same reasons I didn't: we were all silenced by whiteness. Part of the violence is believing racism is subtle, when it's not.

Seeing how many other people were victims of the same self-censoring changed me in some way. It helped me decentralise myself, in a wonderful way. I could understand better how insidious the racism was, finally able to cast off all the 'me' problems and see them for the structural violence they were. It gave me a sharper critical lens to view things through – and the courage to just *be honest* from this point forwards, rather than bend to what others wanted to believe. Amid the outpourings, I was reminded of something I had known about myself long ago: I needed *people.* I thought about Wales. Hadn't I known then the importance of being local with somebody? For years I'd been clinging to the scraps of conversation I had with people. This was so much better.

I decided going forwards I'd lean on my intuition and only chase work that seemed to give me a fair go. My goals went from *survive via any means possible* to *make sure nobody else has to go through this again*. I wanted to better understand the structures at play, and to find more community: I needed community. Maybe I could return to the stuff I actually *wanted* to do. Leaving uni I'd been clear on how I wanted to celebrate my own perspective; yet over the years I'd been ground down into this submissive, conformative, insecure mess. That couldn't happen again. Isn't that why I'd wanted to make stuff in the first place? To catch the ideas that darted around my mind like fireflies and articulate them into something real and tangible; to pour the shimmering contents onto a stage for others; to link it all together, levitate the moments into place, hold that wonder in your hand? To follow that yearning to the ends of the threads and back again; to understand how everything linked and to present the whole myriad constellation of it to other people? For them? If I wasn't doing that, what was the point?

Months passed in an ongoing shuffle of dingy rehearsal studios, copper-potted houseplants and increasingly outlandish UK politics,[1] when my housemates Dom and Seb announced that their mate Jack was visiting. I'd first heard of Jack earlier in the year. I'd been unpacking my suitcase after returning from Japan.

'Lails, what the fuck is this?' asked my housemate Dom, picking up a box at random.

'It's a box of My Melody pancake mix that I got from Sanrio Puroland.'[2]

---

1. No, you're a snap election!
2. Obviously.

It transpired that I couldn't read the Japanese instructions, but Seb had a solution.

'Give it to Jap Jack! He knows the lingo and he's staying here next week.' Whoa! *JAP JACK?!* I couldn't believe Seb had casually thrown out such a pejorative, offensive term. Sure, the boys could be bellends at time – we all could – but this was way out of line.

'What!? Does he know you call him that?'

Dom and Seb snorted. 'Course he does! He loves it!'

Really? I couldn't get my head round that. Dom and Seb liked to mess about, sure, they were always up for a laugh or taking the piss out of each other, mostly in-jokes from their years of friendship, but they weren't cruel or malicious. They were good people, looked out for each other: mates. This did not fit. I knew 'Jap' to be a disgusting, derogatory slur. Hearing it wielded by them was hideous, but they remained insistent that Jack was in on the joke. I wondered if he truly was, or if this was the familiar 'let yourself be a punchline' survival scenario. By the time 'Jap Jack' came to stay, I was half expecting some resentful put-upon guy worn down by banter.

But Jack was not like that *at all*. Jack was kind and charming and sweet, constantly cheerful, helpful to everyone, gentle-hearted in ways that not all of us were. Jack had a warm sunny smile, a calming voice, and was the tidiest houseguest we'd ever hosted. In short, he was joyous. And he really, truly did not seem to care about this nickname, laughing good-naturedly every time Dom or Seb threw it at him.

'Where's your bloody Kitty mix thing, then?' Dom demanded, chucking the box to Jack who scanned the back.

'You . . . add an egg and . . . cook for eight minutes ...'[3] Seb clapped him on the back.

'Jap Jack to the rescue! You'd have been fucked without him!' That word again! I couldn't let this hang: Jack was being so helpful and the boys were literally throwing racial epithets at him in return.

'Oh my God! Stop being such dicks! Jack, thank you, and I can't believe—' I began.

'Stop apologising! He loves it!' Dom interjected, grinning, but I kept my eyes on Jack.

'Nah . . . it's alright really,' said Jack, and he shook his head graciously, smiling.

Still. I didn't buy it, especially not so soon after my blog post and learning how so many people had been self-censoring. Later that week, amid the remnants of a house party ('Things Beginning With C') we reached the point where the night split into two, and I found myself alone with Jack – well, there were about twenty people a foot away from us, but it was just the two of us in conversation. Major Lazer blasted through the house and revved up voices in the kitchen were loudly co-ordinating where to continue the night (*'I am NOT going to Football Crazy Football Mad for the third week in a row, it's a shithole.' 'But it's OPEN!'*) whilst outside, those who opted for a different kind of night settled into quieter activities: discarding bits of costume and chatting, hunched over tinnies in deck-chairs draped with cloud gloves and cat ears. Jack and I were sat crammed in the patio door with somebody's chopping board

---

3. A minor tragedy: it wasn't vegan.

prop as a footrest, Jack still in stripy top and cap (convict) and me in a sparkly gold dress that kept getting caught on the curtains (casino). I decided to ask again about 'Jap' now we were sort of alone. Did he really not mind?

'Nah,' he said. I gave a look. 'Really! They're just dicking around; they're my mates,' Jack explained sincerely. 'No harm. And I am Japanese! Well, half.' *Half.* Half! Oh my God, one of those gorgeous golden moments, kinship, connection, from nowhere, like spotting a shooting star – *half, oh my God we are both mixed!* Delightedly I ran through my life story – not the white person version, but the pitted real one – and Jack regaled me with his: Japanese mum, English dad; spoke both languages fluently; raised in Japan; came here for uni; missed a lot from back there but loved it here too. *I like both.* This was fascinating. I'd rarely met a mixed person who didn't have a longing to find the parts of themselves they knew less well. Jack knew each part equally. I admired the peace he had; a version of mixed existence I hadn't before encountered. We continued chatting, shuffling awkwardly as people walked over us into the house.

'Do you think you'll move back there?' I asked.

'Well, one day . . . I know this sounds weird, but . . . I've always wanted to, like, die in Japan? Like, I want to make sure I go back there when I'm old and . . . yeah.' Jack scrunched up his face. 'I know that sounds weird . . .'

'No, not at all! I really admire that.'

Actually, it seemed an impossibly lovely thing to be sure of. Imagine bookending your life with a clear idea of *home*. He had a surety I had yet to feel in my own life. Could I ever feel a belonging like that? For me, London was home, but growing old in London would be growing old away from family. I was called to spend more time in Mauritius even knowing I'd never be *local* there; and I longed to know more of my American roots but had no idea where to start. Finding 'home' was the old childhood puzzle of juggling different Lailas. Being mixed can leave you with a nagging anxiety over the part of you that you are not engaging with, like something is constantly unattended. Jack had sussed out something I hadn't – how to navigate both sides, find clarity on 'home', and seal it with a promise.

Later, one of my housemates asked if Jack and I were both 'chameleons'; relating to the idea that mixed people both can and do code-switch automatically. The thing is, everyone code-switches, everyone 'switches codes' by pulling on the most relevant parts of their experiences in any given situation. Applying that just to mixed people is bizarre, because what's everyone else then, a . . . crocodile, the same in every circumstance? Maybe everyone else is a gecko, just changing when necessary, or a painted terrapin, only changing to impress, or possibly none of us are reptiles and we're all just different versions of humans lacking a framework to understand each other. Besides, I don't change moment to moment like a chameleon, I'm all those things at once.

By now, I was finding ways to learn: delving through the British Library, YouTube and other people's JSTOR logins. I wasn't annoyed by our housemate asking. The lack of language is stifling. I had no word to define myself apart from 'mixed', less than ideal – I always had the image of two scoops of ice cream melting in a bowl – but the best of a bad bunch. 'Biracial'

didn't work. Bi meant two: *bi*cycle; *bi*annual; *bi*sect – and with
my parents' lives each encompassing more than one culture,
I was more than two. To me, biracial could fit with people
whose parents were of two separate, clearly defined cultural
backgrounds, but I'd never been half-this and half-that. 'Multi-
racial' sounded too clinical, constructed in a petri dish; its relative 'polyracial' was less clinical but somehow mythical, Gre-
cian in scope, some deity with rippling skin changing colour
in the wind. 'Dual heritage' was embarrassing, suggesting the
existence of a 'single heritage' majority who had sprung forth
through cloning or some kind of asexual plant reproduction
or something. Like, what? Most organisms have two separate
parents and therefore two separate strands of heritage. Surely a
vole or a moose or a red slender loris is legitimately dual heritage too? Who's *not* dual heritage – Dolly the sheep?

I could use *Welsh-French-Scottish-American-Indian-Mauritian*,
which was at least correct and covered the most prominent
bases, but who wants to say all that? Just imagining giving that
as an answer to *what mix are you?* I could hear the follow-up:
Wow, that's an interesting mix! which made me want to climb out
the window. Even if you took it back from countries to continents, you had *American-European-Asian-African*, which sounds
more like an international committee or global advisory board
than a single person. So, *mixed*. Just the one word.

Mixed people share considerable discourse on terminology.
Biethnic is favoured by some, or multi-heritage, neither of
which I like due to the 'bi' and 'multi' issues. Many don't like
the term 'mixed race'; it conjures racist ideologies of 'race-mix-
ing' and the 'one-drop rule', but I like 'mixed' more than any of
the other options, though I prefer it without 'race' (though this

does leave open *what* is 'mixed').[4] Some people have reclaimed words like *mulatto* or *mutt* to the chagrin of others. I hated *mutt*, but *mongrel* seemed somehow earnest and cheerful, although maybe that's just the image of smiling street dogs it brings to mind, one floppy ear and one straight.

I liked being able to shut people off with 'mixed' as well. White people were quick to ask where you are from, and quick to tell you how interesting it was that you were mixed. Then, usually frothing up with questions on the topic, never taking into account this was a one-way conversation – an interview, really – because they had nothing to contribute except their own eager questions and maybe some armchair analysis. They had no idea of the hours, years, *lifetimes* you might have spent thinking; processing this topic, trying to figure a way to hold yourself together, no concession to the idea that you might not want to regale them with that entire topic for the sake of small talk whilst you waited for the entrees. They just openly, out loud would say, *but you're mixed, I mean, that must be fascinating!* And if you didn't oblige, they'd add a, *oh I didn't mean to upset you, I just find it so interesting! Because I'm so boring hahaha!* So you were forced to assuage their feelings. And then they'd tell you about their sister's husband or nephew's teacher or cousin's boyfriend's dog who was also mixed. Like, okay, I'll look out for them at the next convention? Christ alive, can't we talk about something else? Using the single term 'mixed' felt like it could shut that down: short, pithy, defiant, finite. 'Oh me? I'm mixed.' End of story, let's talk about something else. Have you ever played *Tekken?*

---

4. Mixed gender? Mixed salad? Mixed materials collage?!

Within the 'mixed' group, I shared more with some people than others. I had lots in common with people who had a white parent and an immigrant parent who'd emigrated in adulthood from a small, formerly colonised island. Even if we'd grown up in different countries and were different ages, friends in this group had almost identical experiences with our parents, right down to sentences exchanged. To see how this experience was so common among people in similar scenarios – crossing generational, gender, locational and class lines – was incredible. Yet with no term to describe us, I couldn't easily ask: 'Are you a PIACIN[5]?' I had to ask: 'So, do you have a white parent and your other parent is a first-generation immigrant who emigrated as an adult from a small, formerly colonised by Europeans island nation?' Quite the palaver. I mean, maybe there's terms I haven't uncovered in some niche branch of cultural anthropology but you shouldn't need an academic career to introduce yourself.

Another distinct yet nameless group: people of colour (mixed or otherwise) who'd grown up in rural (majority white) areas away from cities thriving with diversity, with their own demons to slay. I'd read something that discussed this experience in a journal, but the group the writer discussed in the paper wasn't given a name – couldn't they have offered one? Perhaps, *people in this group could be colloquially described as pebbles*. I wanted a simple term to describe me, in the same way you could use 'musician', 'vegan' – 'pebble' (it would shorten my biography for one). And all other pebble people would immediately

---

5. Parent Immigrated as an Adult from a Colonised Island Nation. See what I did there?

connect and join the dots the same way musicians and vegans would. I hated the ease that was denied us, the clarity of short-hand, a simple, *Oh, you're a pebble? Me too.*

Missing vocabulary is damaging. Existing vocabulary is actively violent. Current terms are framed in a 'white' or 'not-white' binary – emphasising a white majority and defaulting all other groups to 'minority'. Terms like 'BAME' and 'PoC' only make sense if you understand and accept whiteness as the default.[6]

Think of a rainbow. Imagine identifying the colours of a rainbow as 'blue' and 'not-blue'. Blue is still called blue. That's clear enough. Red is now not-blue. Orange is also not-blue. And green, well that's also not-blue, so the same group as not-blue, (or what was red and orange). But green/not-blue is so much closer to blue – closer than red/not-blue or orange/not-blue at least. And red and orange are not exactly the same either; so some not-blue is different to other not-blue – either closer-to-blue, or maybe near-blue? We could call some of the not-blue, near-blue and some far-blue. Or maybe some not-blue is different to other not-blue in ways that cannot be explained using blue and proximity to it. We'd struggle to describe it; *I mean the not-blue that is closest to far-blue, not the not-blue that is more like blue, or, let's change this near-blue not-blue for a less-blue not-blue?* We lose the ability to parse them from one another – they're diminished into one vague approximate mass, where specific shades of not-blue are indiscernible. Huge

---

6. 'People of the Global Majority' (PGM) moves away from the white framing and emphasises being a part of something bigger – the over 80 per cent of the global population who are not white – but it still ends up being a binary term informed by whiteness.

amounts of time are wasted trying to identify them via blue. The only thing all of the not-blue colours have in common is that they are Not Blue, which is truly nothing to do with those colours at all, and tells us nothing about what they actually are, nothing of the character and essence of the colour. How can you understand the difference between red and orange using blue as your only metric? Can you explain what you love about yellow using only the ways it is not blue? Terms like PoC, BAME, non-white, ethnic minority and so on have this effect. All that is understood from these terms is the absence of whiteness and a default white majority. Outside of whiteness, they are meaningless terms connecting only to theories; describing social concepts instead of fixed and factual reality.

Put a tree or a fish or a crescent of the moon in front of pretty much anyone from anywhere, and they'll have a word for it in their language. The same can't be said for the terms we use when discussing race and ethnicity, because they're concepts resulting from our unique history – and I don't mean just those acronyms, but even terms like 'white' and 'mixed' within a race setting don't translate. Even the word 'race': in some languages it is interchangeable with 'ethnicity' or 'nationality' and sometimes none of those terms exist. Because it's a *concept*. We made it up. For some reason, though I already knew that, learning how few of these terms had meanings outside of English really underlined how futile the terms are, and how intangible the whole idea of race is.

That doesn't mean the effects are not real. Such as the language: within English the existing vocab is so limited, half-baked and tethered to oppression, that it's another curse of whiteness; we can't even articulate *who we are*, condemned to lengthy discourse just to identify ourselves. On every conceivable level we lack acknowledgment and space. Though the terms are so uninformative as to be meaningless (universally loathed by the people who are within those groups) it doesn't mean that the effect of trying to understand yourself via a warped lens isn't real. Knowing that the language doesn't serve means I use what I can for now – mixed, PoC – acknowledging the issues without letting it derail me from the actual things I want to talk about, rather than letting language be another factor holding me back.

By 2018, journals and outlets like *gal-dem* and The Other Box existed, alongside books like *The Good Immigrant* and *Why I'm No Longer Talking to White People About Race*.[7] Windows were opening into communities I hadn't known existed. There were more people of colour within pop culture than before; brown men with white women became practically its own trope and TV started featuring more series with PoC protagonists. Blogs were held up as an example of a meritocracy, unlike 'mainstream media'. With blogging anyone could build an audience! This was true enough on the surface but was a different story within the industry. Sure, blogs were written by a wide group of people – but blogging *opportunities* largely went to those who were skinny, white and conventionally attractive. I was by no means a 'big time blogger', with just a few thousand readers – but I befriended other PoC bloggers, all of whom had similar stories of being overlooked by brands. Social media apps like

---

7. Respectively, edited by Nikesh Shukla and written by Reni Eddo-Lodge.

Instagram favoured 'lighter' and 'brightened' photographs – a lot of the default filters made you physically appear lighter – which put dark-skinned creators at an immediate disadvantage. I spent a lot of time organising meet-ups for people I'd met in group chats and comments sections: anything that could allow that sense of community to reach through the screen and be a physical, bolstering presence within life. There was that now-familiar rush of easy intimacy; kinship, unteachable short-hand and comfort.

Mainstream media had begun to fetishise 'the mixed aesthetic', building on the Curly and Candle look from before – going so far as to describe certain celebrities as having the 'mixed look' even when they weren't actually mixed. Though there are literally thousands of ways you can be 'mixed', when it comes to white-dictated western world beauty standards there are just two ways you can *look* mixed. Option one is the 'ethnically ambiguous' tanned skin, thick dark hair, brown eyes, large facial features – the way white people wanted to look (and did, if they could afford it). Option two is an obvious and easily 'decipherable' combination of two or more traits usually associated with different races, (i.e. you had blue eyes and an Afro), which white people could understand as representing 'a mix', because they could clearly break down the mix from looking at you (or so they thought). And that was it.

Everywhere from long-form articles to *Love Island* used 'mixed' to describe somebody's appearance. You'd hear, *I only fancy mixed guys really* or *Yeah, she's got that mixed thing going on.* This was a slap in the face: for years people like me had been invisible, and now everyone wanted to look that way without acknowledging that *we had existed* for years beforehand.

I'd spent years unravelling how isolated society had made me feel – trying to believe I existed. And now that same society had decided overnight it was cool to 'be' mixed without any exploration of what that meant.

In 2017, I decided to open up the question of fake tan with my Instagram followers. At the time, celebrities like the Jenner sisters, Ariana Grande, Rita Ora and half of Little Mix[8] were clearly passing for mixed ethnicity – Arab, Latinx, Black – despite all being white. Responses poured in from PoC who felt invalidated, mocked or robbed of their own appearance by their browned-up white friends – white friends who were responsible for years of microaggressions and upholding racist structures. Meanwhile, replies from white women centred on personal insecurities – a classic white move that effectively stopped them from taking the accountability for their actions as harmful. My white followers sent in these woes and debated what was an 'acceptable level' of fake take. Maybe if an activity requires all this internal debate and imaginary line-drawing it's better just to sack it off altogether.

What the conversation *did* illuminate was why so many problems got projected on to me. When white women demanded to know about the precise machinations of my body – staring at my stomach, scanning my scalp – it came from a place of unsolved insecurity and unexamined privilege. They felt they were entitled to assess me and judge me in ways they had never assessed or judged themselves. My mere existence

---

8. At that point, Little Mix contained four girls; one mixed Black, one mixed white-Arab and two white – all of whom appeared the same colour in photographs.

brought up issues with themselves they hadn't yet contemplated, or were only noticing now. During this time, a lot of pop culture was coming up for reckoning – everyone had a newsletter or a Twitter thread, throwing the word 'discourse' around and re-evaluating *Friends* for cultural appropriation. Why now? Had the S Club Juniors fallen so far from collective memory?

On occasional weekends home to visit my parents, I'd do very little – sleep in, idly watch Dad watch CNN, or amble to the kitchen and try Mum's latest cookies. Now with some of my own incessant 'identity quest' over, I could consider things differently, unravel some of the more difficult times we'd shared. It was clear that how we understood identity was different. Though Mum was white, in a white majority country, she didn't have the same 'white' mindset as she'd grown up an outsider – as a minority in sub-Saharan Africa. In a way, my own confusion at being outside of mainstream society was more similar to her than to Dad, although she (obviously) bore white privilege I didn't access. Dad and I, on paper, were more similar – PoC, in white countries. But Dad had never voiced confusion over his sense of belonging because, presumably, he'd never had any – until he came to the UK as an adult, he'd been the majority. Dad is from Mauritius – an African country – but was born in a British colony – India – before he and his family made their way back to another British colony – Mauritius. At the end of his teens, he moved to the UK. He said he was British with no addendums or fuss, the same way he was Mauritian and Indian.

What about Mauritius itself? After the colonisers left and the dodos died and the forests were cleared for crops, what remained? People. Few came voluntarily – plantation owners, their slaves, indentured labourers, captured prisoners. The events that caused people to be in Mauritius are so recent that everyone is 'from' somewhere else if you go back a couple hundred years. Mauritian society contains multiple different identities; different groups based on different social aspects with varying correlation and overlap between them. In an anthropology book in the British Library, I found a study that gave several pages to diagrams on Mauritian society and its construction. The diagram looked like an intricate spider web (especially compared to the three-line triangle that showed the construction of Western society). None of the usual societal hallmarks created a single group – language, religion, ethnic background, culture – instead, groups spilled into each other.[9] Mauritius is a place where multiculturalism is not a goal so much as the default state of existence.

When we drove down the streets, we passed temples next to mosques next to churches. Some people were first-generation

---

9. Overwhelmingly from India, Pakistan and Sri Lanka, but the British also took people of Chinese, Malay, Malagasy and origin to Mauritius. Previously, during Portuguese and French rule, slaves had been brought over from Madagascar, Mozambique, and Zanzibar. Today the population is further augmented with expats, deposed Chagossians and foreign workers from Southeast Asia. According to the 2011 census, 85 per cent of people speak Creole and the largest religious group, Hindu, is around 45 per cent. Around two thirds of Mauritians are Indian or of Indian heritage – although without an ethnicity question, this is a composite group. Clearly these stats don't indicate one definitive majority group who share language, heritage and religion.

immigrants and some sixth, seventh, eighth. People talked about London as a diverse utopia, and maybe it is on paper, but you could just as well group the ethnicities by postcode in London. In Mauritius *where are you from?* wasn't a vocalisation of perceived racial isolation, it was a logical greeting, the same as asking your name.

Dad explained even as a child he had an understanding of being as equally Mauritian as his classmates, despite all having separate backgrounds in terms of religion, culture and ancestral country. It wasn't discussed, he said, you just knew where people were from based on other cues, like their name. This had rarely happened to me; every once in a while an Uber driver or airport security person would ask if I was Muslim based on my name, and Jaya had recognised my name immediately – but most of the time in the UK my name was not emblematic of my heritage. It was a burden, a spelling to fall over. This was not how Dad grew up.

'You know, everyone is from somewhere, but everyone's Mauritian as well. We're all here together. Like me. I'm Mauritian, but my mother was from Goa.'

'That's what you said to me when I was younger,' I said, recalling the confusion that had caused years before when I'd brandished my homework.

'Yeah, I remember. You didn't understand me, though, you were thinking in halves. It doesn't work like that.'

This exchange struck me. *It doesn't work like that.* Well, maybe that's true *here*, in Mauritius, where society is able to acknowledge the complexity of human identity – but try saying '*it doesn't work like that*' to the ruthless 2001 census. The UK was light years behind. We'd introduced the ethnicity question explicitly in 2001. Mauritius has not included an ethnicity question on the census since 1972 – so, just once since independence (I like the idea of some people in an office deciding, *this is pointless, the British can sod off and bloody well take their weird fixation on ethnicity with them*). Meanwhile, politicians in the UK toss off words like *multicultural* and *global society* without ever once acknowledging the racist structures the country is built on. It was hard to imagine us ever achieving the kind of post-colonial system that Mauritius had. Theresa May gave an infamous 2016 speech stating that a 'citizen of the world' – yes, do go on – '[is] a citizen of nowhere'. Oh. Huh. And yet, whilst I was growing up, thanks to the absence of context, targeted censorship of history and whitewashing of representation all wrought by UK society, understanding myself as a citizen of the world had been one of the only structures that allowed me to feel connected to the human race.

When I turned my attention to my wider family I could better see the issues I faced *because* of them. I'd become better friends with my white cousins, able to visit with them and chat regularly (online, of course). The two halves of my family were not well integrated in terms of religion and culture. Any attempts to integrate seemed to have been abandoned years before my arrival, resulting in Mum's family feeling like hers and Dad's family feeling like *his* without anything feeling like *mine* or *ours*. Discrepancy over how my two sides operated cropped up *all the time*. For example, my brown family were full of congratulations when I went to university, even though they didn't understand how I could be studying music. All of my white cousins had gone to college and they turned up to my graduation recital and knew to bring flowers, dress smart casual, thank the accompanist and so on. If my brown relatives had come – which they couldn't, because of money/passports/etc – they would not have known any of the general classical music protocol and might have felt uncomfortable. Some part of *me* felt uncomfortable, playing music by dead white men, entrenched in the academic system. Shouldn't I have been tackling systemic poverty or ending world hunger? Who did I think I *was* to fanny around interpreting sonatas?

The main approach to me was wholly ignoring I was mixed. On my brown side, there were concessions to my white Westernness. My relatives greeted me and my mum with English (varying from fluent to single words), bought us *Western* presents (i.e. t-shirts and Western-style tops rather than the salwars and saris they wore) and catered to our more Western-centric diet (more salads, and in later years, my veganism). On my white side there were zero attempts to integrate: in terms of learning the language, studying the culture, understanding Islam. Even small actions implied the brown part of our family wasn't acknowledged; like when I was a small child watching Mum making separate sandwiches for her and me in my grandparents' kitchen, because we couldn't eat their food, and it was on us to *avoid* what didn't align with our different diet.

My dad had historically opted out of white-side gatherings because of work – but stayed absent after retirement. Hass never came either. If you wanted to be involved it had to be within the white framework of the family, aligning to *their* world instead of meeting in the middle. They were friendly and eager to host, sure, but it was different. I'm not suggesting white relatives should have completed a degree in Creole to make Dad feel welcome or whatever, but between small things like house rules and menus, and bigger things like conversation topics, the overall cumulative effect, as far as I could tell, is that my white side just did not acknowledge any strand of non-whiteness in the family. As that 'strand' is largely my dad; essentially, in some crucial way, from my vantage point, it seemed they did not acknowledge him.

On some level I'd realised this as a kid: the lack of anywhere for Dad to stay; his absence in the mantelpiece photos. The subconscious attitude was 'you can do that side of culture with the other side of your family', rather than any form of integration. The issue is that families are then inadvertently putting all the responsibility of integrating the two sides of family on to the child. The need to do this becomes internalised early on, and you grow up continually code-switching from side to side: a constant state of unnoticed low-level stress and anxiety, a heightened variant of the expectations usually found in white circles. As an adult, my mum's parents and siblings would sometimes make sniffy comments about my dad not attending family meet-ups, apparently viewing my mum as a tragic victim of her unsociable and unsupportive husband – but it's not for the guest to make themselves feel welcome.

One time my mum mentioned how many times Dad had previously been invited to stay with her in the small rural US town her relatives lived in. I pointed out I barely wanted to go and I'd gone twice. Sure, the scenery is lovely, and who doesn't love a good chipmunk sighting, but outside of that . . . did she not know how awkward it was in those tiny towns? The hassle of being pulled aside in an airport, the white-bread milieu, the deluge of *oh wow what an interesting name* every five minutes?

It only got weirder as I got older. One time we had Indian food with my white relatives because ostensibly 'your uncle likes curry', like that was the only connection to India within the whole house. Instead of cooking or going to a restaurant, Dad was dispatched to collect takeaway from Southall like it was some daring quest only he could complete. He didn't even take orders, like he implicitly knew what to get and it was taboo to suggest otherwise. My uncle chatted about the cuisine he liked with zero input from my dad who had quite literally chosen and brought the food home. Another time I was in a conversation with Mum and other relatives, everyone swapping stories: about my aunt and uncle who had briefly lived in Bangladesh; a white cousin who was dating a guy of Bengali heritage; my white great-grandparents who were in India for several years. There were comments like, *isn't it interesting how our family seems to have this connection to that part of the world* and *I'd love to go visit one day*, whilst I sat there staring at my clammy hands. It was like being six again and wondering if I existed: was I . . . in the room? Could they see me? It was thoroughly meta, like I'd fallen out of a different storyline into this conversation. Surely I was both *family* and *that part of the world*, and not in some figurehead mascot-type way but just . . . by default, due to my heritage. As they continued to talk about the family threads that continued to lead 'us' on a journey 'back' to 'there' I wondered if they considered me part of 'us' or part of 'there', or, if, like my white uncle, they didn't consider me at all.

Incidents like this were bizarre. Maybe I'd done such a good job of code-switching that they genuinely had not understood who I was, or maybe they'd only accepted the parts of me that aligned with them. Maybe they were too invested in keeping the apparently faraway 'part of the world' far away instead of allowing it into the room. Below the awkwardness, I knew a growl of anger deep within me: resenting the implication that 'that part of the world' was some exotic nostalgia, rather than a recently colonised country devastated by our common ancestors, especially whilst I was right there in the room carrying around the memory of said devastation in my flesh and blood. If they'd looked over, they'd have seen the flash of fire in my eyes, a seldom-used inheritance from my dad.

Somehow, this jarring dichotomy never played out in public and was left going back and forth inside me. It stopped my family from knowing me, in some ways. When extended relatives on my mum's side commented on me, my nature, their understanding of me as a person – but viewed only through the prism of what they could directly understand: whiteness – I'd read their words and feel half-full of love and pride, but half-empty, thinking *but you don't know me really*. You've never seen me in a context where I'm the majority. You have no idea what colour I turn when I belong, how much more nourished my soul is in the sun.

Reaching my late twenties, I knew now that identity was not some magical location I was trying to reach but an ongoing, ever-changing journey. I understood the confusion born from a perspective that had never been presented to me. Society doesn't offer examples, or celebrate, or even *validate* the sense of a kaleidoscopic existence – like my everyday perspective. Lives are framed in a singularly forward stance, like the way we limit time to clocks: all linear A to B, one experience laid out neatly after another, instead of a series of stars forming constellations, with each individual moment overlapping and colliding, launching off fragments like meteorites. That framework of understanding means little when you're levitating between the different layers of your life, leaping from Laila to Laila, accessing all things in all ways at all times.

That was why I'd found it easier to relate to self-reflexive work, pieces that expanded tenfold and reached outwards in some dynamic collision of disparate forces. Huge complex productions with dozens of moving parts, the more the merrier – those are the places that felt calm and safe. Those moments of everything coming together unendingly, of home.

After I had come to terms with this, I thought I could put myself down. But there was something else, something further down, that nagged me, called to me, haunted me. I had heard this low rumble before – it crept up behind me in dark and quiet moments, but I thought it was part of my central quest and confusion to find myself. Except now I had, and it was still there, something different, something bigger than my own problems that was lurking, waking up. I could answer the call now. I was ready.

And so I delved deeper. It was buried, somewhere beneath the lantern and the comet, deep down in the centre of my soul. I descended further. Under all the layers of myself, I found the things that came before me – and then I found the issue, the problem, the thing that refused to be solved. Some ancient conflict that had been waiting, and was now provoked; something old and forgotten and yet very much alive.

A trip to Mauritius in my late twenties: the familiar feeling that somebody had turned the saturation up and chickens fleeing nervously as we opened the heavy steel door to my cousins' yard. Instead of several days we had several *weeks*. Each evening, I sat on porous volcanic rocks in the sea, they stayed warm for hours, soaking the sun up as though remembering when they had first left the molten mountains. Sat there, alone, the ocean was endless, shot through with the silver threads that were really fish, and all around stretching outwards until it seamlessly stitched into the sky. I could dive into my thoughts, finally granted enough space for the swarm of sparks I carried around in my mind. I'd spot baby starfish waving from gaps in the rocks, massive bats darting in and out the mangroves and, one day, to my shock, around dusk, I watched the waves drop small fish on the rocks next to me, where they *stood up* and *walked*. Skittering this way and that, sometimes hitching a ride a couple of waves later to land back in the water, but sometimes not, staying on the rocks, taking small careful steps and staring at me suspiciously. I was awestruck − cast back to childhood enchantment, like every moment was remaking reality, *fish that walk*, and it was calming to know wonders never ceased, and that even at this big age the world could strike me sideways.

For years when I'd asked about Dad's relatives, he'd told me that the things I wanted to know were, 'in the box at Iqbal's house'. Our trips never allowed time to investigate, but now, with *weeks* . . . One calm afternoon, finally, Iqbal obligingly fetched the box, passing carefully preserved documents across the lace tablecloth. Afternoon sun hit the floor in front of us and a plate of gateaux piments sat next to an unopened bottle of Coke, the only sound the fan churning overhead and the gentle coos from the yard.

A photograph of my grandmother. The second I'd seen. I was confused why she had a different name recorded on the back – a Portuguese name. Dad looked at me; she was from Goa. *Don't you know the history?*[10] But he wasn't angry. He laughed, always in a better mood on holiday. Next, a passport that had belonged to *my grandfather.* This passport was the only thing of his I'd ever seen other than his son. I tried to grasp meaning from each trace left of my grandfather. His birthday! His height! The curly way he signed the W in his signature! Still musing, I turned the fragile page carefully and my heart yelped in my chest with excitement and joy: so it was that I first saw my grandfather.

Triumph! It was a shock to see not just my nose, but my eyes, my brow line, the whole top half of my face rendered back at me. The expression on my grandfather's face – relaxed yet direct, nearly a grin, some glimmer of a secret in the eyes – was one I was well familiar with, because I had seen it in hundreds of photos of me: in candid snaps, posed photos, headshots, even photos where I was merely in the background talking to other people. I pulled the exact same expression all the time. Internally I cheered, greeted him, *I have the same listening face as you. I like music too. Did you know? I'm your poti. Thank you for the nose.*

---

10. Clearly not and we'll thank the haphazard chaos of the curriculum for that.

'Dad! Why didn't you tell me I look like Grandad?' Dad turned around, distracted.

'What? I did! I told you — Grandad Woozeer's nose!'

'Yeah, and also his exact expression! And his eyes! And the whole top half of his face!' I held up the passport.

'Oh, okay,' Dad said, which made me think *I didn't* — but I was holding the photo! I had proof! Dad examined the small black and white rectangle. 'God, he looks young here.' But I was overjoyed. Dad didn't understand what this meant to me — I didn't look like my dad, but I looked like *his dad*. I looked like *a Woozeer*, unequivocally *part of the family*.

As the afternoon rolled blissfully on, Iqbal and my dad's explanations were punctuated by my questions, Poupa nodding wisely in the corner, and Iqbal's kids curled up on all available laps like kittens. Mum sat redundantly off to the side. It was a new way of learning about family — not just Dad and I hacking through things back and forth, increasingly agitated, but all of us together, sharing.

The last item we found in the box was a very old piece of paper.

It was a contract.

'He was an indentured labourer. That's what they call it.'

A contract. My great-grandfather's contract.

Something rose in my throat. I knew all about these contracts. These contracts, written in English and dispersed to those who could not read them, the millions of innocent people who were tricked, threatened and coerced into signing them. Signing these contracts meant signing your life over — or, more accurately, thumb-printing your life over, as education was denied. I knew official punishments for being unable to produce the contract included docking pay, jail and being banned from returning home; unofficial punishments weren't listed but historians agreed they were numerous and violent. If you lost or damaged your contract it was impossible to get a replacement or copy, leaving you essentially up for extortion.[11] I knew of the millions of people who'd been systematically sent away from *their land* by the people who had *stolen* it, an act that forced a population into a diaspora – all because of these contracts. I knew all about the British behaviour that left a civilisation slashed into threads and scattered to the world like tiny fish in the bottomless sea. Here was a remnant of just one. A thread that tangled all the way down to me.

It felt jarring that the only part of my great-grandfather left was that same contract. No photos, no items, no letters, just this single document, protected so resolutely during his life-time that it had survived intact all the way through to mine, a century after it would have last been legally required. Apparently, the contract we were passing around was a photocopy, the original was 'kept safe' in a plastic wallet. Still safe, just in case – why risk the brutality of the British? What is a century to them, or a law, or a life? We know what they are capable of.

I felt some thread come loose, a thread which seemed to shake itself out, and come alive – like a thread that wasn't a thread at all but was really a fish, tugging urgently on the loose end, darting through the years. If I follow the fish far enough,

---

11. We're talking a literal sheet of A4 paper here, signed in ink. That contract has to survive your voyage over and then stay on your person at all times during your fourteen-hour days of manual labour in the hot and sweaty fields. Even the contract details (i.e. the ink) not being clear could lead to penalty.

will I find a finite end? I read the contract slowly; not trying to gather clues or search for traces of myself, as I had done with the photographs and the passport. All I tried with my great-grandfather's contract was to read the words. To make sense of something which made no sense at all, to accept into my conscious something unconscionable, to hold the proof that something that should never have happened, had. And as I read, I felt the rumbling within me, held the hot storm at the centre of my soul, heard the low, raging roar of something so deplorable it only grew in pain. And somewhere, far below, that hideous conflict deep in the smoky heart of me suddenly stirred, growling, and soon it would lurch forwards, and pounce.

EMIGRANT EMBARKED AT CALCUTTA,

27th June, 1875.

NAME: *Woozeer.*
AGE: *11*
SEX: *Infant boy.*

I confirm that the Infant Boy above described, Emigrant, who I have engaged as a Labourer on the part of the government of Mauritius, has appeared before me and declared his willingness and desire to proceed to for Hire in the Colony of Mauritius.

Chapter Ten

A Ceaseless Sequence of Stars

Two fish, swimming in opposite directions. Two small souls, unknown to one another but starting from the same point: India. Two rippling strands in the Indian Ocean, ripples that are not equal in tenor or range but will resound through the following years and centuries until they finally collide, leading to one single life: to Laila. For this is the tale of my two great-grandfathers, and the strands of their once living stories, stories that became threads, which became entangled down into me.

One fish moves towards an unknown future it has no possible comprehension of, under false terms, hasty contracts, and sinister enterprises. According to the contract he keeps safe – so safe it will last a century – the small boy declared a *willingness* and *desire* to proceed, but clearly those words have been warped beyond any extant meaning, because who, if they had a choice, would choose this: a terrifying one-way journey with their mother on an overcrowded and disease-riddled ship. Stripped of home and humanity, crammed in like cattle, forced into fear, where there are worms in the drinking water and death in the dorms; where circumstances are murky, where nobody knows, and nobody cares, and everything you thought you'd one day know is lost and gone, mere tatters and scraps in the sea. The legacy of this life is stolen, delivered again to the oldest injustice the world knows, returned to nothing, to the ground, where the dead things dwell and only the earth turns, and even that is tired.

What of the other thread, what was the story when it was alive? The other fish sails away from India in entirely different circumstances, upon a ship of glorious triumph, a reunited couple sailing home, after years apart they are together once more – and now three! With a baby in tow, sailing back as a burgeoning family to the welcoming Highlands of home, leaving an adventure and a life worth recalling. And here, at the start of this triumphant journey – which is also, imminently, the end – sailing home, a tragedy occurs. Passing a small island of jungle and orange quartz, the reunited couple part for the last time, a widow leaving what will become the lost grave of a dead man and a pause in the past, a split branch of the story dislocated from its start – but at the time in the present is simply a grieving woman. Still a mother, no longer a wife. The widow and child head towards colder climes and heavy waters and the harsh winds of the British coast. The man was headed home from India to Scotland before he became ill, died, and was laid to rest at the next port by his grieving widow. Ostensibly she buried him so he could be found, to leave something of him for someone other than fishes. He could have been buried at sea – but she chose land. She chose gravity, and earth, a place down in the soil among the quartz. She chose a funeral with two strangers; a corner of a cemetery in Sri Lanka; and a *somewhere*. And she noted down the precise location of the grave for her infant son before taking him back to the UK where he grew into my grandfather, and could one day return.

Except he never went back to the grave, and neither did his children. And as decades slipped by, the legacy of this dead man cast a long shadow over all who came from him. What a bitter vein: the grief of my great-grandmother, widowed in her thirties; the reclusive nature of her fatherless child, and the detached patriarch he became. The sense of vague unknowns and insecurity he passed on to his family; the tip toeing conversations his children – like my mum – have had since, and their continuing avoidance of anything other, like a different coloured daughter. All the way through this vein reverberates that weird sense of not knowing; of not trusting my mum for the answers; of all the problems that were mine and mine alone; the strange fog I'd always sensed seeping into the cracks of the family, like the way a cloud curls around a moon between phases; a trench of trauma that reaches all the way back through the questions and distance and fundamental, foundational *not knowing* to a young mother and her baby mourning her dead husband on the deck of a ship in the middle of nowhere, waves breaking ceaselessly on the prow, thinking you were all finally headed home to *begin*, and now all of a sudden it is the *end*, and you are left, quite alone.

May 2018. Ninety-two years after he died, my cousins (on my mum's side) found themselves headed from America to India for a wedding. Realising this is the nearest anyone has been to Sri Lanka in a century, they have decided to answer the call, and I'm going too! We're journeying to Colombo, Sri Lanka, to try and find the long-lost grave of our great-grandfather, Johnnie, whose life we never knew but whose death has reverberated. The trip is thrown frantically together in just under a week – lots of late-night logistic phone calls and eager involvement from the family at large. Though nobody knows about my great-grandfather Johnnie as a person, we know a lot about his widow, Mina. When Mum first came to the UK at the age of seventeen, Mina – then a prim elderly lady – was the only member of family she had in the country. Mina died long before I was born, but some of her possessions are in the attic. Mum shows them to me the weekend before I travel to Sri Lanka; me saving pictures on the Photos app to show the others. Through these items, I imagine Mina: eclectic, inquisitive, regal. Mum says she was tall and striking with dark hair, large features and toothy smile, all of which fits. There are letters from her time working with the Prussian royal family, a pink glass sugar bowl (this I spirit away to my house for propagating plants), a midnight blue silk kimono, a small empty compact, and – oh! – two brass candlesticks: coiled snakes holding thistles in their mouths. Mina's candlesticks from India. The same candlesticks I'd seen in childhood that everyone found creepy. Seeing them again, I am struck by the strange combination of snakes and thistles (India and Scotland?), by how heavy and solid they seem and how much more detailed they are than in my memories. But mostly I'm struck by how they look like the two rescue snakes my house ended up with. These candlesticks are not a design of grandiose cobras or fearsome pythons, as snakes are often depicted, these ones look like mine:

all tentative sniffs, curious glances and Labradorian hunger. The candlesticks I take as well, to live on top of the snakes whose likeness they bear.

Mina is known. Johnnie, not so much. His life is mostly a mystery. He is most notable for his death, the grave nobody visited and the closest co-ordinates being 'Colombo'. Extended family have come through with all manner of documents for us to peruse, most of which I had no idea existed: notes from Mina's life, laboriously typed up in the 70s; a photocopy of some ancient hundred-year-old book that mentions our great-grandfather's grave[1]; holey samples of the family tartan; an explanatory essay on our clan. I pack Johnnie's book of Scottish folk songs and research traditional Scottish funeral rites, which he was unlikely to have had at the time of burial – sourcing seeds, shortbread, whisky (Heathrow airport's finest). Mum sends me an A4 page of printed photo scans: Johnnie, Johnnie with Mina, even a photo of Mina with *her* father, my great-great-grandfather, almost so far back as to be totally abstract. He died in New Zealand, where another branch of the family live – but that's another story.

My cousins and I had five days together to locate Johnnie's grave and close this chapter. On the first day, we meet in Sri Lanka and board a noisy train that winds through misty mountains and delivers us to a guesthouse surrounded by rainforest. On the second day, we explore tea-planting country – verdant furry mountains sprinkled with colonial buildings. On

---

1. I'm not making this up; a British reverend wrote his collected memories about his time living in Sri Lanka and includes several paragraphs about the lonely Scotsmen (our guy and another) buried in the cemetery after a tragic death at sea, plus a very blurry photo of their graves.

the third day we visit small towns, with shuttered buildings painted in bright colours. All the while we use every available moment to scour the ream of papers; jumping on patchy Wi-Fi to google the cemeteries of Colombo; taking notes from the documents; teaching (me) and learning (my cousins) one of the Scottish hymns in Johnnie's volume; deciphering scans of old books; and assessing the best guesswork of our collected mothers recalling their grandmothers' stories they'd last heard fifty years ago. The constant question, *where is he?* hangs over us, the unshakeable knowledge that he is *somewhere*. I mean, he must be. He was buried on land, so he is somewhere, we just have to find him. Finally, the day before we are due to leave Sri Lanka, we head to Colombo, and the cemetery we think he could be buried in.

This is not one of those stories where everything unfolds as if charmed by a benevolent narrator. Problems abound from the off. We leave the hotel late. The taxi driver gets lost. He stops for directions. We arrive at the cemetery an hour before closing time. The central office is shut. We hurry around, googling frantically, until we eventually find a person. We find the records room. The translator's shift is over. We outline our story with nervous gestures and sweat. Nobody recognises the area in the photograph. The plot number our great-grandmother so carefully recorded is part of a system no longer in use (and by the way did we know the cemetery is closing in an hour). The records of *that* system were lost. The extant records have been eaten by whitefly.

Here, we are led outside to the impossibly sad sight of several huge books, two feet tall, with thick, stiff pages covered in intricate script – I am forcibly reminded of a prop we made for a WOLF PACK:TEXT concert – their pages pockmarked with holes so as to be unreadable, the brown leather covers crumbling, threads dangling in the afternoon sun. My cousins and I exchange tense looks, not wanting to admit we may have come all this way and worked so hard to find somebody who remains lost in obscurity.

Still. As our spirits tank, others have become invested; the guys in the office, two of the gravediggers. A mystery! That's exciting! Two of the office men zoom off on the moped to a further away corner; three more hover over to examine our assorted documents. Eventually it is clear we have just one option: head to the section of the cemetery most likely to hold Johnnie – the 'Christian (other)' section – and traipse around. By now the whole venture was unprecedented. The motley group of onlookers in the office decide to abandon their watch there, lock up the small room and join us on the hunt. Two guys on a moped, another on a bike, four more on foot and several more who join us en route (plus an enthusiastic puppy). The cemetery is so large we spread out on individual paths, completely unseen from each other, and begin trawling through the heat and avoiding stinging plants, row after row, all simply trying to *find him*.

As I trudge hopelessly through clusters of tombstones, swatting away insects, sweat trickling down my back, my mind starts to wander. Row after row of grey stones. Is the heat getting to me or have I been here before? Some innate sense of belonging . . . I *knew* I had never been to Sri Lanka before, yet I felt like I was walking through a familiar dream; the soft breeze through the trees; something in the hot dust; the obnoxious cawing of the crows; the clinging heat and syrupy smell. At some point

I pass a surreal sight – a completely white cow, untethered, watching me curiously and idly perched by a gravestone – and I realise it is a vague feeling of home and belonging I sometimes feel in new places. Though I don't look like the locals we meet – too tall and a lighter shade of brown – next to my cousins I'm by far the shortest and roundest, the only non-white and non-blonde person in our merry band. People here take in the three of us, deduce I am local, and then aim greetings at me in a language I don't speak. I am used to this, it's happened in so many places, and I like it – always some guilt over not answering in turn, but the warmth from strangers is pleasant and not something I ever feel in my own country. It's comfortable here; I like the heat, enjoy the porous nature of the nights. I like the animals chattering away and the heavily scented flowers. It's curious, I've spent my whole life on motorways and in cramped buildings, or literally underground in dirty tube stations, so why do I feel like I'm being welcomed home in this faraway and unfamiliar place? But there's something else familiar, something about the lack of gravity and the curious weightlessness of the air and the stoop of the trees growing up between wedged stones that makes me think of the winding off-roads in Mauritius, and the Welsh woods I wandered as a small child. The trees here know things, see things, and though rationally I suspect I'm dehydrated or plain exhausted from the stress of the day, I can hear something in the wind, feel some palpable energy from the lost souls resting here, pushing me forwards, *nearer, nearer, your ancestor is here, waiting for you.* He is *somewhere.* Or maybe it's magic older than my small life; maybe it comes from long before me and is a remnant of my ancestors who trod in these places. Maybe somehow, whatever is left of his spirit can sense, *finally, kin*, or maybe the day my great-grandmother was here – surely one of the worst days of her life – was so searingly branded into her memory that some residual trace of that day has trickled down the strands of DNA that lie in me, now gently stirring, coaxed into recollection. Or maybe some combination of both; some remembered fragment that makes it down to me, that makes itself known in these strange moments where I am between lost and found, between foreign and family, cautiously searching a cemetery for a sorry ceremonial ghost.

A shriek shakes me from this reverie. My cousin. One of the gravediggers has found Johnnie. I hear excited and grateful shouts from different corners of the cemetery. I dash over to the source of the noise, where everyone is laughing and jumping and the dog is running in excited circles. This is probably the most life the cemetery has seen in a while. We exchange thanks and take pictures, and then the assembled group leaves us and we curl up around the grave and do what we set out to. Grieve.

We spend the rest of our time with Johnnie, thanking him, scattering seeds and whisky and occasional bits of shortbread (to the delight of the crows), and we leave behind a section of the family tartan looped around the storm-weathered tombstone. Back at the hotel, knackered, the rest of the family send us an outpouring of gratitude and grief from their respective time zones (all awake watching Harry wed Meghan). They felt we'd righted a wrong – *finally* somebody visited Johnnie's grave to pay their respects. We'd allowed something collectively to come off pause and move forwards. We shared tears down the phone, shock and awe in shaky tones, because something that was unravelled was now safely sewn shut, and the past could slowly start to heal.

Later, back in the UK, my grandfather watched just thirty seconds of the footage of his grandson eulogising his father before saying he'd had enough; it was too emotional, too powerful, too much. I didn't fully understand what was at play until later when I realised it wasn't just Johnnie we'd found, it was everyone we'd lost to the obscurity of the past. Not just finding closure but finding the possibility of closure, the chance to right a regret, to recover.

Interacting with the past in this way reminds us we are never truly that far from it, that time works not just how we suppose it to − in seconds and minutes − but in how it is felt. How it wraps around us, occasionally pulling us forwards or sending us back. We can move away from the relentless ennui of being ourselves and for a moment re-examine something ruptured in our shared history. Maybe we can never fully tie it together again, but even acknowledging this brings us to some level of resolution That's the best we can manage.

The echo of Johnnie's death still reverberates through our family today − an intergenerational trauma, to reference the scholarly term, and an unprocessed, upsetting legacy. It is theorised that intergenerational trauma can take five to seven generations to fully exit the feedback loop of suffering, and studies suggest intergenerational trauma affects us not just in behaviours, learning patterns and relationship dynamics, passed down through our actions and beliefs, but on a cellular level. Right down to our DNA and the way our brains are formed, something that exists not just for humans but many other animals, whales and mice and small coiled snakes. Finding Johnnie's grave and easing the collective family guilt over losing him twice over became something in my life that I achieved for both myself and my family. The experience validates me in the same thrilling way I discovered some abstract link to Wales as a kid. It's easier to connect to the dead – they're not around to piss me off, for starters – and knowing *somebody* was here on this rainy, moody island before me and my parents is some source of comfort.

I thought once I had reached a point of belonging and happiness – my twin goals for as long as I could recall – I could set aside the questions and analysis. I thought things might be more straightforward, or at least optional. Like, okay, let's go find a grave! We found him, I belong, end of. What do you do when you've solved the mystery? The credits roll. That's it. You're done.

Except when you're not, and something else lurks below, something still unsolved and unexplainable. What is this source of fury and fear, this constant conflict in my heart?

I found it, finally found the bottom and the source of all the anguish, excavated a tomb where something supposedly dead was still very much alive. Waiting. Inside me, two big cats prowl, stalking each other: a leopard and a tiger. They circle each other endlessly, menacingly, doomed. That low rumble I hear sometimes, when I try and think of myself, I know now what it is: that is when I hear them growl. It is the tiger who is stronger, the tiger who will emerge the winner, though the tiger is older, scarred, glaring, rarely edging fully into view out of the shadows. Their story and their fight is never fully played out, continuously colliding in this hearth and falling further into this fiery festering pit, deep inside my dull bones.

On my white side, the leopard, the trauma is traceable. I can scan the legacy all the way back through the ages to the baby and the widow on the ship. On my brown side, the tiger, it is not. I cannot even bring myself to mention the trauma without knowing a tremendous heaviness.

Because the intergenerational trauma on my brown side is a cancerous mass, an unknowable, dangerous thing that ties up all of our vital strands of life into its blank, unknowing reach. When I try to visualise the 'family tree' on this side, I see not a tree but a vast grey land, pockmarked with holes, hard things embedded in the ground, and damp swamp amid the otherwise dry and dusty land. And in the middle of this is some charred stump, some withered and blackened hunk of coal. In this vision, I am stood in front of it wondering how the hell anyone could think a tree could grow in these conditions, in this place that has known such violence and loss and disturbance. If we on my brown side could know the simplicity of the trauma on the white side – to have the ability to track a single traceable vein of bitterness to its source! If only. To track the trauma is, on my white side, to track a creek up a mountain; on my brown side, to track a drop in the ocean. There is no start. Every single life on my brown side brings with it tragedy, illness, loss, and the collective trauma is different – ongoing, weighty, heavy, too much to bear or even begin sifting through; far too much for one mind, for one lifetime, for one family. It's too momentous to even contemplate, even the air feels heavier, and you don't

want to take a single step further lest you become further ensnared – because it already feels too vast and too wide and too
utterly wrecked.

There's the systematic trauma, like colonisation, child labour,
forced deportation and relocation. The suppression of culture
and religion. The outlawing of beliefs and culture.

The loss of personhood and history and identity. There's the
trauma that came from the lifetime of hard labour. The cruel
and mass exodus of people. The proximity to death and toil
and illness. The coercion, the denial of education, the effects
of a life lived entirely in systemic oppression. There's the re-
sultant trauma of those things, too. Poverty. Sickness. Grief. I
see the effects of trauma on my brown side not as displays of
behaviour or nebulous actions, but as reality-shattering events
that cause numerous more bleak offshoots of trauma in their
wake. Malnutrition. Addiction. Insecurity, emotional and social
withdrawal, several generations of dying young; the impact of
that loss on the still living, depression, anxiety, panic attacks,
and what (to me at least) seem like several lifetimes' worth of
mental health issues that only now in my time can reach various stages of acknowledgment. Not processing, not releasing,
not solving; merely *acknowledging*. Just trying to keep above water long enough to scream for help.

And then there are the smaller, individual traumas that leak
out from those bigger ones, tiny channels seeping into individual lives: the loss of family members means you lack the
support of a parent or sibling; the broken family structure and
the cruel knowledge of that grief, the sense of a terrible unknown – and not just one unknown, but a huge, vast, collective
unknowing about somebody. About all the unknown trauma

that came before you; and all the relatives you don't know, and all the lost strands of your family that were cruelly severed by something else. It's absolutely impossible to see where this trauma began, how it connects and how we might move past it, because there's just *so much more* of it.

As well as there being considerably *more* trauma, there is *less* ability to deal with its effects than on my white side. On my brown side, we face loss of information – from being forcibly moved, losing connections to other relatives, unable to keep in touch with the community, to having less physical *stuff* (which means less to pass down), to even something as simple as less space to recall memories with one another, because every spare moment is spent on survival. On my white side, we had personal recollections of Mina, efforts to keep her memory alive. We solved that quest using truths known to us from our still living relatives. On my brown side people died younger – literally less life to recall. Those left behind were, accordingly, younger – fewer memories to recall, less time spent learning to remember. On my brown side we didn't have heirlooms, or grave plots, or records of burials. Most indentured labour was improperly documented and nothing like a clear record of where you came from existed – the British rarely even spelled your name correctly as they shipped you elsewhere, erasing you into 'theirs'. The trauma on my white side is a fault line through the family, something seen and observed, like a strip of quartz in a mountainside. But the trauma on my brown side? That trauma is an ancient beast that lives deep in our bones, hackles raised, tortured into complacency by time and hard work, but still there, waiting to pounce.

This huge discrepancy is most fully realised in my life, combining as it does both sides of the chasm. Of course, you can say on paper *the descendants of colonised individuals are less likely to have documentation of their family* and that seems straightforward enough to understand. Is it upsetting, unfair? Sure. But it's also just a fact; unfortunately, that's just how things are, right? Some people have more than others. Life sucks until it doesn't.

But in my life – in me, explicitly – those two discrepancies are pitted against one another; two circling cats. It is a conflict that began long before me but exists right in the very core of my existence: the low growl of the tiger and its ruined paws across my heart. I cannot mourn my great-grandfather Amir Woozeer in the same way I can mourn Johnnie. They are equally my great-grandfathers – equal parts of my tapestry – and yet one of them has all these memories and stories and strands that have been passed down, somehow only further enmeshed by tragedy. And of the other we have nothing. No, worse, we have a document saying the British sent him thousands of miles round the world to labour in a sugar cane field when he was eleven. And then we have nothing. The same British that Johnnie had gone to India with, where he was planting tea, and Mina – whose kimono I wear, whose candlesticks I polish – that same Mina, was, according to her notes, reliant on the local 'coolies', who were 'amenable' and 'round-faced', who were, I have to imagine, sometimes terrified eleven-year-olds being sent to Mauritius.

How can I reconcile that? Amir is an abstract, unknowable figure to me – and yet I swell with righteous fury; a tiger's thundering roar, an indignant outcry for justice when I think of this *child* sent away from his home, of the jagged, fractured, forcible movements his descendants would be shunted into. Johnnie *chose* to go to India for work and adventure – and our family had the audacity to celebrate that.

Because I'm not able to process these sides in similar fashions it makes me feel unequal and off balance. On some days, I resent my white side; how could they have the *effrontery* to be affected by this one unfortunate death? How could they have the gall to let it torture them for so long? The nerve, it was criminal, the near-sighted narcissism afforded to them. On other days, I am needled with the knowledge of how much more I know of processing and absolving this trauma due to my white side, and that I cannot bear the burden in the same way for my brown family. Having discovered some tools for healing and reconciliation, I carry them around with me – but can only use them on my white side. On my brown side, I cannot get a handle on where the trauma reaches. I cannot shimmy off to a forgotten grave, compile some notes, and help us release some of the unending, throttling violence we have survived. I cannot do anything except leave futile tears in the ocean.

I still have conflicted feelings over how frustrated I should be that privilege and historic actions have resulted in me having so much *more* in terms of my white family. Which one is the norm? Should it be the typical experience to have an understanding of your relatives, maybe an item or two from their lifetime – in which case, I am justified in my grief for my brown side, who do not have this and are instead ensnared in post-colonial hardships and structural racism. Or should it be typical to know nothing, to have had the family branches severed systematically and all the terrible consequences that splinter from that – in which case, I am justified in my anger at the white side, who are either directly responsible, complicit in the system, or ignorantly benefitting from it (most likely, a combination of all three). Then I feel guilty over the resentment: my brown relatives *only* have the lack of family I feel for them. I should be grateful to have connections and ties to any family at all, grateful for the tools and access I have (this guilt I think of as my white guilt, and when white people do not discuss this it shows me they have not processed theirs). Then I feel disgusted at thinking such awful things over history I carry with me at all times.

This constant conflict is par for the course when one part of you is colonised and the other coloniser. I was born with my sin. The cats circle each other, constantly, a dance far older than my tiny life, a war that has been waged for centuries locked inside me. Even as a child, I would wonder (often resentfully) what my life would have been like to have known my dad's parents instead of my mum's. Imagine relatives I looked like. Maybe on that trip when I was seven my grandfather would have put me on his knee and made a joke about how I'd stolen his nose, like my dad did. Maybe my grandmother would have brushed my hair gently and said soft sentences in my ear, the calming tones you use with children. She would have known how to brush it. Maybe I'm over-romanticising and they would have felt as distant and impenetrable to me as the grandparents whose lives did overlap with mine. But, either way, I can say with some certainty their house would have been warmer. And they would have been in Mauritius, the magical place I so love. And I would have known for sure.

Where does that grief *go*? Somehow even the trip to Sri Lanka – a trip to explicitly quell one of the beasts – fed the gnawing conflict at the centre of me; like making a bed for the leopard provoked the tiger. As we sat on a train to Kandy through jungle-covered mountains I looked out of the window. I realised the truth that the privileged get to write history; not just in broad strokes, (whose experiences are documented and who crafts a curriculum), but even on micro levels, from one generation to the next. We had no memories from any of my father's relatives because they'd lived lives of loss and hardship, so what meagre scrap could you salvage and how?

Johnnie's death was one of the overarching family events that had gone on to shape our particular branch of the tree; like a knot in the trunk we had eventually grown around. On my brown side, tragedy is the norm, there were a dozen such tragedies at every turn, family being lost forever. *That* family tree, if I were to visualise it beyond the withered stump: lopped off branches; charred, brittle bits of bark that crumble into nothingness; empty space where leaves should have grown. A tree that well recalls the axe.

Life felt less like something to invest in, and more something to endure. Survival was a relay baton being handed down; my great-grandparents, suffering forced moves and hardships and the British, but surviving and whispering, *here, go, do your best*, to their children, who in turn travelled when they had to and crossed the world to work and saved everything they could, surviving, passing it down to their sons and whispering, *here, go, do your best*, at which point my dad came to England and worked through it all: driving between jobs and contorting into opportunities and surviving and turning to me, passing everything he had and saying, *here, go, do your best,* and then I decided to . . . spend a lot of time playing empty gigs and reformatting tags on blog posts? No, I mean that is true, but – I made a choice. I made a choice because I was the first one to have a choice. That is the real legacy of all of those people doing their best, that I was given the privilege of choice. And what did I choose? Happiness.

Sometimes I think this is unbearably selfish of me and other times I think it is the logical conclusion, because how far higher could I ascend, how much faster can you run? Survival, for so long a target chased, in my life has become a given. I can take my eye off surviving and reasonably expect that it will continue to happen whilst I pursue other things. Thriving – or, at least, imagining what thriving might be. Every day as the sun rises, I think of how it must have felt beating down on my great-grandfather's back as he toiled in the fields; I wonder if he even saw the sun as they left India, or on the boat as it moved backwards through the sky. I think of how I know the sun to shine different colours in Mauritius than in England, than in Sri Lanka, and I wonder if they knew that too. Did they think about it, long for home the way I longed for Wales? Did they yearn to be back where they started? Did they have time, or were they too exhausted? Did they *know* that one day I would choose? Because I feel their unanswered questions and corralled achievements and their wants and their drive, and it shoots through my life surer and stronger than anything I alone could experience, like a comet through my days. And if anything makes me remarkable at any point, I know it is all them, for I am just an ember in a comet's trail.

Shortly after returning from Sri Lanka, I tried to reach for balance: attempting the same coda on my brown side. I asked my dad if next time we went to Mauritius we could find the graves of my grandparents, auntie and uncle. Already there is a discrepancy between my two sides – the graves I want to visit on my brown side are two generations more recent. There are access issues: Dad isn't sure when we could go back, or where they're buried, or if we would have time on a trip to Mauritius to source this. And then my dad said something that stopped me in my tracks. He added, *anyway, my brother is buried in North London.*

What? It had taken one mention of *one* of my cousins going to a Sri Lanka-adjacent country for the whole family to become involved in this quest to get us three cousins there and find Johnnie. That's how stark the legacy of Johnnie was in the collective consciousness even ninety-two years after his death; just waiting in the wings to be called upon. Meanwhile, I had *lived* in North London for seven years at the time my dad told me my uncle was buried there. At no point had my dad made that connection. Unlike Johnnie's funeral, only attended by Mina, three generations away – my dad was *at* his brother's funeral. He organised it. It wasn't some long-ago thing, it was a lived experience. And it didn't come up once.

When I googled it, it turned out to be a thirty-minute drive to the cemetery – less than half the time it takes me to get to my dad's house. I could not believe how far away that tragedy felt compared to Johnnie, like it was centuries ago, ancient history even though it was within my dad's lifetime. It's not that my brown family cares *less* about my uncle's tragic early death, but that there has been so much *more* to endure since – more

death, more trauma, more illness, more fresh wounds to deal
with. My uncle's death and burial don't loom in everyone's
mind the way Johnnie's has. I pressed Dad for more – another
crack of the whip across my heart: the reason my uncle is buried in North London, several hours away from where both he
and my dad lived, is because it was the only place that would allow a Muslim burial. Dad says this matter-of-factly, a *well, that's
life isn't it*, but that's not life for everyone (well, death) because
Mum's relatives could be buried wherever they wanted. In fact,
numerous discussions had been had on this topic – they had
plots both here and in the States, for when the time came – and
choices (again, available) made over everybody's ideal resting
place. On Dad's side you were laid to rest wherever would
take you. I thought of my adult mum on the phone to her
also adult sisters and the long back-and-forth over my grandmother's final resting wishes. And then I thought of my dad in
his twenties, alone in the UK, organising a funeral somewhere
he'd never heard of because he had no choice but to bury his
brother there.

The contrast of my dad working extra shifts to fund an un-
planned funeral in an unfamiliar country that shunts you clear
across two counties to grieve, and of my white side, where my
still living grandparents a whole generation up have chosen
plots where they would like to be buried. I can not compute
the injustice and it just sits there, awkwardly on my consciousness, never understood or accepted. This contrast is so huge
and hideous and *unbearable*. The shame it causes me feels like
some cruel joke from an uncaring God who is looking the
other way.

I know the tiger wins, but the cats still prowl ominously. Mina had a dead leopard skin on her sofa, a souvenir from India that terrified her grandchildren (Mum said they always squabbled over sitting at the opposite end of its head). It was shot through the eyes so the skin could remain perfect – without the 'flaw' of a mortal wound – and this was deemed to be a specific skill, which made for a prized gift. But every time I've seen that leopard skin I feel a yearning for her to be home in her country. Somehow that glassy-eyed stare, locked into that cruel moment of death feels like another tragedy for my *brown* side, even though the leopard is an heirloom on my *white* side, because it makes me think of the grotesque needlessness and macabre horrors enacted on the whims of the British towards both my ancestral plains and people and the leopard.

I remember as a small child, the first round of divvying up my grandparents' possessions at their poky old house in Wales, with my mum and my two aunts. The same day as the snakes. When we reached the leopard, they told me the story and how they had all been scared of it. Nobody really wanted it in their homes but it was agreed it was not something one could easily donate. I knew a great sorrow in my soul, eclipsed only by how urgently I wanted that leopard. I was seven and therefore not an active part of proceedings, just *there*, and I voiced my desire but it transpired that maybe they would send it to my uncle – the racist one, although maybe not racist, then – as he'd received the least heirlooms. Mum told me they weren't sure about the customs situation and logistics of transporting a pelt over international lines, and if they couldn't get it to him, I could be next in line.

As an adult, I wonder why I was so desperate, what drew me to that leopard and the golden coiled snakes, the items that had so creeped out everyone else? Why did they beckon me and me alone? These are not normal kid objects. I liked animals but had no particular affinity towards either leopards or snakes at that point. At the age of seven I was still confused over who I was: only cognisant of 'Welsh' and 'American' via Mum, no notion of India or any links to it; but I still felt such a pull towards those two objects, like they spoke to me, something emanated from them that only I could hear. Maybe because I was a lonely child who preferred animals to people. Maybe because among the floral plates and annotated Bibles and printed dresses, the leopard and the snakes were the unwanted, unplaceable parts of the family, and I saw myself in them. Maybe because all of us – the candlesticks, the leopard and me – had, in some way, started off in India and ended up here, united in a cold Welsh sitting room and a room full of white people. I don't know. Maybe this is just wishful thinking. I probably just wanted them to be contrary – seeking attention from a family focused elsewhere. I just know I wanted them, deeply, badly, some pull behind my navel that these items should be with me and not the charity shop, and that I felt more of a connection to the leopard and the snakes than practically anything else in that house, save for my grandmother's piano.

Many of my mixed friends process variations of what I do: they face silent inner sharks waiting to strike, or enormous jellyfish who tangle their tentacles across your twenties, or two-faced owl butterflies constantly metamorphosing and swooping through time. But those are not my stories. Only I know the kneading of a gnarled paw on my heart. And whatever way you look at it, in choosing to contemplate our identity, it is clear we have been gifted *choice*. Though I hold this huge chasm within me, this endless battle passed down through history, nobody knows. Nobody sees it. To everyone, we are a normal family. My parents are married, living the same life, part of the same class: equals. Family friends don't see the disparity, they see two equal people with equal backstories. Like so many things before, it is an issue for me and me alone. I integrate those elements on some molecular level; the tiger and the leopard stitched into my soul. Though they are different in magnitude they are equally endless, equally mine. I have to find a way to hold it all within me; not just carry it but keep it under control as I go about my life. Some tragedies are more broken than others and it doesn't diminish the pain or trauma my white side face to say my brown side face more. However high I soar I will always have this fight playing out inside of me.

It's all too tremulous for me to hold in my head, that dizzying feeling I had as a child. I see the different ways life allows us to grieve, the space life offers us, and I can't ever make peace with the fundamental cruelty of it. I reach a state of precarious balance – moving my focus away from the prowling cats and out into the light, the lantern, the capacious world around me – but they will still be there. It's not something that can be rectified, at least not solely by me, in this one lifetime.

What about at the top of the garden? That, I think, is the only place that could hold this constant circle of conflict, that place where I lie and watch the clouds. Sometimes they move so fast you can feel blurry and dizzy even just lying perfectly still. And on my left side is the apple tree by the swing, when you push your legs off the floor it feels like you could launch into the sky; and further on my right at the end of a wobbly path is the huge mound of soft deep brown mulch and matter, where the bugs live, where we throw the ends of the vegetables and the egg shells and the fragments of the burned cookies for the birds to take (the early ones, I presume), and the bugs get the rest and they eat it up into bits of earth. And then those same fragments go back into the ground, and start again, as soft shoots of grass that greet the morning or tiny daisies that greet the children. Or maybe they go deeper, where the worms are, and the chunks of quartz in the ground, and the unknown parts stay hidden. That is the place where if you open your eyes wide when your head is laid down, all you can see is the swirling sky above, hear the roar of the turning world; and that is where, if anywhere, I can set the cats free to roam alone, and empty them out of the centre of me, and know peace. There, if anywhere – though I have not succeeded yet, and they prowl still. Maybe they always will, a problem not for me but for time, for my descendants, and for the skies who have to hold it all together.

I can never not know the experience of being both many and of being a single entity, nor would I want to. The plurality helps me make sense not just of myself, but of *everything*: art, music, gender, love, sex, humanity, fate and time; how each moment connects to the next, how the end is also the beginning, how many lives can lie in just one, how there are more stars in the sky than grains of sand on the shore. It was hard to navigate this when I was younger – not just how to know everything at all times, but how to *experience* it – how to exist right there in the eye at the centre of it. But now I know. And I am aware that others may not understand this, but they do not need to, because *I* know, and that is enough.

As a teen, my safe 'space' was retreating into small solitude from an otherwise difficult and negative world. Now that space is my existence and with the precious light I've found, I set my whole life ablaze. I think of my great-grandfather toiling under a foreign sun, infant labourer; and my grandmother cleaning and sweeping and saving every penny; and my dad, tracking the M4 every other week between two jobs in two countries; and of myself, small and strong, staying awake into the night, and grinning at myself in every mirror I've met, and getting lost in my lyrics on a soft dusty stage, and planting my two feet where the oceans overlap, and reaching for my hair as I fall safely asleep. All the parts of me that exist and have always existed and are yet to exist, and all the lives that live within mine: lives yet to be born from me and lives that culminate in me; two fish swimming in opposite directions, two separate strands inextricably linked, bound together in taut ribbons, from the hair on my skin to the song in my soul.

I hear the rush of a comet and a thousand long-lost winds whispering, *here, go, do your best.* My younger self stays with me, tools hung on the wall – the Laila who pulled together a sum of many scattered parts – so that I know if I need to I can do it again. Increasingly, I refer back to myself; placing hidden tributes and tiny secrets through my songs and scores and writings. Why not? Who else would look for a trace of me? I contribute to myself as I go; it's not intended to be found by anyone except myself, to bolster myself, to say to myself, *that happened, you did that, you were here, you are here, you are always always here and besides, you did your best.*

Epilogue

For Fur

And what of you, dear reader, what will you do? Maybe you are like me, and found in this tale some adjacent moonlight lighting your way. Maybe you are not. Maybe you came to this book in search of a window; maybe you found it, and, if so, I wonder what you saw when you looked. Maybe you are in the future, and found some small fragment of something you'd forgotten. Or maybe you are not – maybe you are still young, in which case I pass on this cherished map to find yourself with.

You can't thrive if you're lost at sea; you just hope for it to pass, wait to wash up somewhere on a sandy shore and see what survives. I wish you board and lodging, love and shelter, and a soft place to spend the night until a better morning dawns. I wish you solidity on all sides, and the choice to walk out of the sea and onto the shore. The business of being yourself, of being true to those who came before and of following the directions they laid down to you: it is the easiest thing in the world, like a leaf caught in the wind, until it's not. Some days there simply is no breeze. I wish you a tender embrace, and an unending will to *keep going, do your best, pass it on.* I wish you love like a comet through your days.

Lives are no more than a single petal that flutters to the ground, and I am far more minor still. Sometimes it's tiring to be a battering ram, or a small stone in a shoe, trodden on irritably, knowing you are not where you should be, knowing you are placed where it is impossible to thrive. Even the rocks need to feel soft sometimes; finding themselves unburdened as they descend into the ground to be cradled by the earth, rolled over and suspended in soil too thick to sink into, or maybe sinking through the sea and sleeping in the sand. Depends on where they get tossed.

You do not have to carry the hardness around. On many days I have needed to recall that I can be small and nascent – that I can unfurl too. To know I can curl up into all the things I am, nestle like a sleeping serpent in the warm serene sand. Seek out the soft places. That I can take all that is wondrous and magical about myself and hold it close, protect it, appreciate it and cherish it. It's a triumph to know your soul so well you can cup it in your hand, carefully, tenderly, listen for that tiny victorious heartbeat, a million miraculous murmurs of a life well-lived. I take this tiny precious nugget into my gently cupped palms where it murmurs back at me, soothing me, reminding me, of everything that was, everything that will be, everything I am in every moment that I am. *You are safe. You are loved. You are here.*

You can hold it in yours, too.

Afterword

LETTER FROM LAILA

Dear readers,

Thank you so much for holding this book in your hands. I'm so thrilled that this book has reached you! From the earliest days of *Not Quite White*'s existence I had hoped it would reach the US, and about the only thing everyone agreed on was how extremely unlikely that was. To be writing this letter to you all knowing it will be included in the US edition is remarkable. I hope you will recognise the references, connect to the culture, discover the joys of British slang, and above all, enjoy the work.

As I move further away from both the version of me that wrote *Not Quite White* and the version of me written *into* it, I find the two strangely entwined. While writing, I employed all sorts of trickery to cast my mind into the past, and now those same methods help me remember who I was when I began the process of creating this book. The story of the book ends in the same year I began writing it and revisiting these words is like opening an old save file.

Author Laila creating the book in 2018 is as equally alive in its pages as the book version of Laila they were articulating. Among the various supporting materials I made along the way (for the curious among you, these are all collected online – scan the QR code at the front and go from there), you'll discover echoes of those two versions of Laila side by side. The playlists of music Book Laila listens to are assembled next to playlists Author Laila kept on repeat while writing and editing. Lists of books Book Laila is inspired by are lined up next to books Author Laila studied and researched when creating this one.

I've often been asked if it was cathartic or emotionally challenging to write this book. If I had not emotionally processed the incidents in the book I would not have been able to write it. The challenging part happened years before, largely in going to therapy but also in difficult conversations and finding ways to process – all things which had to happen before I could think about creating this story. I truly believe if I had *not* gone to therapy I would not have been able to write this book. Perhaps another, but not this one.

When writing, I wanted to make sure each word connected not just to the rest of the story but beyond the book, pointing towards other works and ideas: if it didn't connect further it got cut. I knew that the answers of the book had to be present from the start even if they weren't "revealed" until the end, the way it is in life.

I have always enjoyed repeatedly revisiting my favourite works to search for minor details. It is my dearest hope that people will reread this story, play the game, and find the clues and allusions I hid throughout its pages – forming a line that will lead you elsewhere if you wish. If you should follow the trail you will illuminate further parts of the constellation: the song lyric appearing here as a chapter title; the Instagram post masquerading as a metaphor; the literal act hiding in plain sight, pretending to be a simple poetic aspiration.

Thank you for being here,

I hope to see you in the sequel.

And what of your stories? I hope to read those too.

Laila
Autumn 2023

Appendix

THE SNOW QUEEN

There are two things to know about the day I was born. One is that it was the coldest, heaviest snow fall that Britain had seen on that day for decades; it would remain the coldest on record until that day this year. Two is that it should not have been the day I was born at all; I was supposed to arrive in a younger month. But I held off, arriving instead with the unseasonable snowstorm in unfamiliar times. Today it is my birthday. The current climate here in London (blizzard of snow) marks the first year of my life when the cold temperature and constant snowfall has matched the bitter North Wind I arrived with.

In this cold country of my birth, I'm well aware that people like to associate me with warmer climes. I am told often how I remind people of the tropical and exotic, of places we might readily associate with the sun. Sometimes I think of my ancestors, out there in the northern plains of Africa; the dusty plains of Southern Asia; the wide expanse of pre-America 'America'; the warm islands of the Indian Ocean. How absurd it would have seemed to them to imagine snow at all, much less a direct descendant born amid a blizzard. (Climate change and immigration; the dual factors of my existence.) Even one generation ago we were deep into sun-drenched territory: my own two parents born in Uganda and Mumbai. My heritage truly does lie where the sun shines.

People love the snow; are attracted by its seemingly pure state, it's newness and cleanness, unending beauty and peace. You see the snow from afar and you want to partake in its loveliness. To experience the snow up close is another story. The snow is deceptive and cruel; hiding deadly, invisible sheets of ice; rendering the world you know an illusion; smiting you with invisible winds that rip through your bones. You go out to greet the snow in all its splendour and the snow comes for you. Never as nice as you imagined. A solitude broken. Better to have left it alone.

Leave the snow to its own devices and it's a force like no other. Like a silent, deadly version of its alter ego: water. A tsunami will crash upon you, encroaching, destructive and deadly; a storm will rain down around you, surrounding you, dangerous and calamitous. But snow falls softly. You wake up in the morning and it's a surprise. The world has become a barren, confusing landscape — even a familiar street looks completely different under thick snow — and, with the ice sneaking into your veins, a cold you had forgotten. Perhaps you thought you had understood the situation; you didn't, the snow has decided otherwise. Or maybe you thought you knew how you were getting to work today; no, the snow had other plans. You want to meet your child, but the snow has fallen. And so you adapt to the snow.

When the snow envelopes the world and creates such a harsh landscape, the best you can do is survive. But thoughts of anything else — of growing and blooming and thriving — seem impossible amid such unforgiving terrain. Those indigenous to such lands tell us that one never truly lives with the snow; the focus is to survive, to adapt and to withstand. And for years I felt this way. In the wilderness I grew up in, I merely existed alongside the impermeable frost. Playing a waiting game with the snow; who will disappear first? This birthday the Arctic winds reign upon us again, showing their might, and for me too, this birthday is a remarkable one in many ways. Not once did I think I would make it this far. I was so focused on surviving that I failed to imagine what I might do should the snow actually thaw. Because who knew if it actually would? But this year and this age brings a change. Spring is in sight.

Because snow does thaw. The blizzards will pass. I look to the skies and ask that the snow that arrived when I did will finally blow over; ask that this blizzard can bookend the first chapter of my life, instead of continuing to underpin it. The skies agree. Rain is already beginning to fall; the snow is morphing into something more manageable. This ice, too, shall melt. And the sunflowers are mere husks now, seemingly dried up and dead in their pot. But the wise winds will tell you that hope is not lost. Because with the melted ice, and the warmth of the new sun, and just a little bit more time, they will grow.

Adapted from the original version of this blog, first written and published in 2018.

ACKNOWLEDGMENTS

For Maggie (who waited) and Michael (who went).

In memoriam to everyone who died whilst I wrote this: Grandma, Sally, Maggie, Michael, Uncle Wahab, Auntie Jo, Granddad and Clarissa. And for Stuart, in the pages.

Huge love to everyone mentioned in this book; thank you for shaping my life. Thank you to those who read and fact-checked individual episodes, including Nick, Jeremy, Charlotte, Sam, Tom, Ollie; and to those who graciously allowed me to directly mention them in this book, including Andrew, Nilo, my brother "Hass", "Jaya" and "Jack", with additional thanks to "Jack" for your signature warmth and the impromptu nostalgia trip. Pints on me for all of you.

Many thanks to all of the editors, agents, assistants and other lovely souls who have worked on publishing this book, and especially to Kaiya Shang for your clarity, editing and feedback. Thank you to the wonderful Rukhsana Yasmin for your much-needed editing, guidance and support. Thank you to Dr Elen Ifan for the insight and offerings regarding the section on hiraeth. Thank you to Micaela for understanding the cover and Martin for understanding the words – and thank you to Zekra and Dani at Colour PR for understanding *me*. You saw this story and I so appreciate you! Thank you, Heavy Entertainment, for recording the audiobook: having my parents voices authentically in the audio has made this story alive in a way it never could be in text. Thank you.

■ For the US edition I am delighted to have a whole new paragraph of people to thank! Thank you to Dan Crissman and everyone at Indiana University Press for offering *Not Quite White* a home across the pond. Huge thanks to everyone who helped me through the thickets of US publishing (and beyond), including Cailey, Will, Jackson and John. A massive thank-you to Annie Hwang for your time, wisdom and extraordinary generosity. Shout-outs to the US Laila Lot who have had my back for years, and to Becky (and her book clubs) for the incredible support. Lastly, a huge, gigantic thank-you to everyone Stateside who shipped, scavenged, sent-via-relatives, and by all other means procured the previous non-US edition, thereby proving there *was* an American audience – you are truly my people!

▥ Big thanks to the exceptionally kind folk who offered me advice, insight and connections as I navigated this convoluted industry, including: Angelique Tran Van Sang, Rachel Mann, Aimée and Dee from Knights Of, Jess, Anna, Lubna, Layla, Gina, the MTM gang, Amber and the CNF crew, and Nikesh.

And the same but even bigger thanks to Philly for telling me to write a book in the first place.

■   To everyone who read this book, pre-ordered this book, reviewed this book, told a friend, shared it online and so on and so forth: my endless gratitude, truly. What a thrill to exist on your support. What a thrill to exist in a world where I can give my art to you.

🌳   Thank you to my family, my beloved big brother, my cherished cousins. To decades of second parents and found family and extra siblings; and always to my ancestors who shaped the world I find myself in. Thank you for your guidance and legacy and love.

🍃   To my Mum and Dad: thanks for the (almost) total lack of objections and enduring the stultifying weirdness of *gestures around* this whole thing. Mum, you are so gracious and I am grateful for your words in these pages. Dad, please know you are my hero. Thank you for committing your voices into these words and then the recording, and most of all thank you for being there.

♫   Thank you to Lou for reflection, insight and support – so much has become possible for me through your help. I am so grateful for you.

✦   THANK YOU to the good people of the LailaVerse: the gig-goers who allowed me to grow; the Laila Lot (you are all lovely); and everyone who ever supported my work over the years. Whether you sat in a show, shared a post, or simply got in my notifications with a timely Captain America gif: thank you! You are the reason I pay my Wi-Fi bill each month. And the largest, most endless gratitude is for the Patreon patrons: without you I simply would not be here. You support me in ways I didn't know I needed and you give me a safety net over what was an endless void to nothing. Thank you for being in the most precious pocket of my work.

🐌   A huge and heartfelt thank-you to my dear friends who read, listened, commiserated and generally kept me going. All things which had to happen.

🐚   Shouts to my CREWS past and present: the Studio 87 paldem, "we're going to goldsmiths", baba head BAH, plant yoga crew, ADHD Wasians, and all my mates not already mentioned. Where did you people come from and why?! I love you all endlessly and I'm taking you with me so stay the fuck ready and let's fucking goooo! And to everyone who came through for the London book launch – you are appreciated! Plus: anyone adjacent to the collected larks in this book, my comrades and cohorts from years gone by – Stumble Trip, #crapbloggers, Rhum & Clay, Quizcats, Gold Skull Gig gang, Mondays MT, monson massive, TMT legends, and everyone I ever lived with down SchoRo. Thanks for keeping me going long enough to get here.

💜   Massive love to Mariya Takeuchi for gifting the world with Plastic Love, and my endless undying appreciation to anyone who has contributed a mash-up, remix or edit to the discourse and unknowingly sponsored all of my breaks throughout the vampire marathon and beyond.

All my teachers, who provided life rafts and windows and doors and so much more. Thank you. To my many instrumental teachers, especially Elena, whose lessons I still learn now, and Sally, who taught me far more than song. To Mrs Pitts, Mr Leadbetter, Miss Frawley, and my secondary school music department. To Anna for being a teacher, boss, mentor and friend. And to Professor Alexander Ivashkin aka Sasha, who first told me to write; I try my best.

And finally: Bruce, Todd, Emily, Lucas, Toby, Lou, Harry, Milton, Ginger, Nugget, Sabrina, Penny – how I love to be here with you all! – Clarissa, Cloyd, Michael, Kish – how blessed I have been! – Peter, AC, Tony, Dmitri, Virgil, Johnny, Tanya, Robin – how life goes on! And finally to Darth, for proving it. And the only reason I wrote a book at all, dearest cherished precious Maggie. I wanted to give you a home but I'd have given you the world if I could. How I wish you knew. How I miss you so. ♥

Laila Woozeer is a writer, musician, and performer, born and based in London. Laila's work has been published in the *Guardian*, Mashable, and *Stylist*. Notable projects include producing and directing the award-winning contemporary music performance collective *WOLF PACK* and authoring the blog *TAPE PARADE*. *Not Quite White* is Laila's first book.

www.lailawoozeer.com

FOR INDIANA UNIVERSITY PRESS

Tony Brewer *Artist and Book Designer*
Dan Crissman *Editorial Director and Acquisitions Editor*
Anna Francis *Assistant Acquisitions Editor*
Anna Garnai *Editorial Assistant*
Brenna Hosman *Production Coordinator*
Katie Huggins *Production Manager*
Dave Hulsey *Associate Director and Director of Sales and Marketing*
David Miller *Lead Project Manager/Editor*
Dan Pyle *Online Publishing Manager*
Pamela Rude *Senior Artist and Book Designer*